Karen Bro[...]

SWITZER[...]

2009

Romantik Seehotel Sonne

Küsnacht am Zürichsee

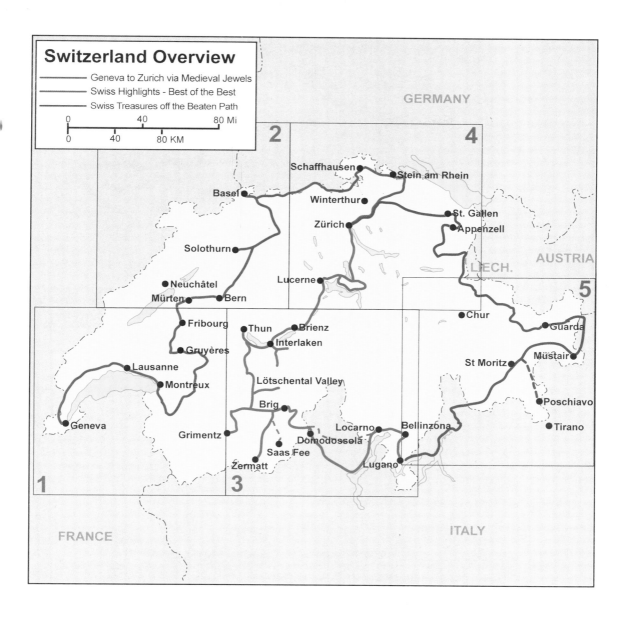

Switzerland Overview

- Geneva to Zurich via Medieval Jewels
- Swiss Highlights - Best of the Best
- Swiss Treasures off the Beaten Path

0	40	80 Mi
0	40	80 KM

GERMANY

AUSTRIA

LIECH.

FRANCE

ITALY

2

4

5

1

3

Schaffhausen

Stein am Rhein

Basel

Winterthur

St. Gallen

Zürich

Appenzell

Solothurn

Lucerne

Neuchâtel

Chur

Mürten

Bern

Guarda

Fribourg

Thun

Brienz

Interlaken

Müstair

Gruyères

St Moritz

Lausanne

Lötschental Valley

Montreux

Brig

Poschiavo

Geneva

Grimentz

Locarno

Bellinzona

Tirano

Domodossola

Saas Fee

Zermatt

Lugano

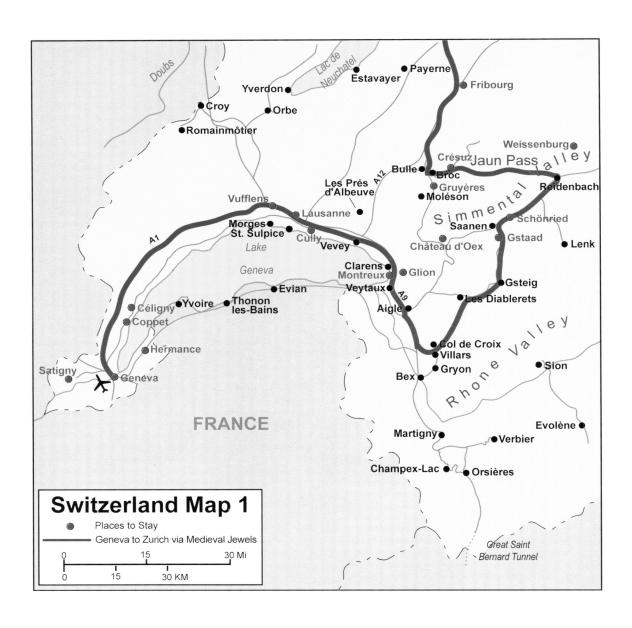

Switzerland Map 1

● Places to Stay

━━━ Geneva to Zurich via Medieval Jewels

0   15   30 Mi

0   15   30 KM

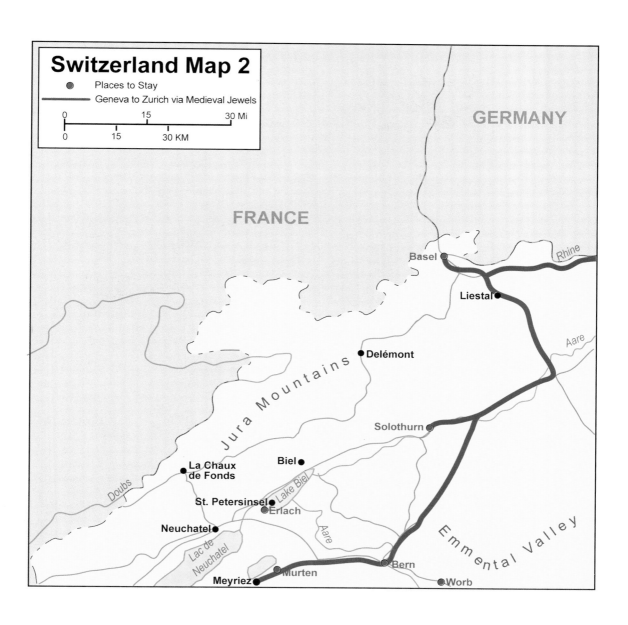

Switzerland Map 3

- ● Places to Stay
- ── Swiss Highlights - Best of the Best

| 0 | 15 | 30 Mi |
| 0 | 15 | 30 KM |

ITALY

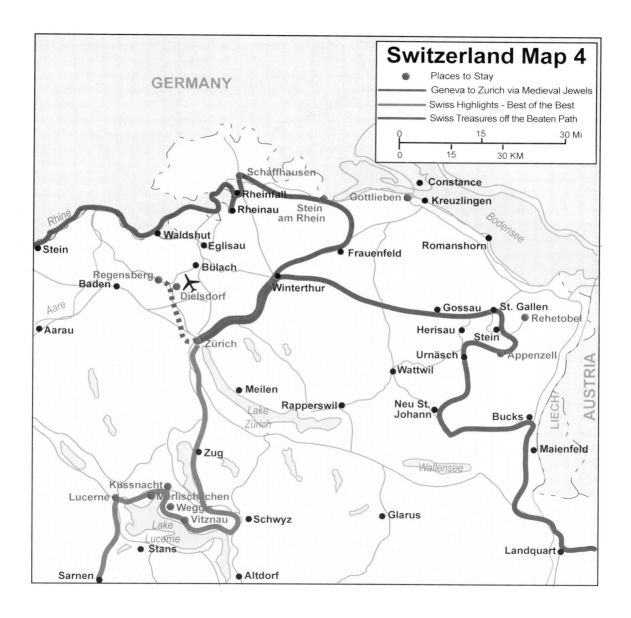

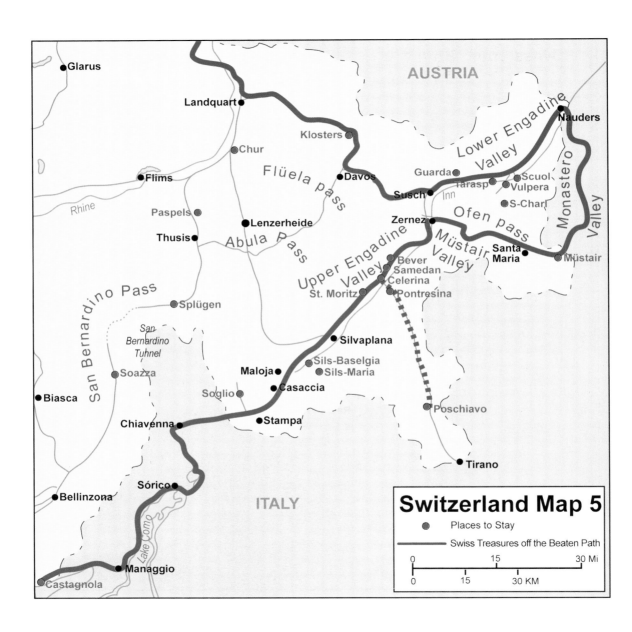

Switzerland Map 5

- Places to Stay
- Swiss Treasures off the Beaten Path

0   15   30 Mi
0   15   30 KM

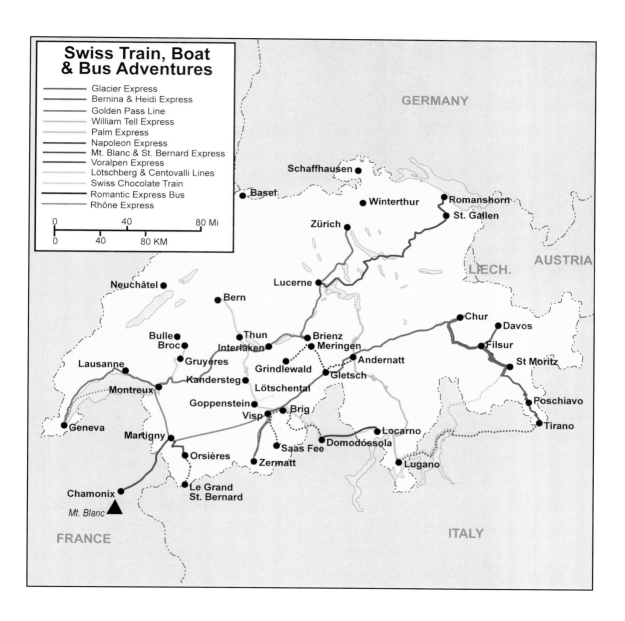

Contents

In memory of
Michael
You will always be in our hearts

2009 Cover Painting: Romantik Seehotel Sonne, Küsnacht am Zürichsee

Photographs front: Lauderbrunnen and Murten

Authors: Clare Brown, Karen Brown and June Eveleigh Brown.

Editors: Clare Brown, Karen Brown, June Eveleigh Brown, Kim Brown Holmsen, Debbie Tokumoto, Melissa Jaworski, Terri Jo Woellner.

Illustrations: Barbara Maclurcan Tapp.

Cover painting: Jann Pollard.

Maps: Rachael Kircher-Randolph.

Technical support: Andrew Harris.

Email: karen@karenbrown.com.

Distributed by National Book Network, 15200 NBN Way, Blue Ridge Summit, PA 17214, USA.

Tel: 717-794-3800 or 1-800-462-6420, Fax: 1-800-338-4500, Email: custserv@nbnbooks.com.

A catalog record for this book is available from the British Library.

ISSN 1532-8791

Introduction

Switzerland is a country of incredible beauty: rugged mountain peaks enhanced by delicate, wispy clouds; velvety green meadows tucked high on mountain ledges; dramatic rivers rushing through narrow gorges; tiny blue lakes sparkling like jewels in their mountain pockets; postcard-worthy villages made up of toy-like chalets. The country is almost too perfect to be real. For centuries Switzerland has inspired poets and artists who have advertised her glories on paper and canvas and her reputation has attracted visitors from all over the world. Switzerland's tremendous growth in popularity as a tourist destination stems from the 19th century when the ever-hearty British, challenged by tales of unconquerable mountain peaks, ventured to Alpine villages in search of adventure. These sportsmen returned to England, spreading the word of the glories of Switzerland. One of these was Edward Whymper, a young English gentleman, who on July 14, 1865, at the young age of 20, came to Zermatt and conquered the summit of the Matterhorn. Whymper's enthusiasm is captured in his words of praise for the beauty of Switzerland:

"However magnificent dreams of the imagination may be,
they always remain inferior to reality."

About Switzerland

The Swiss call their country Helvetia and all federal documents bear the seal of the Confederation Helvetia, CH, or Swiss Confederation. Swiss independence dates from the days of William Tell when the magistrates from three cantons, then under Hapsburg rule, met to courageously and successfully oppose the hand of the ruling landholders. It was in 1291, on a meadow near Lake Lucerne, at the Rutli, that the magistrates set the seal to the new Confederation Helvetia. Those original three cantons, Uri, Schwyz, and Unterwalden, have expanded over the centuries into 26 cantons (23 if you do not consider the semi-cantons of Appenzell, Basel, and Unterwalden). Each jealously guards its autonomy and separate identity. The canton of Bern is the capital of Switzerland and serves as the seat of the federal government. However, the Swiss have historically shunned centralization of power and so, rather than have too many federal branches in one city; they maintain the supreme court at Lausanne.

Although Switzerland is a small country (barely 323 kilometers wide and 161 kilometers north to south), it has a compulsory military service, being determined to protect its hard-won independence, national character, and peace. Every young Swiss man must enlist at the age of 20 and complete 17 weeks of basic training. Then, until the age of 50 or 55 he is responsible for participating in a few weeks of annual "refresher" courses. This military force is always ready to defend the country and can be coordinated into action at a moment's notice. We often encountered such training groups who were "stationed" at our hotel. They would practice maneuvers by day then return to the hotel in the afternoon and often spend their leisure hours washing their Mercedes cars. Where else but in Switzerland?

Contrary to the Swiss people's reputation of being somewhat aloof, we find them to be exceedingly cordial and hospitable. Not with a back-slapping brand of friendliness, but a friendliness wrapped in reserve and dignity—no less real though quite "proper." Perhaps the Swiss dedication to hard work, their total commitment to providing excellence of service, and their respect for privacy have been misinterpreted as "coldness."

Cantons of Switzerland

AIRFARES

Karen Brown's Guides have long recommended Auto Europe for their excellent car rental services. Their air travel division, Destination Europe, an airline broker working with major American and European carriers, offers deeply discounted coach- and business-class fares to over 200 European gateway cities. It also gives Karen Brown travelers an additional 5% discount off its already highly competitive prices (cannot be combined with any other offers or promotions). We recommend you make reservations by phone at (800) 835-1555. When phoning, be sure to use the Karen Brown ID number 99006187 to secure your discount.

CAR RENTAL

Readers frequently ask our advice on car rental companies. We always use Auto Europe—a car rental broker that works with the major car rental companies to find the lowest possible price. They also offer motor homes and chauffeur services. Auto Europe's toll-free phone service, from every European country, connects you to their U.S.-based, 24-hour reservation center (ask for the Europe Phone Numbers Card to be mailed to you). Auto Europe offers our readers a 5% discount (cannot be combined with any other offers or promotions) and, occasionally, free upgrades. Be sure to use the Karen Brown ID number 99006187 to receive your discount and any special offers. You can make your own reservations online via our website, *www.karenbrown.com* (select *Auto Europe* from the home page), or by phone (800-223-5555).

CURRENCY

The Swiss franc (CHF) is the official currency of Switzerland. An increasingly popular and convenient way to obtain foreign currency is simply to use your bankcard at an ATM machine. You pay a fixed fee for this but, depending on the amount you withdraw, it is usually less than the percentage-based fee charged to exchange currency or travelers' checks. Be sure to check with your bank or credit card company about fees and necessary pin numbers prior to departure. Visit our website (*www.karenbrown.com*) for an easy-to-use online currency converter.

DRIVING

Roads, like everything else in Switzerland, are efficiently marked. Once you get used to the excellent color-coded sign system, directions are easy to follow: green signs indicate motorways, blue signs mark regular roads, white signs depict the smaller roads, and yellow signs mark walking paths or roads closed to vehicle traffic. Most of the roads are excellent, but some of the smaller roads in remote areas (i.e., narrow, twisting, mountain passes) are not recommended for the faint of heart. It is also notable that certain passes close during the winter months. To inquire about road conditions while driving in Switzerland, you can reach a hot line by dialing 163.

DRIVER'S LICENSE: A valid driver's license from your own country is sufficient when driving within Switzerland.

DRUNK DRIVING: The penalties for driving while under the influence of alcohol are very severe. Do not drink and drive.

GASOLINE: The price of gasoline in Switzerland is very high so be sure to budget for this when making your plans. If you find yourself short of cash, many of the service stations (such as BP, ESSO, and Shell) will accept payment by a major credit card. Some of the service stations have an efficient system whereby you put coins into an appropriate slot and can pump your own gas—day or night. Some service stations are even more automated and you can purchase gas by inserting your credit card directly into the indicated slot. Service stations off the major freeways frequently close for a few hours in the middle of the day.

MOTORWAYS: Switzerland does not collect tolls on its motorways—instead, motorists must buy a permit (to be displayed on the windshield) in order to drive on them. If you rent a car in Switzerland, the rental company will have done this for you. If you are arriving from another country, you can buy a permit (called a *vignette*) at the border.

ROAD CONDITIONS: Highways link Switzerland's major cities and are kept in remarkably good condition. No sooner are the snows melting in the spring sun than maintenance crews begin repairing damage done by winter weather. Many villages are tucked away in remote valleys linked to civilization by narrow little roads, but even these are well tended by the efficient Swiss and are usually in good condition.

ROAD SIGNS: If you are driving, prepare yourself before leaving home by learning the international road signs so that you can obey all the rules and avoid the hazard and embarrassment of heading the wrong way down a small street or parking in a forbidden zone. There are several basic sign shapes: triangular signs warn that there is danger ahead; circular signs indicate compulsory rules and information; square signs give information concerning telephones, parking, camping, etc.

SEAT BELTS: Seat belts are mandatory when driving within Switzerland. It is also the law that babies and small children must ride in proper car seats.

SPEED LIMITS: There are speed limits throughout Switzerland: motorways—maximum speed 120 kilometers per hour (kph); highways—maximum speed 80 kph; towns and built-up areas—maximum speed 50 kph.

ELECTRICITY

If you are taking any electrical appliances made for use in the United States, you will need a transformer plus a two-pin adapter. A voltage of 220 AC at 50 cycles per second is almost countrywide, though in remote areas you may encounter 120V. The voltage is often displayed on the socket. Even though we recommend that you purchase appliances with dual-voltage options whenever possible, you will still need the appropriate socket adapter. Also, be especially careful with expensive equipment such as computers—verify with the manufacturer the adapter/converter capabilities and requirements.

FESTIVALS

Proud of their local traditions and cultures, the Swiss observe many festivals and events that serve as reminders of the past. They range from centuries-old ceremonies commemorating national victories to popular pageants and processions. Colorful costumes, often unique to a particular canton, are frequently worn on Sundays and festive occasions. Music and theater are important in Swiss life—from the theater and symphony in the larger cities to the local band or yodeling society in the villages, throughout the year the Swiss host numerous festivals incorporating music. Festivals and traditions inspired by the seasons are also plentiful and fun to experience. To name a few: in early summer farmers in traditional costumes parade their herds of cows, adorned with bells and decorated with flowers, through the villages to higher summer pastures. When cold weather approaches, the cows are brought back down the mountains, again with great ceremony. In the fall, gaiety prevails with the grape harvest in the numerous wine regions. In summer, special sports contests take place, such as Alpine wrestling, tugs-of-war, or *hornet*, a team game in which a vulcanite disc is "swatted" with a wooden racket. Political meetings are also staged as a traditional event. In spring, there are open-air cantonal meetings, *Landsgemeinden*, held by citizens in the cantons of Appenzell, Glarus, and Unterwalden. In the town square of each canton, elections take place and issues are debated and voted upon by uplifted hand. Switzerland Tourism, organized by the Swiss Tourist office, is an excellent source for festival information, see page 15 for more details.

FLY RAIL BAGGAGE

In a total commitment to ease the way for the traveler, Swissair has devised an ingenious, outstanding, and convenient method for the handling of your luggage which they call "Fly Rail Baggage." From any North American airport you can check your luggage all the way to one of 60 train stations. Imagine being able to check your baggage from your departure airport in the U.S. and not have to see it again until you reach your final train destination. The cost is nominal and is per piece of luggage (approximately $15 each piece). Please allow sufficient time—inquire at the airport about time requirements for checking in your luggage.

FOOD & WINE

Switzerland is bordered by Germany, Austria, Italy, and France. Culinary specialties from each of these countries have been absorbed into the Swiss kitchens where talented chefs interpret these various foods into gourmet delights.

Many guide books imply that Swiss cooking is mediocre—that it has no character or style of its own. We feel that this is totally unfair. The high degree of training stressed in the Swiss hotel schools contributes to the consistently fine food and service that is found not only in the elegant city restaurants, but also in tiny restaurants in remote hamlets. Usually every entree is cooked to order—rarely will you see a steam table. For a grand finale to your meal, Swiss pastries and desserts are world-famous.

You will find throughout your travels in Switzerland delicious fruits and vegetables from the garden, a marvelous selection of fresh fish from the rivers and lakes, outstanding veal dishes, and wicked desserts including an assortment of local cheeses.

To satisfy the morning appetite, the breakfast repast is usually a continental offering of rolls, bread, butter, jelly, cheese, and Muesli, served with coffee or tea. At larger hotels, you can often order as a supplement, and for an additional charge: juices, eggs, and breakfast meats.

The following list of Swiss specialties is not comprehensive—it is merely a sampling of some of the delicacies we most enjoy while in Switzerland. The fun of completing the list is left to your own culinary adventures.

BRATWURST: I am sure the Swiss would chuckle to see included such mundane fare as Bratwurst in a specialty food list. However, there is nothing more delicious than the plump grilled veal Swiss hot dogs smothered in onions, topped by mustard, and accompanied by fried potatoes. A cold beer makes this meal memorable.

BÜNDNERFLEISCH: In southeastern Switzerland, the Grisons area, an unusual air-dried beef or ham cut into wafer-thin slices is served as a delicacy.

CHEESES: Switzerland is famous for her cheeses. Appenzell and Gruyères are but two of the many towns that produce these mouth-watering cheeses. You will find that each area seems to produce its own variety of cheese.

CHOCOLATE: This list would not be complete without the mention of Swiss chocolate. Nestlé, Tobler, or simply "Swiss" are synonymous with the world's best chocolate. Rarely does a suitcase return home without a candy bar or two tucked into the corner.

FONDUE: The Swiss specialty of fondue has gained popularity all over the world. Melted Gruyères cheese, white wine, garlic, and kirsch are brought hot to the table in a chafing dish and diners use long forks to dip squares of bread into the delectable mixture. Fondue Bourguignonne, chunks of meat skewered on forks, fried in oil, and seasoned at will, is also popular throughout the country.

FRITURE DE PERCHETTES: Nothing could be more superb than the tiny, mild fillet of fresh perch fried in oil found on most menus during the summer in the Lake Geneva area. Be sure to try this outstanding gourmet delight.

GESCHNETZLETS: Veal is very popular in Switzerland. Perhaps the most famous and delicious method of preparation is small pieces cooked in a white wine sauce with mushrooms. This is frequently called Veal Zürich on the menu.

HERO JAM: This divine jam comes in many delicious fruit and berry flavors and is traditionally served with little hard rolls that break into quarters.

LECKERLI: This is a spicy, cake-like, ginger-flavored cookie covered with a thin sugar icing. To be really good, the cookie must "snap" when broken.

RACLETTE: Raclette is a fun dish, a countryman's dinner and feast. A block of Bagnes cheese is split and melted over a fire. The softened cheese, scraped onto your plate, is most often served with potatoes and onions. Sometimes variations in the accompaniment are offered, such as the addition of mushrooms, tomatoes, ham, and sausage—almost as you would order variations of an omelet or quiche.

ROSCHTI or RÖSTI: These delicious fried potatoes are served throughout Switzerland, often accompanying sausages and roasts. The potatoes are diced and lightly browned in butter—frequently with the addition of diced onions.

WINES: To complement the meal, Switzerland produces some exceptional wines that are rarely exported—a definite loss to the rest of the world. Many of these wines are made from grapes grown in the Rhône Valley and have a light, slightly fruity taste and a tinge of effervescence. Be sure to take the opportunity to sample Swiss wines. If you want to economize, ask your waiter if he has an *offenen wein,* an "open" wine served either in a carafe or a bottle without a cork.

GEOGRAPHY

The unique geography of Switzerland lends itself to breathtaking beauty. In the northwestern section of Switzerland are the Jura Mountains, while 60% of the southeast of the country is dominated by the Alps. In between these two mountainous areas, the verdant lowlands sweep from Lake Geneva diagonally across the country to Lake Constance. You return home with the impression of precipitous Alpine peaks, deep mountain gorges, beautiful mountain valleys, glaciers gleaming in the sun, glorious blue lakes, spectacular waterfalls, gently flowing rivers, soft rolling hills, picturesque villages, toy-like churches, and quaint chalets. Every turn in the road offers postcard vistas for your scrapbook of memories.

Languages of Switzerland

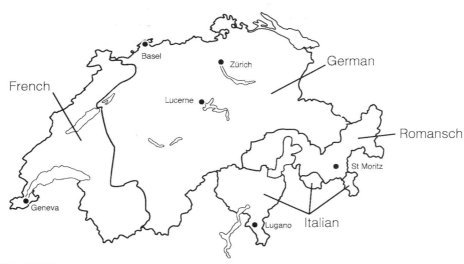

LANGUAGES

Switzerland is a country of four languages: German is spoken all over central and northern Switzerland; Italian is spoken in the south; French is spoken in the west; and Romansch is spoken by a small number of people in the southeast. English is usually spoken in the hotels and shops in tourist centers. In remote areas you might need to communicate using a dictionary and a smile.

If you enjoy diversity, in the course of a day you will find your skills challenged with multiple languages. Quite surprisingly, you can travel a distance of just a few kilometers, from one village to the next, and find yourself in a new region and encounter a complete change in language. If you are uncertain upon arrival in a given town as to whether to use your French or German skills, road and town signs are excellent clues.

RESTAURANTS

Switzerland boasts some of Europe's most outstanding restaurants. An exceptionally high degree of professionalism and excellence is maintained in even the simplest of restaurants, and the presentation and quality of food rival any in the world. Many restaurants in Switzerland serve food piping hot from a cart—a nicety usually encountered in only the most exclusive restaurants elsewhere. Then, when you have finished your entree, you are presented with a comparable second portion, brought to you on a clean warm plate with the same skillful delivery.

Many inns have two restaurants. Frequently there is a central entry hall with a somewhat formal restaurant on one side and a "pub-like" informal restaurant on the other. The latter is called the *stubli,* and if you are in the countryside, this is where the farmers gather in the late afternoon for a bit of farm gossip and perhaps a card game of *jass*. Locals gather after work in the *stubli* for relaxation, and in the evening families congregate for a glass of beer, wine, or a thimbleful of kirsch.

SHOPPING

Switzerland has a tempting array of products to entice even the reluctant buyer. Shopping in Switzerland is fun: the stores are pretty and the merchandise is usually of excellent quality.

Many larger towns have stores that feature an exceptional selection of art and handicraft items, referred to as *Heimatwerk*, from the surrounding region. (While in Zürich visit the *Schweizer Heimatwerk*, a marvelous store that features crafts from all regions—you will find it on the Limmat Quai just across from the train station.) In Switzerland the prices are usually set, so there is no bargaining, and tax is included.

Some shopping suggestions: watches, clocks, mechanical toys, wood carvings, hand-painted pottery, cow bells, Swiss army knives, chocolates, cheeses, kirsch, antiques, Saint Gallen lace, hand-embroidered items, fine cottons, children's clothing, and ski wear.

SPECIAL TID-BITS ABOUT COWS

It is almost impossible to visit Switzerland without being captivated by her cows—gentle, brown-eyed beauties grazing peacefully in lush pastures with their bells harmonizing as they munch the wildflowers. Sometime between the end of May and the third week in June, farmers with their families and neighbors (dressed for the festive occasion in colorful embroidered vests, knickers, blouses with puffy sleeves, and alpine hats) lead their cows up into the hills for the summer. The lush mountain pasture is called an "alp." If in your travels you spot a sign with a name such as Fafleralp, Grimmialp, Axalp, or Ebenalp, the road (which usually narrows to a path) probably goes to a mountain meadow.

Every region has its own special customs, but overall the scene is similar as the farmers (wearing traditional costumes) lead their cows (richly adorned with garlands of flowers) up into the hills. Frequently the lead cow proudly displays the most lavish bouquet and wears a large ceremonial bell. When grazing, each cow wears its own bell which has a unique ring. Amazingly, the farmer can quickly identify each cow by its melody. While in the high pasture, the farmers live quite simply. They milk their cows, boil the milk in huge cauldrons over an open fire, and produce wheels of cheese in the same way their families have done for many generations. Supposedly, the quality and flavor of these alp-cheeses can never be duplicated in the lower pastures. Although the work is arduous, families seem to look forward to their summers when they all work together in the mountains. When autumn approaches, the process is reversed as the cows, once again gaily adorned, are brought back down to the valley.

It is possible to visit an alp and see how cheeses are made. Local tourist offices can advise you of particular places where visitors are welcome—often for a fee. You need to walk to most of these, but a few are accessible by car. A convenient choice is the Fromagerie d'Alpage in Moléson-sur-Gruyères, located near Gruyères (for details, see our itinerary *Geneva to Zürich via Medieval Jewels*).

To supplement their income, a few farmers offer a program where you rent a cow for the summer. The enterprising Agenstein family in the Diemtigval (a pretty valley southwest of Lake Thun) goes all out to introduce you to the ultimate cow experience. For CHF 280 you can select your own cow, or if you prefer, one will be chosen for you. You receive a photo of your cow and at the end of the season a certificate. The cow is "yours" for the summer and you can visit it, milk it, work with the farmers for half a day, and enjoy a snack on the alp. If you are in Switzerland after the cows have been brought back down to the valley, you are invited to join the festivities when the most beautiful cow in the village is chosen, and if you like, to purchase some of your cow's cheese. (*www.rent-a-cow.ch*)

Introduction–About Switzerland

SPORTS

Sports are part of the lure of Switzerland. The mountains have been tempting climbers since the middle of the 1800s when Edward Whymper crossed the Channel from England to be the first to reach the top of the famous Matterhorn. Ski areas such as Zermatt, Saint Moritz, Davos, Wengen, Klosters, Villars, and Verbier are world-famous. Mountain lakes such as Lake Geneva, Lake Lucerne, and Lake Zürich are ideal for boating, fishing, and swimming. Marked walking trails beckon hikers from far and near and the skies of the mountain valleys are often colored with the canvas of hang gliders.

SWITZERLAND TOURISM

Switzerland Tourism, previously known as the Swiss National Tourist Office, is an excellent source of information. If you have any questions not answered in this guide, or need special information concerning a particular destination within Switzerland, they will be glad to assist you. Also, you can visit their web site: *www.myswitzerland.com.*

Switzerland Tourism, Head Office
P.O. Box 2077
CH-8027 Zürich, Switzerland
tel: (01) 288-11-11; fax: (01) 288-12-07

Switzerland Tourism, International
Worldwide toll-free number
tel: (011) 800-100-200-30
email: info.int@switzerland.com

Switzerland Tourism, USA
608 Fifth Avenue
New York, New York 10020-2303
tel: (877) 794-8037; fax: (212) 262-6116
email: info.usa@myswitzerland.com

Switzerland Tourism, Great Brittan
Swiss Center, 30 Bedford Street
London WC2E 9ED, England
tel: (020) 7420-4900; fax: (800) 1002-0031
email: info.uk.myswitzerland.com

TELEPHONES

CALLS TO SWITZERLAND: If you want to make a call to Switzerland from the United States, dial 011 (the international access code), 41, Switzerland's country code, then the city code (dropping the initial 0), and then the local telephone number.

CALLS WITHIN SWITZERLAND: There are many public telephone booths conveniently located throughout Switzerland. To use a public phone you need to purchase a Taxcard priced at CHF 5, 10, or 20 at a post office, rail station, newsstand, gas station, or hotel. Instructions for using the card are displayed in the phone booths. For calling a local number, omit the city code (the numbers in the parenthesis). For calling a long-distance number, dial the city code, complete with the 0, and the number.

CALLS FROM SWITZERLAND: Long-distance calls from Switzerland are expensive. Use your telephone credit card such as AT&T or Sprint to make calls to the United States. Before leaving home, find out the telephone number in Switzerland that connects you directly to the United States.

CELLPHONES: Cellphones are wonderful to have as some hotels do not have direct-dial phones in the guestrooms. Also, cellphones are enormously convenient when you are on the road and want to call for directions or advise of a changed arrival.

Cellphones can be rented through your car rental company and at the airport or train stations, or you can purchase an international phone once overseas. If you are considering taking your cellphone from home, be sure to check with your carrier to make sure that your phone even has international capability. Sometimes it is necessary to make arrangements in advance of your departure to activate a special service. We would also recommend getting international phone access numbers and inquiring about international access charges or rates so there are no billing surprises.

TRANSPORTATION

Although cars afford the flexibility to deviate on a whim and explore enticing side roads or beckoning hilltop villages, Switzerland's transportation network is so superb that you can travel conveniently by train, boat, or bus throughout the country—from the largest city to the smallest hamlet. So, if you were ever thinking of a vacation without a car, this is the place to try it. The ingenuity of the network is almost beyond belief: the schedules are so finely tuned that buses, trains, and boats all interconnect. Not only do the time schedules jibe perfectly, but usually you can walk from where the boat arrives to the train or bus station. It is like a puzzle, and great fun.

Should you be planning an extensive holiday using the Swiss public transportation system, there is an invaluable set of books called the Official Timetable, published once a year, which contains a wealth of information, outlining every timetable within Switzerland for boats, trains, and buses. There are other train guides published, but this official guide is the only one we found that shows access by public transportation to every town—no matter how tiny or how isolated. Unfortunately, you can no longer purchase the Official Timetable in the USA; however, it is available at train stations and kiosks in Switzerland. The Eurail Timetable Guide is available free of charge through Rail Europe—visit our website, *www.karenbrown.com*, and click on *Rail Europe.*

BOATS: Switzerland is a land of lakes and rivers and to travel the country by its waterways affords an entirely new and enchanting perspective. Often a river boat or lake steamer will depart from a dock just a few meters from a hotel, enabling you to journey from one destination to another or continue inland by connecting with either a train, bus, or hired car. Concerned with preserving their heritage, the Swiss have

refurbished a number of beautiful and graceful lake steamers and ferries so that you can not only see Switzerland by water, but also experience some nostalgia.

BUSES: Boasting more mileage than the Swiss railway itself, the postal bus lines originated after World War I with the primary purpose of transporting mail. In conjunction with the entire network of railway lines, every village in Switzerland is serviced by postal bus—providing Switzerland with one of the most exceptional transportation networks in the world. Depending on the demand, there are 4- to 5-person limousines, minibuses, or the ever familiar buttercup-yellow buses. In addition to the mail, the bus lines are responsible for transporting about 15 million passengers. Their dependability and excellence of service is impressive.

Postal Bus–Palm Express

Introduction–About Switzerland

In Switzerland, the position of postal bus driver is very prestigious. Those chosen for the job are unmatched in driving ability. In addition to excellent driving techniques, the drivers also play an important role in the community—usually they are well versed on the local news and social activities and familiar with the most recent wedding, gossip, or current business venture. Bus drivers must know every millimeter of the road, and their training is exacting and stringent. Thousands apply each year for positions available to just a few. To qualify, an applicant must be no older than 28, have completed his military duty, pass a rigorous physical exam, and be able to speak three languages. They undergo years of specialized training before taking position behind the wheel. Their first assignment is to drive a postal truck, then a bus in the lowlands, and as a finale they must negotiate a bus up a treacherous, narrow, mountain road, and then successfully complete a seemingly impossible U-turn, observed and judged by a busload of veteran bus drivers. Justifiably, those who achieve the position of postal driver have command of the roadways and other vehicles are expected to yield. It is not uncommon to see a postal busman assisting a petrified driver who has encountered difficulty on a pass or a narrow bend and who is too frightened to move. The sound of their horn, as the postal buses wind up the incredible mountain passes, warning other vehicles of their approach, may seem familiar. Indeed, it is a melody from Rossini's *William Tell Overture*.

TAXIS: Unless money doesn't matter, try when possible to avoid taxis while in Switzerland—they are very expensive. Frequently you can take a bus or tram from the train station almost to the door of your hotel. If you are on a tight budget, when you make your room reservation, ask the manager or owner if there is a direct bus or tram from the station to your hotel. If so, ask the number of the bus or tram, name of the place to get off, and how many stops it is from the station. If you have a map and luggage on wheels that you can pull, another alternative is to walk.

TRAINS: Switzerland has one of the most remarkable rail systems in the world, with more than 5,500 kilometers of track. Just over half are operated by the Swiss Federal Railway system while the others are privately owned. However, they are all integrated and connections are scheduled to synchronize both efficiently and conveniently. Their timetable is patterned after the perfection of the Swiss clock—trains depart on the scheduled second.

If you are flying into either Zürich or Geneva, you will find a beautifully geared network: from either of these airports you can board a train directly to many of the tourist destinations throughout Switzerland. The entire setup is wonderfully convenient for the traveler. As you exit the baggage claim area, there is a counter where you can check your luggage right through to your destination and climb aboard the train completely unencumbered. If you really want to spoil yourself, when the train arrives at your first night's stop, you can take a cab to your hotel, give the baggage claim ticket to the receptionist and ask him or her to send the porter to the station for your bags.

The train stations, often chalet-style buildings, are spotlessly clean, and quite frequently double as a residence for the station master. You often find evidence of domesticity— flowers cascading from the upstairs window boxes and laundry hanging on the line. Station masters are handsome in their uniforms and most speak some English.

Introduction–About Switzerland

Train Tips: It is very important to be able to quickly find "your" train as the schedules mesh like clockwork. Once you have the system down pat, you won't panic when you see that there are only a few minutes to get from one train to the other. You will know that this has been established as enough time to make the connection. In every station a large yellow poster with black print lists all the outgoing trains according to departure times. You need to study your own map because where you want to disembark might not appear on the sign—you might need to look at a major city beyond where you plan to get off. Along with the schedule, the yellow sign also states the number of the track from which each train

will depart. Large white signs with black print show the arrival times of trains. When you go to the departure track, there is a diagram showing the alignment of the cars so that you can stand at the proper spot for first- or second-class cars. This diagram is very important because on certain routes, trains split and different cars go to different cities.

If you plan to travel by train in Europe, you can research schedules and fares and even purchase tickets and passes online. (Note that many special fares and passes are available only if purchased outside Switzerland.) For information and the best possible fares, and to book tickets online, visit our website, *www.karenbrown.com.*

TRANSPORTATION PASSES

Public transportation is easy and economical to use. It is an absolute joy to be able to just climb aboard a train on a whim or to hop on one of the numerous boats that ply

Switzerland's many lakes. Even if you are traveling by car, you might well want to take some sightseeing excursions by train since they whisk you right to the center of the towns. From Zürich take a quick trip to Schaffhausen to see the Rheinfall, or an excursion to Winterthur to see the superb Oskar Reinhart museum.

There are train passes that can be purchased outside Switzerland through travel agents. All passes are priced for either first- or second-class travel. If you are not on a tight budget, you might want to go first class since these sections are less crowded and more comfortable. Swiss rail tickets and passes are available through Rail Europe, visit *www.karenbrown.com* for more information. The following are some of the available passes—one surely tailored with you in mind.

SWISS PASS: The Swiss Pass entitles you to unlimited trips on the entire network of the Swiss transportation system covering 14,500 kilometers of railroad, boat, and postal bus routes; as well as streetcars and buses in 36 Swiss cities—plus a 25% discount on excursions to most mountaintops. The pass is available for 4, 8, 15, 22 days or 1 month of consecutive travel.

SWISS FLEXI PASS: The Swiss Flexi Pass might be perfect for you if you are on a driving vacation. It has the same benefits as the Swiss Pass, but is more flexible. You can choose any three days of travel within a one-month period.

SWISS CARD: The Swiss Card, valid for one month, entitles you to a transfer from a Swiss airport or border point to any destination in Switzerland, and a second transfer from any destination in Switzerland to a Swiss airport or border point. It also allows unlimited trips on all other train, bus, and steamer services at half fare. (This card is not quite as convenient because you need to purchase a ticket before boarding your train, bus, boat, or tram.)

SWISS SAVERPASS: Offers a per person discount based on groups of 2 or more traveling together. The pass is available for 4, 8, 15, 22 days or 1 month of unlimited travel.

SWISS TRANSFER TICKET: Offers easy transfers from any Swiss airport to any destination and back.

TRIP CANCELLATION INSURANCE

Because unexpected medical or personal emergencies—or other situations beyond our control—sometimes result in the need to alter or cancel travel plans, we strongly recommend travel insurance. Prepaid travel expenses such as airline tickets, car rentals, and train fares are not always refundable and most hotels and bed & breakfasts will expect payment of some, if not all of your booking, even in an emergency. While the owners might be sympathetic, many of the properties in our guides have relatively few rooms, so it is difficult for them to absorb the cost of a cancellation. A link on our website (*www.karenbrown.com*) will connect you to a variety of insurance policies that can be purchased online.

WEATHER

For such a tiny nation, Switzerland offers an amazing variety of climates: the brisk mountain weather is quite different from the milder temperatures encountered near Lake Geneva or the balmy Swiss-Italian Lake District. Because of the sudden, unpredictable weather changes, it is highly recommended that you use the so-called "onion principle" in clothing. Wear layers of clothing, like T-shirts, sweaters, and jackets, which you can take off or put on at any given time to adjust to the weather conditions. Also be sure to pack good, comfortable walking shoes (lots of cobblestoned streets) and suntan lotion for summer and winter vacations.

Introduction–About Switzerland

The seasons in Switzerland are varied and all are lovely. Winter beckons the sports enthusiasts with excellent downhill ski slopes, beautifully marked cross-country trails, skating, and curling. Winter is also for those who simply love the charm of picture-book villages wrapped in blankets of snow. Spring is my favorite time of year. Weather in late spring can be absolutely glorious—the meadows are a symphony of color with a profusion of wildflowers, and the mountains still have their winter cap of snow. Summer is the most popular season. The days are usually mild and sunny and the mountain passes are open so you can explore all the isolated mountain villages. Autumn is lovely, with the first snowstorms leaving the mountains wearing new bonnets of pristine snow. The trees and vineyards are mellowing in shades of red and gold and the flowers are at their peak of bloom in every window box. There is a hint of winter in the air, except in the Swiss-Italian Lake District where the weather is usually still balmy.

About Itineraries

In the *Itineraries* section we feature four itineraries. Each of the first three itineraries links to the one that follows, enabling you to make a loop of the entire country. The fourth itinerary, *Swiss Train, Boat & Bus Adventures*, has twelve excursions that cover most of the country by public transportation.

Geneva to Zürich via Medieval Jewels takes a leisurely, scenic route between Geneva and Zürich. Along the way you will visit romantic medieval villages, explore wonderful walled towns, go over spectacular mountain passes, travel along tranquil valleys, visit fabulous castles and discover interesting museums.

Swiss Highlights—the Best of the Best is our recommendation if this is your first trip to Switzerland. This itinerary introduces you to many well-known destinations and gives a tantalizing taste of dazzling mountains, beautiful lakes, lovely rivers, splendid cities, and romantic villages. The itinerary begins in Zürich, goes to Interlaken and the Jungfrau region, includes Zermatt to see the famous Matterhorn, and ends by the Italian border, in the romantic Lake District.

Swiss Treasures off the Beaten Path features some of our favorite places in Switzerland. You might never have heard of all these treasures (such as Soglio, Guarda, and Tarasp) but if you delight in places a bit off the beaten path, you will love them. This itinerary starts in the Southern Lake District, goes north through the Engadine Valley, loops through scenic Appenzeller Land and ends in Zürich.

Swiss Train, Boat & Bus Adventures gives details for twelve itineraries where the transportation is by train, boat, or bus. The names alone are enticing: *Glacier Express*, *Bernina & Heidi Express*, *Golden Pass Line*, *William Tell Express*, *Palm Express*, *Napoleon Express*, *Mont Blanc & Saint Bernard Express*, *Voralpen Express*, *Swiss Chocolate Train*, *Romantic Route Express, and Rhône Express*. You can't help but find in this rich selection one or more that will enchant you. Perhaps you might want to visit a chocolate factory, go to a high mountain hospice to admire cuddly Saint Bernard dogs, take a ride a nostalgic paddle steamer, or go by bus on a backroad to Grindelwald. Certainly you can find a tour, or a combination of tours, that is perfect for you. If you have any doubts about driving, Switzerland is the finest country in the world for travel by public transportation.

With the exception of *Swiss Train, Boat & Bus Adventures*, these itineraries are designed to be traveled by car—there is no better way to explore the countryside, to really understand the depths and reaches of a valley, to fully comprehend the dimensions, magnificence, and power of lofty Alpine peaks, and to experience the beauty and grace of lakes and rivers.

Each itinerary is preceded by a map showing the route. These maps give you a preview of the route, but are not intended to replace detailed commercial maps. We recommend the Michelin overview map of Switzerland, Michelin Map 729 (1 cm = 4 km) and suggest you use highlight pens to outline your route. You can purchase Michelin Maps from our website, *www.karenbrown.com.*

In the front our guide we have a set of five colored-maps that indicate with a red dot the towns where we recommend hotels. All of these places to stay are described in the back of the book, listed alphabetically by town. These five maps also have a colored line for each itinerary. Our sixth map is an overview for the *Swiss Train, Boat & Bus Adventures* itinerary. This map does not indicate hotel locations, but shows a color-coded line for each of the twelve train, boat, and bus excursions.

Introduction–About Itineraries

About Hotels

Charm and old-world ambiance are used as the basis for the selection of hotels in this guide. Some of our recommendations are luxuriously elegant, while others are quite simple. Some are located in the center of cities, while others are tucked into remote mountain villages. Our hotels vary also in quality. Frankly, some are better than others because in a few instances we have chosen a hotel not on its merits alone, but so that you would have a place to stay in a region or village we considered so spectacular that it warranted an overnight stay. We have indicated what each hotel has to offer and have described the setting for your consideration. We believe that if you know what to expect, you will not be disappointed. Therefore, we have tried always to be candid and honest in our appraisals. The charm of a simple countryside chalet will beckon some while a sophisticated, luxurious city hotel will appeal to others. For a few lucky travelers, price is never a factor if the hotel is outstanding. For others, budget will guide their choice. Read each description carefully so that you can select the hotel that most suits you.

If you really want to "rough it" Switzerland offers a program called *Schlaf im Stroh, Aventure sur la Paille*, or Sleeping in the Hay. The name says it all. Hundreds of farmers throughout Switzerland open their barns in summer for overnight guests. For a minimal cost (about CHF 18 per person—which includes breakfast) you can stretch out in your own sleeping bag in a freshly prepared, pristine bed of straw. At the moment, we haven't featured any of these barn stays in our guide, but we'd love to get some feedback.

CREDIT CARDS

Whether or not an establishment accepts credit cards is indicated in the list of icons at the bottom of each description by the symbol [CREDIT]. We have also specified in the bottom details which cards are accepted as follows: AX–American Express, MC–MasterCard, VS–Visa, or simply, all major. Note: Even if an inn does not accept credit card payment, it will perhaps request your account number as a guarantee of arrival.

DATES OPEN

Under each hotel's description we have indicated when the hotel is open. Some hotels close the end of July until the middle of August—more commonly, many close during the spring and again in the fall. This is especially true in mountain resorts that are open for skiing in the winter then close for maintenance in the spring in anticipation of the influx of summer tourists. A word of caution: Even though many hotels quote a certain date to open or close, in reality it might fluctuate by a day or two, perhaps because of weather and occupancy. So it is always wise to contact the hotels if you are traveling footloose and without reservations to confirm that they are open before you head over that mountain pass on the assumption that you'll find a bed—particularly if your travels coincide with the beginning or end of a season.

DECOR

Regardless of the category of Swiss hotel, service and quality of cuisine are generally stressed over the importance of decor. The old-world charm is usually allocated to the public and dining areas, while the bedrooms are simple and modern, with light knotty-pine furniture. Rarely do you find an inn with antique decor in the bedrooms.

Often the most appealing room in the inn is the *stubli*, a cozy dining room where the local villagers congregate in the evening for a drink and conversation. As a general rule, the *stubli* oozes with the charm of mellow wood paneling, rustic carved chairs, and pretty country curtains.

DINING OPTIONS

Many of the inns featured in this guide have a restaurant (sometimes just for the use of guests) and offer the option of demi-pension, which means that breakfast and dinner are included in the price of the room. We recommend that you accept this meal plan whenever it is available. Naturally, the nightly rate is higher, but, almost without exception, it is a very good value. When making a reservation ask if you can have demi-pension and the price. (Remember that usually demi-pension is quoted per person, so be sure you understand whether the rate is for one or two persons.) Each hotel has its own policy: some will provide demi-pension only with a minimum of a three-night stay; others offer the option from the first night—especially if requested in advance.

The type of menu with demi-pension varies: most hotels offer a set menu each night, but a few (usually the more deluxe hotels) offer a choice for the entree. There is sometimes a separate dining room for house guests who are staying on the demi-pension plan. Usually you have the same table each night, which is an advantage as you can get to know your neighbors. Another advantage—if you don't finish your bottle of wine, it will be saved and appear at your table the next night. Note: There are a few hotels in our guide that offer *only* demi-pension and, in that case, we have indicated that under the hotel's description. Although most hotels quote demi-pension on a per-person basis, for consistency purposes, we quote the per night cost for two persons sharing a double room.

ICONS

Icons allow us to provide additional information about our recommended properties. We have introduced the following icons in this guide to supplement each property's description. For easy reference, an icon key can also be found on the inside back cover flap.

Services:

❋ Air conditioning

⊥ Beach nearby

▬ Breakfast included

🐾 Children welcome

♨ Cooking classes offered

▭ Credit cards accepted

⛰ Dinner upon request

☎ Direct-dial tel. in room

🐕 Dogs by special request

🛗 Elevator

🏋 Exercise room

@ Internet for guests

🍹 Mini-refrigerator

⊘ Some non-smoking rooms

P Parking (free or paid)

🍴 Restaurant

⚘ Spa (massage etc.)

🏊 Swimming pool

🎾 Tennis

📺 Television with English channels in guestrooms

💍 Wedding facilities

♿ Wheelchair friendly

W Wireless for guests

Activities:

🏌 Golf course nearby

🥾 Hiking trails nearby

🐎 Horseback riding nearby

⛷ Skiing nearby

🚣 Water sports nearby

🍷 Wineries nearby

FINDING HOTELS

To assist you in determining the general region in which a town where we recommend a hotel is located, one of the last lines of each hotel description refers to the town's canton (listed as "region"). At the beginning of this section, on page 3, you will find a map outlining Switzerland's cantons. In the front of this book are a series of color maps; a key map of Switzerland followed by five regional maps pinpointing each recommended hotel's location and lastly a map outlining the *Train, Boat & Bus Adventures* itinerary. The pertinent regional map number is given at the right on the top line of each hotel's description. The hotel's location with reference to neighboring, larger cities is indicated at the bottom of each hotel's description.

Introduction–About Hotels

HOTELIERS

From large hotels to small inns, the owners' dedication and personal involvement in the management of their hotels are astounding. No job ever seems too small or inconsequential to merit attention. It is not unusual to find hoteliers supervising both the hotel and the restaurant—more often than not, we would discover the owner in the kitchen, dusting flour off his apron before extending a welcoming handshake. Swiss hoteliers, many having studied in their country's own prestigious hotel and restaurant schools, take great pride in their profession, and ownership is often passed down within a family from one generation to the next.

MEMBERSHIP AFFILIATIONS

A number of the properties recommended in our guidebooks also belong to private membership organizations. These associations impose their own criteria for selection and membership standards and have established a reputation for the particular type of properties they include. Three affiliations that are very well recognized throughout Europe are Relais & Châteaux, Romantik Hotels and Swiss Historic Hotels. Swiss Historic Hotels is a fine organization that includes some of Switzerland's most treasured historic properties that provide a unique cultural experiences and top notch cuisine.

If a property that we recommend is also a member of the Relais & Châteaux, Romantik Hotels or the Swiss Historic Hotels group, we publish the reference at the bottom of the description page.

RATES

Rates, in Swiss francs (abbreviated to CHF), are those given to us for the 2009 season. Switzerland is not part of the European Union and therefore does not use the euro. We quote the range of rates for two people sharing a double room, including taxes and service charges. If breakfast is included you will see the ☕ symbol in the list of icons at the bottom of each description. We point out the few cases where you are also required to eat dinner or lunch in house (demi-pension). Please use the rates we give as a guideline and be certain to ask what the rate is when you make a reservation. Please visit our website (*www.karenbrown.com*) for an easy-to-use online currency converter.

RESERVATIONS

HOTEL RESERVATIONS & CANCELLATIONS: Whether or not you opt to secure reservations in advance depends on how flexible you want to be, how tight your schedule is, during which season you are traveling, and how disappointed you would be if your first choice is unavailable. Reservations are confining and usually must be guaranteed by a deposit. Refunds are difficult should you change your plans—especially at the last minute. Although reservations can be restrictive, it is nice not to spend a part of your vacation day searching for available accommodation, particularly during the peak summer months and holiday periods, and since many of the hotels in this guide are in remote areas it would be frustrating to arrive after hours of driving to find the only inn already full. Also, hotel space in the major cities is usually very scarce—even in the "off season" city hotels are frequently booked solid.

Should you decide to make reservations in advance, several options are discussed below. However, in each case, when making a reservation be sure to state clearly and exactly what you want, how many people are in your party, how many rooms you require, the category of room you prefer (standard, superior, deluxe), and your date of arrival and departure. Be sure to **spell out the month** since Europeans reverse the American numerical month/day order—to them 9/6 means June 9th, not September 6th as in the USA. Inquire about rates—which might have changed from those given in the book—and deposit requirements. It is also wise to advise them of your anticipated arrival time; discuss dining options if so desired; and ask for a confirmation letter with brochure and map to be sent to you.

The hotels appreciate your visit, value their inclusion in our guide, and frequently tell us they will take special care of our readers Many offer special rates to Karen Brown members (visit our website at *www.karenbrown.com.*) We hear over and over again from hotel owners that the people who use our guides are wonderful guests!

EMAIL: This is our preferred way of making a reservation. All properties featured on the Karen Brown website that also have email addresses have them listed on their web pages on our site (this information is constantly kept updated and correct). You can link directly to a property from its page on our website using its email hyperlink.

FAX: Faxing is a very quick way to reach a hotel. If the hotel has a fax, we have included the number in its listing. As you are communicating with a machine, you also don't have to concern yourself with the time of day or worry about disturbing someone's sleep.

LETTER: If you have ample time before your departure, a letter is an inexpensive, though less efficient, way to request hotel space. Allow four weeks for a reply.

TELEPHONE: A call to the hotel is a very satisfactory way to make a reservation. You can immediately find out if space is available and, if not, make an alternative choice. For each hotel we have given the telephone number, including the area code. From the United States you dial 011 (the international code), then 41 (Switzerland's country code), then the city code (dropping the initial zero), and then the local telephone number. (Note: The zero before the city code is dropped only if calling from the United States—it must be included when dialing within Europe.)

WEBSITE

Please visit the Karen Brown website (*www.karenbrown.com*) in conjunction with this book. It provides trip planning assistance, new discoveries, post-press updates, the opportunity to purchase goods and services that we recommend (rail tickets, car rental, travel insurance, etc.), and one-stop shopping for our guides, associated maps and prints. Most of our favorite places to stay are featured with color photos and direct website and email links. Also, we invite you to participate in the Karen Brown's Readers' Choice Awards. Be sure to visit our website and vote so your favorite properties will be honored.

WHEELCHAIR ACCESSIBILITY

If an inn has *at least* one guestroom that is accessible by wheelchair, it is noted with the symbol ♿. This is not the same as saying it meets full disability standards. In reality it can be anything from a basic ground-floor room to a fully equipped facility. Please discuss your requirements when you call your chosen place to stay to determine if they have accommodation that suits your needs and preference, be sure to ask for written confirmation.

Sightseeing Reference

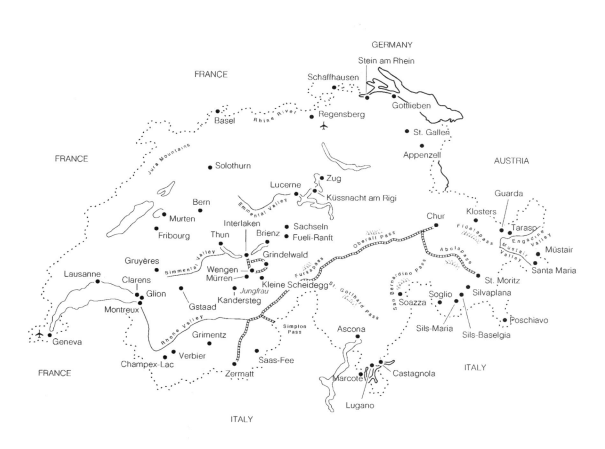

GERMANY

FRANCE

Stein am Rhein

Schaffhausen

Gottlieben

Basel

Rhine River

Regensberg

St. Gallen

FRANCE

Solothurn

Appenzell

AUSTRIA

Lucerne

Zug

Guarda

Bern

Emmental Valley

Küssnacht am Rigi

Klosters

Tarasp

Murten

Interlaken

Sachseln

Chur

Flüelapass

Fribourg

Thun

Brienz

Fueli-Ranft

Oberalp Pass

Engadine Valley

Müstair

Gruyères

Simmental Valley

Grindelwald

Furkapass

Abulapass

Mustair Valley

Santa Maria

Lausanne

Wengen

Kleine Scheidegg

St. Gotthard Pass

St. Moritz

Clarens

Mürren

San Bernardino Pass

Soglio

Silvaplana

Glion

Jungfrau

Soazza

Sils-Maria

Montreux

Gstaad

Kandersteg

Rhone Valley

Simplon Pass

Ascona

Sils-Baselgia

Poschiavo

Geneva

Grimentz

Verbier

Saas-Fee

ITALY

FRANCE

Champex-Lac

Zermatt

Marcote

Castagnola

Lugano

ITALY

Sightseeing Reference

Switzerland offers a rich selection of picturesque villages and enchanting cities—some well known, others not as famous but also treasures. Our itineraries feature as many outstanding places as we could squeeze into the routes. To help you choose which destinations you want to include on your holiday, we give below a quick preview of some of our favorites and indicate in which itinerary they are featured. For orientation, see the *Sightseeing Reference* map on the previous page.

APPENZELL

Appenzell, a charming village with colorfully painted buildings, is located in an idyllic region of rolling hills, lush pastures, picturesque farmhouses, and splendid mountains. The area is famous for its delicious cheeses and handicrafts—especially fine embroidery. Folk customs are prevalent and it is not unusual to see the women wearing traditional costumes. Itinerary: *Swiss Treasures off the Beaten Path.*

ASCONA

Ascona, nestled on the shore of Lake Maggiore, is located in the southern part of Switzerland in a canton called Ticino. With the Italian border so close, it is no wonder that Ascona reflects the romantic ambiance of Italy. This is a gem of a small town with colorfully painted houses, great food, boat rides on the lake, and mild weather. Itineraries: *Swiss Treasures off the Beaten Path; Swiss Train, Boat & Bus Adventures* (*William Tell Express* and *Lötschberg-Centovalli Express*).

BASEL

Because Basel is a major commercial center, it is sometimes forgotten as a tourist destination. However, it is a delightful city. Particularly charming is the old part of town with its many historic buildings, colorful squares, and excellent museums. Basel is located in the northwestern corner of Switzerland, bordered by France and Germany. Itinerary: *Geneva to Zürich via Medieval Jewels.*

BERN

Bern, a charming medieval city brimming with colorful buildings, whimsical fountains, and arcaded walkways, is justifiably a favorite tourist destination. Beautiful churches, fascinating museums, and excellent shopping make the city even more enticing. Itineraries: *Geneva to Zürich via Medieval Jewels*; *Swiss Train, Boat & Bus Adventures* (*Lötschberg-Centovalli Express*).

BRIENZ & BALLENBERG

Brienz is a beautiful village with a stunning setting at the eastern tip of Lake Brienz. Boats glide up to the dock, picking up passengers for fun excursions. In addition, there is a little red train, the Brienz Rothorn, which chugs up to the top of the mountain where the views are glorious. Ballenberg, an outstanding open air museum with typical houses brought from all over Switzerland, is nearby. Itineraries: *Swiss Highlights–The Best of the Best; Swiss Train, Boat & Bus Adventures* (*Golden Pass Line*).

CASTAGNOLA & GANDRIA

Castagnola and Gandria are two tiny villages on Lake Lugano, just a few kilometers east of the town of Lugano. Castagnola (only accessible by boat or on foot) is made up of a strip of small hotels and restaurants that line a trail that runs along the hillside above the water. Gandria, a colorful old fishing village snuggled on a steep hill above the lake, is linked by a scenic path to Castagnola. Itineraries: *Swiss Treasures off the Beaten Path; Swiss Train, Boat & Bus Adventures* (*Bernina Express, William Tell Express* and *Lötschberg-Centovalli Express*).

CHUR

Dating back to medieval times, Chur is the largest city in eastern Switzerland. Because it is a major rail terminal, linked by expressways to Zürich and Lucerne, many people start their sightseeing excursions from here. Cobbled streets with historic houses and colorful squares add an old world ambiance. Itinerary: *Swiss Train, Boat & Bus Adventures* (*Glacier Express & Bernina Express*).

CLARENS

Clarens is a pretty lakefront suburb just north of Montreux. A romantic promenade, enhanced by gardens, stretches along the edge of the lake. Many of the homes (some of which have been converted into small hotels and restaurants) are very attractive. The views across the lake are spectacular. Itinerary: *Geneva to Zürich via Medieval Jewels.*

FLÜELI-RANFT

Although you might never have heard of Flüeli-Ranft, the tiny village is very well known to devout Catholics, many of whom come on pilgrimage to pay homage to Saint Nicholas of Flüe, who was born here and spent many years in a hermitage nearby. Even if you are not drawn to Flüeli-Ranft for its religious significance, the town is well worth a visit for its stunning scenery. If you want to spend the night, the large, Victorian-style, Hotel Paxmontana captures magnificent views in every direction. Itinerary: *Swiss Highlights– The Best of the Best.*

FRIBOURG

Fribourg is a charming city that makes a convenient stop en route between Montreux and Bern. The Sarine River forms a loop around the town, adding to its romantic appeal. The newer part of Fribourg (which isn't that "new" since it has many outstanding historic buildings) sits high on a bluff overlooking the river. The ancient part of the city, which is exceptionally attractive with its colorful squares and cobbled streets, sits below the bluff, hugging the banks of the Sarine. Itinerary: *Geneva to Zürich via Medieval Jewels.*

GENEVA

Geneva is one of Switzerland's most elegant cities with pretty parks, fine museums, splendid gardens, gorgeous views, and a superb lakeside setting. The Rhône River splits the town in two—the section to the north of the river is newer, the section to the south of the river is the historic heart of the city. Geneva offers excellent shopping and many things to see and do. Not to be missed is a romantic boat ride on the lake. Itineraries: *Geneva to Zürich via Medieval Jewels; Swiss Train, Boat & Bus Adventures* (*Golden Pass Line* and *Rhône Express*).

GLION

There is no finer spot to enjoy breathtaking views of Lake Geneva than the small town of Glion, which is perched in the hills above Montreux. You can drive up to the village or take a tram from Territet (located just south of Montreux). Combine a trip up the hill with lunch at the Hotel Victoria. Itinerary: *Geneva to Zürich via Medieval Jewels.*

GOTTLIEBEN

Gottlieben is a small, picturesque village hugging the water's edge on the Unter See, a small lake linked to Lake Constance by a canal. The town is as an excellent base from which to explore the region by water rather than by road. From Gottlieben you can take ferryboats to Stein am Rhein and Schaffhausen or you can travel by boat to Lake Constance. Closest itinerary: *Swiss Treasures off the Beaten Path.*

GRIMENTZ

For a picturesque, off the beaten path destination, nothing can surpass Grimentz, which is located at the end of a box canyon accessed via the d'Annivieres Valley. With its cluster of weathered, age-darkened farmhouses clinging to the edge of the mountain, Grimentz seems lost in time. Itinerary: *Swiss Highlights–The Best of the Best.*

GRINDELWALD

If you want to drive as close as possible to start the Jungfrau excursion, Grindelwald is the place to go. Perched on a mountain ledge high above the Lauterbrunnen Valley, the town bustles with activity. Many come to hike and enjoy the glorious mountain scenery, but the trip to the Jungfraujoch is the one excursion that no one wants to miss. Itineraries: *Swiss Highlights–The Best of the Best; Swiss Train, Boat & Bus Adventures* (*Golden Pass Line* and *Romantic Express*).

GRUYÈRES

Located just a short drive north of Lake Geneva, the enchanting medieval village of Gruyères is easily accessible by either train or car. Its setting, cresting the top of a small hill, is something out of a fairy tale and the surrounding mountains and lush rolling hills add to the picture-perfect scene. Although a very popular tourist destination, most people come just for the day, so plan to spend the night and enjoy the tranquil beauty of the village after the last busload of tourists rolls down the hill. There are many interesting towns and beautiful places to visit nearby, making Gruyères an excellent hub for sightseeing. Itineraries: *Geneva to Zürich via Medieval Jewels; Swiss Train, Boat & Bus Adventures* (*Chocolate Train*).

GSTAAD

The village of Gstaad, which exudes a charming country ambiance, is not only one of Switzerland's most attractive ski towns, but is equally enchanting as a summer resort for hiking and mountain climbing. Gstaad is centrally located and easily accessible by car or train. Itineraries: *Geneva to Zürich via Medieval Jewels; Swiss Train, Boat & Bus Adventures* (*Golden Pass Line*).

GUARDA

The Lower Engadine Valley is glorious and features many picturesque towns. One of the most stunning of these is Guarda, which enjoys a breathtaking perch high on a mountain shelf. The main recreation here is simply being out of doors exploring the beckoning mountain paths and soaking up the sensational beauty of the nearby mountain peaks. Itinerary: *Swiss Treasures off the Beaten Path.*

INTERLAKEN

Interlaken, which sits on a thread of land that separates Lake Brienz and Lake Thun, has been a popular tourist destination since the 19th century. The views of the mountains are sensational, plus the town offers shopping and romantic excursions on the lake. Interlaken is also popular as a starting point for the Jungfraujoch excursion. Itineraries: *Swiss Highlights–The Best of the Best; Swiss Train, Boat & Bus Adventures (Golden Pass Line).*

JUNGFRAUJOCH EXCURSION

The Jungfraujoch excursion is one of the highlights of Switzerland. This is a trip that combines a series of trains that climb ever higher up into the mountains, with its final leg tunneling through a glacier to the Jungfraujoch, Europe's highest train station. On clear days the views are amazing. You can begin the trip in Interlaken, or in one of the towns en route, such as Lauterbrunnen, Grindelwald, or Wengen. Itineraries: *Swiss Highlights–The Best of the Best; Swiss Train, Boat & Bus Adventures (Golden Pass Line).*

KANDERSTEG

If you want to take a short cut from the Simmental Valley to the Rhône Valley, there is a train tunnel, which begins in Kandersteg and cuts through the mountains. Even if you are driving, you can take advantage of this route since the train also carries automobiles. However, Kandersteg offers far more than just its strategic location. It is a lovely small town set in a meadow wrapped by majestic mountains. Itineraries: *Swiss Highlights–The Best of the Best; Swiss Train, Boat & Bus Adventures* (*Lötschberg-Centovalli Express*).

KLEINE SCHEIDEGG

Kleine Scheidegg is a cluster of buildings set in a barren, windswept plateau where you board the train for the last lap of your Jungfraujoch excursion. From Kleine Scheidegg a train tunnels through a glacier, popping out on the other side at the highest train station in Europe. Itineraries: *Swiss Highlights–The Best of the Best; Swiss Train, Boat & Bus Adventures.*

KLOSTERS

The architecture in some of Switzerland's famous ski areas is quite modern with high rise buildings replacing the original chalets. Happily, this is not the case with Klosters, where the buildings (both new and old) reflect charming, old world flair. Popular both in winter and summer, Klosters, which is set in a beautiful valley embraced by mountains, has chic boutiques, upscale hotels, and wonderful restaurants. Itinerary: *Swiss Treasures off the Beaten Path.*

KÜSSNACHT AM RIGI

Küssnacht am Rigi, located on the north bank of Lake Lucerne, is an especially pretty village and makes a great place to stop for lunch when you take a boat ride from Lucerne. The ferry pulls up right in front of the Hotel du Lac Seehof where you dine on a tree-shaded terrace overlooking the lake. After lunch, you can wander through the village, which has some colorful historic buildings. Itinerary: *Swiss Highlights–The Best of the Best.*

LAUSANNE

Lausanne is one of the most popular towns that dot the northern shore of Lake Geneva. The oldest part of the city, with its fabulous churches and many historic moments, lies on a crest of a hill, quite a hike up from the waterfront. Most tourists stay along the lake in an area called Ouchy, which used to be a small fishing village but now has grand hotels, lovely parks, a large marina, and a delightful lakeside promenade. Itinerary: *Geneva to Zürich via Medieval Jewels.*

LUCERNE

Lucerne, which in spite of its size has the enchanting ambiance of a small town, is one of our favorite places in Switzerland. Its location, snuggled on the banks of Lake Lucerne, is stunning. The River Reuss cuts through the center of town, crisscrossed by a series of intriguing bridges. The historic heart of the city is like an outdoor museum with quaint squares, painted buildings, and a maze of cobbled streets. Ferries (including nostalgic old paddle steamers) are docked at the waterfront, waiting to take you on excursions to enjoy one of Switzerland's most beautiful lakes. Itineraries: *Swiss Highlights–The Best of the Best; Swiss Train, Boat & Bus Adventures* (*Golden Pass Line, William Tell Express* and *Voralpen Express*).

LUGANO

Lugano is an enchanting village on the shore of Lake Lugano. The weather here is milder than in the rest of the country and the flavor is delightfully Italian. Pastel-hued houses line the square that is fronted by a lakeside promenade. The scene is so romantic that it could be the stage set for an opera. Boats glide in and out from the dock, offering enticing possibilities for exploring. Itineraries: *Swiss Treasures off the Beaten Path; Swiss Train, Boat & Bus Adventures* (*William Tell Express* and *Palm Express*).

MONTREUX & THE CASTLE OF CHILLON

Montreux is a sophisticated city at the eastern end of Lake Geneva. Its setting is superb and its view across the lake to snowcapped mountains memorable. There are many grand hotels in town plus a casino. One of Montreux's sightseeing highlights is a visit to the Castle of Chillon, which is tucked on a tiny island just 3 kilometers south of town. This romantic castle (attached to the mainland by a bridge) is open as a museum and certainly should be on your list of places to see. Itineraries: *Geneva to Zürich via Medieval Jewels; Swiss Train, Boat & Bus Adventures* (*Chocolate Train* and *Rhône Express*).

MORCOTE

Morcote, a tiny lakeside village south of Lugano, is a photographer's dream with its colorful, arcaded houses clinging to a wooded hillside that rises abruptly from the water. Morcote is a great destination, either for spending the night, or as a place to come for lunch at one of the charming restaurants perched over the lake. Itineraries: *Swiss Treasures off the Beaten Path; Swiss Train, Boat & Bus Adventures* (*Palm Express*, *Napoleon Express* and *Lötschberg-Centovalli Express*).

MÜRREN

Mürren, tucked high on a mountain ledge overlooking the Lauterbrunnen Valley, is so precipitously perched that its only access is by cable car. The views from here are incredible and the hiking superb. Mürren has no direct access to the Jungfraujoch, but offers its own adventure—a trip by a series of cable cars that climb further up the mountain, ending the Schilthorn, where a revolving restaurant makes a great luncheon stop. Itinerary: *Swiss Highlights–The Best of the Best.*

MURTEN

Murten is a picture-perfect walled village that snuggles next to Lake Murten. As you enter through the gate, you step back into medieval times. Colorful 15th-century buildings, small squares, cobbled streets, clock towers, and ramparts add to its fairy tale charm. Boat rides around the lake are available from the dock at the foot of town. Itinerary: *Geneva to Zürich via Medieval Jewels.*

MÜSTAIR

Müstair is a small village that lies at the eastern end of the Müstair Valley, just before the road runs into Italy. This is a very historic town with some of its buildings dating back to the 12th century. There is little in the way of commercialism to spoil the old world charm of the town. Itinerary: *Swiss Treasures off the Beaten Path.*

POSCHIAVO

In the southeastern corner of Switzerland, the Bernina Pass goes over the mountains and drops down into the beautiful Poschiavo Valley. The only significant town along the way is Poschiavo, which is a gem. This medieval town, unspoiled by time, has many historic buildings, fine churches, and beautiful old mansions. The border with Italy is just a few kilometers to the south, which undoubtedly gives the town its romantic Italian flavor. Itineraries: *Swiss Treasures off the Beaten Path; Swiss Train, Boat & Bus Adventures (Bernina Express).*

REGENSBERG

If romantic walled villages enchant you, there is none finer in all of Switzerland than Regensberg. Surprisingly few tourists have discovered this jewel—perhaps because it's so tiny. The hamlet (which is about a 20-minute drive north of Zürich) crowns the top of a small hill that is adorned with vineyards. There is a wonderful small inn here, the Rote Rose. Itinerary: *Geneva to Zürich via Medieval Jewels.*

SAAS FEE

From Visp a road leads south from the Rhône Valley, heading directly to the mountains. After a short distance, the road splits: the right branch going to Zermatt, the left branch going to Saas Fee. While not as quaint a village as Zermatt, Saas Fee has a marvelous location on the side of the mountain with stunning views over the Saas Valley. Skiing in winter and hiking in summer are what attracts the many tourists who come here on holiday. Itineraries: *Swiss Highlights–The Best of the Best; Swiss Train, Boat & Bus Adventures* (*Napoleon Express*).

SACHSELN

Sachseln, a small town on the main road between Lucerne and Interlaken, is famous for its church where the beloved Saint Nicholas of Flüe is buried. The town has a pretty setting near Lake Sarner. Itinerary: *Swiss Highlights–The Best of the Best.*

SAINT GALLEN

Saint Gallen, a moderate-sized city that lies in the northeastern part of Switzerland, has an attractive medieval section. However, its main claim to fame is its stunning Cathedral and Benedictine Abbey which houses an awesome Baroque library, one of the finest in Europe. Itineraries: *Swiss Treasures off the Beaten Path; Swiss Train, Boat & Bus Adventures* (*Voralpen Express*).

SAINT MORITZ

Everyone has heard of Saint Moritz, a chic resort catering to skiers from around the world. The town also shines in the summer when tourists come to enjoy the lake, hike in the beautiful surrounding mountains, shop in fancy boutiques and dine in great restaurants. Itineraries: *Swiss Treasures off the Beaten Path; Swiss Train, Boat & Bus Adventures* (*Glacier Express* and *Palm Express*).

SANTA MARIA

As you travel through the Müstair Valley, which is located in the eastern part of the country, one of the most picturesque places along the route is the village of Santa Maria. What make the town special are its lovely old Grisons-style buildings. Itinerary: *Swiss Treasures off the Beaten Path.*

SCHAFFHAUSEN & THE RHEINFALL

Schaffhausen is a colorful, medieval town that gained importance due to its strategic location on the Rhine River, just a few kilometers above the mighty Rheinfall (Europe's largest waterfall). A dramatic castle looms on the hill above the town, adding to its charm. From the dock in the center of town, you can board a boat to take you to the charming town of Stein am Rhein. Itinerary: *Geneva to Zürich via Medieval Jewels.*

SILS-BASELGIA, SILS-MARIA

Located about 10 kilometers south of Saint Moritz, Sils-Baselgia and Sils-Maria blend into each other via interconnecting streets. The pretty villages have a supreme setting on a thread of land that runs between Lake Silvaplaner and Lake Silser, two beautiful lakes that are embraced by majestic mountains. Itinerary: *Swiss Treasures off the Beaten Path.*

SOAZZA

Soazza, a tiny hamlet with only about 300 inhabitants, is perched on a sunny terrace overlooking the gentle, verdant Mesocco Valley, which leads north from Bellinzona to the San Bernardino Pass, a route that has possibly been used since prehistoric times. This picture-perfect village is enhanced by a lovely 13th-century church perched atop a knoll overlooking the town. Handsome stone houses, which appear untouched by time, line the narrow, cobbled streets. Closest Itinerary: *Swiss Treasures off the Beaten Path.*

SOGLIO

We fell in love with Soglio from our first glimpse of this unbelievably picturesque town, perched on a mountain ledge high above the splendid Bregaglia Valley. Although located a bit off the beaten path, this jewel is well worthy of a detour, particularly if you are captivated by ancient villages untainted by any hint of commercialism. Not only is the town charming, but its views are amazing. Itinerary: *Swiss Treasures off the Beaten Path.*

SOLOTHURN

Solothurn is one of Switzerland's most beautifully-preserved towns. Its walls are still intact and enclose a charming historic center that turns back the clock to medieval times with a maze of cobbled streets, picturesque houses, stunning clock towers, lovely churches, and painted fountains. Itinerary: *Geneva to Zürich via Medieval Jewels.*

STEIN AM RHEIN

Stein am Rhein is a jewel—one of Switzerland's most picturesque towns. Snuggled next to the Rhine River, the village oozes old world charm with its quaint cobbled streets, houses adorned with fanciful paintings, pretty churches, and quaint fountains. Adding to the fun, boats pull up at the dock where you can hop aboard for an excursion on the river. Itinerary: *Geneva to Zürich via Medieval Jewels.*

TARASP

Located in the Lower Engadine Valley, Tarasp is a jewel that enjoys one of the most beautiful settings in Switzerland. The village is snuggled in a gorgeous meadow that sweeps out to majestic mountains. A pretty lake and a picturesque castle add to the perfection of the scene. Itinerary: *Swiss Treasures off the Beaten Path.*

WENGEN

Wengen is an enticing village hugging the mountainside above the Lauterbrunnen Valley. Part of its charm is that no road leads up to it—the only access is by train. Because of its high perch, the views out over the valley and beyond to backdrop of towering mountains, are unforgettable. On a clear day, there is no vista anywhere in the world more gorgeous. Walking trails lead off in every direction, but the most exciting excursion is to board the small train that climbs even further up the mountain to make connections to the Jungfraujoch. Itineraries: *Swiss Highlights–The Best of the Best; Swiss Train, Boat & Bus Adventures.*

ZERMATT

Everyone has heard of Zermatt, which first gained fame in the 1800s when the British adventurer, Edward Whymper, came here and climbed the Matterhorn. At that time, Zermatt was just a sleepy village of blackened-with-age, wooden farmhouses. Some of these rustic farmhouses can still be seen, but today most have been converted to boutiques, souvenir shops, restaurants, and hotels. Hiking in the glorious mountains is still a treat and the Matterhorn is as magnificent as ever. Zermatt is a pedestrian-only town, which further heightens its appeal. Itineraries: *Swiss Highlights–The Best of the Best; Swiss Train, Boat & Bus Adventures* (*Glacier Express* and *Rhône Express*).

ZUG

Zug, one of Switzerland's oldest towns, makes an interesting stop as you travel between Zürich and Lucerne. Bypass the new part of the city and head directly to the lake where you will find its historic center, snuggled next to the waterfront. From the lake, a maze of cobbled streets, colorful houses, and quaint squares stretch back to its ancient walls. It won't take you long to explore this section since it is like a tiny town within a modern city. Itinerary: *Swiss Highlights–The Best of the Best.*

ZÜRICH

Zürich, which is a main hub for airlines and trains, is frequently the first destination for tourists when they arrive in Switzerland. Happily, no one is disappointed because the city is very beautiful and has excellent museums, fabulous shopping, enchanting boat excursions, and a delightful medieval section. Zürich's setting is extraordinary—the Limmat River intersects its historic center and romantic Lake Zürich stretches along the lower part of town. Itineraries: *Swiss Highlights–The Best of the Best; Swiss Train, Boat & Bus Adventures* (*Golden Pass Line* and *William Tell Express*).

Sightseeing Reference

Geneva to Zürich
via Medieval Jewels

FRANCE

GERMANY

Schaffhausen

Rheinfall

Stein am Rhein

Basel

Rheinau

Regensberg

St. Gallen

Zürich

FRANCE

AUSTRIA

Biel

Solothurn

Neuchâtel

Lucerne

Chur

Bern

Murten

Sachseln

Fribourg

Thun

Brienz

Broc

Gruyères

Spiez

Interlaken

Lausanne

Molèson

Gstaad

St. Moritz

Montreux

Gsteig

Soazza

Aigle

Villars

Brig

Geneva

Locarno

ITALY

Martigny

FRANCE

Zermatt

Lugano

ITALY

● Sightseeing/Orientation

—— Itinerary Route

- - - Suggested Side Trip

51

Geneva to Zürich via Medieval Jewels

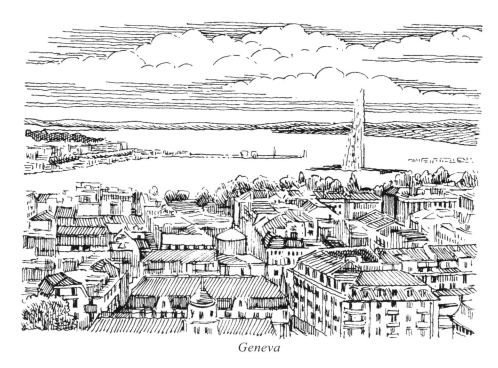

Geneva

Switzerland has some of the most enchanting, remarkably well-preserved, medieval villages and cities in all of Europe, whose character and charm suggest a style of life that slipped by many centuries ago. In these towns you find ramparts enclosing a maze of cobbled streets, enticing buildings, painted fountains, intricate clock towers, turrets, and a wealth of history. Sometimes capping the crest of a hill, perched precariously on a valley's ledge, or snuggled next to a river, these walled villages and cities captivate the imagination and are fascinating to explore.

This itinerary wanders from Geneva to Zürich (or if you prefer, instead of Zürich as your destination, you can choose Lucerne, which is just a short drive beyond). It is possible to zip between the cities in just a few hours via the fast freeway system, but if you have the luxury of time, this leisurely route introduces you to places you might not otherwise see—leading you through glorious countryside, over breathtaking passes, and to romantic medieval towns.

RECOMMENDED PACING: We recommend a minimum of six nights for this itinerary. This does not include the nights you choose to spend in Zürich.

THREE NIGHTS in Geneva: You need three nights in Geneva in order to have two full days to visit its museums, stroll through the cobbled streets of its delightful old town, and—not to be missed—enjoy a boat ride on the lake.

TWO NIGHTS in Gruyères: One day is needed en route to the walled town of Gruyères. If you were to drive directly there, the travel time would be very short, but instead we suggest you make a large loop—visiting along the way a couple of superb castles, enjoying some cute villages, and winding your way over several splendid mountain passes. Then you will need two nights in Gruyères to give you one full day to savor the charm of this adorable village, visit cheese factories, and tour a chocolate factory.

ONE NIGHT between Gruyères and Zürich: We suggest that you choose one more stopover en route to Zürich, such as Fribourg, Murten, Bern, Solothurn, Basel, Schaffhausen, or Stein am Rhein. As you read on, choose a place that most appeals to you.

ITINERARY ENDS in Zürich. If you are planning to extend your trip, the following itinerary, *Swiss Highlights, the Best of the Best*, dovetails seamlessly with this one.

NOTE: This itinerary includes so many sightseeing suggestions along the way and we are aware you won't have time to include them all. We describe our favorites so that you may choose those that seem most appealing to you.

GENEVA

You will be captivated by Geneva with its sophisticated beauty and international air. As you meander through the parks and promenades, you could be anywhere in the world—you see all nationalities and hear all languages.

Geneva is frequently thought of primarily as a modern city—an international center for banking and commerce with splendid hotels, fine restaurants, a wealth of museums, and superb shopping. All this is true, but Geneva also has one of the most attractive medieval sections in Switzerland.

OLD GENEVA: The old part of Geneva is located on the south side of the Rhône River. Here the hills rise steeply from the shore of the lake and the streets twist and turn in a maze of fascinating little boutiques, hidden courtyards, fountains, flower-filled squares, and picturesque buildings. The heart of the old town is called *Place du Bourg-de-Four*, which was the marketplace in the Middle Ages. The plaza, graced by a fountain and many colorful 16th-century buildings, is especially charming. Many of the most famous buildings in Geneva face the plaza, including the Palais de Justice (a 17th-century building which was the court of law), the Hotel de Ville (an 18th-century building with a Renaissance façade that was originally the city hall), and the Ancien Arsenal (the place where weapons were stored in the 18th century).

NEW GENEVA: On the north side of the Rhône, circling around the lake is the newer part of Geneva. In this area there are peaceful lake promenades punctuated with splendid flower gardens, stately hotels, small squares, and elegant shops. In the spring Geneva becomes a small Holland with glorious tulips blooming in every little park. Like the medieval section of the city, the newer part is also perfect for strolling. Within walking distance are many museums and interesting places to see.

TOURIST OFFICE: When you arrive in Geneva, make a beeline to the tourist office to pick up some city maps and ferry schedules, and find out what events are scheduled during the time of your visit. Geneva abounds with cultural possibilities such as concerts, theater and opera. In addition, many of the museums feature special exhibits that might appeal to you. Note: Be aware that most of the museums close Monday.

SIGHTSEEING HIGHLIGHTS IN GENEVA

Walking Tour: One of the best ways to get the "feel" of a city is on foot, but often you miss something along the way without a guide. The Geneva Tourist Office offers a two-hour walking tour of the old part of the city with a guide who will lead you back through history as you discover hidden courtyards, fountains and picturesque squares, plus a glimpse into the Cathedral and the Town Hall. You can return later on your own to revisit in depth some of the places that most appeal to you. The tour departs at 10 am every day except Sunday, from June to September. The departure point is the Geneva Tourist Office. If you have a group of five (which often is possible if traveling with friends or family), the tourist office can put together a special tour, tailor made just for you.

Audio Self-Guided Tour: In addition to its guided walking tour, the Geneva Tourist Office offers a self-guided audio tour that covers 24 points of interest and takes approximately 2½ hours. On this tour you receive a portable cassette recorder, headset, and a map showing the locations of places described. The rental period for the headset is a maximum of four hours.

Saint Peter's Cathedral: The medieval part of Geneva is crowned by the 12th-century Saint Peter's Cathedral, which dominates the old town. Within the church you find a triangular chair supposedly used by Jean Calvin when he preached at the cathedral and the tomb of the Duc de Rohn who was the leader of the French Protestants during the time of Henry IV. Perhaps the most spectacular feature of Saint Peter's is the climb to the top of the north tower (there is a small fee for this) where you have a panoramic view of Geneva and beyond to the lake and the majestic backdrop of the Alps. After visiting the church, wander down the little twisting streets, exploring small antique shops and back alleys—you cannot get lost because it is all downhill and when you are at the bottom, you are at the lake.

Palais des Nations: The Palais des Nations is one of the largest conference centers in the world. It was built in 1936 as home to the League of Nations, which at the time was optimistically the World's hope for world peace. It is now the seat of the European branch of the United Nations. The palace is set in a park called *Parc des Nations*, which is enhanced by sculptures. (Open daily April through October. Closed Saturday & Sunday November through March. Guided one-hour tours—available in 15 languages).

Petit Palais Museum: The Petit Palais Museum, housed in a beautiful 19th-century palace, features French painters from the end of the Impressionist period. Included are works by such renowned artists as Monet, Picasso, Renoir, Chagall, and Cézanne. (Open daily except Monday mornings and holidays.)

Museum of Old Musical Instruments: The Museum of Old Musical Instruments displays a fascinating collection of European musical instruments.

Patak Philippe Museum: Since you are in Switzerland, home to the finest clockmakers in the world, it is fascinating to visit the Philippe Museum, which displays a fabulous collection of timepieces that span 500 years of clockmaking. Not only Swiss clocks are featured, but also those from all over Europe.

Jardin Anglais: The Jardin Anglais (English Garden) snuggles on the edge of the quay, at the foot of the old town. Highlighting the lovely gardens is an intriguing clock that keeps perfect time. Made of 6,500 plants, which are changed according to season, the clock is placed in the garden to honor the clockmakers of Switzerland.

Maison Tavel: The oldest house in Geneva is the Maison Tavel. It was built in the early 1300s by the Tavel family whose coat of arms still graces the Gothic turret.

Musée du Vieux Genève: the Musée du Vieux Genève (Museum of Old Geneva) is housed in the Maison Travel. It features exhibits showing the daily life in early Geneva, including 12 rooms furnished as they would have been in the 17th century. On the top floor is an interesting model showing how Geneva looked in days of yore, before the walls were torn down.

Jet d'Eau: when exploring Geneva you cannot miss the Jet d'Eau (located on the south bank of the lake), which is a huge spout of water that soars into the sky. Originally it had a utilitarian purpose—a practical way to release the extreme water pressure. However, everyone was captivated by the plume of water, so it was decided to turn it into a permanent fixture of Geneva. Today floodlights accent the fountain at night, enabling it to be seen from afar.

Musée International de la Croix Rouge: The Red Cross (an international organization whose mission is to alleviate suffering throughout the world) was started by a Geneva banker, Henri Dunant, in 1863. The Musée International de la Croix-Rouge, a modern concrete and glass building, was built to honor the great works accomplished by the organization.

Musée d'Art et d'Histoire: The stunning Musée d'Art et d'Histoire (Museum of Art and History) houses an awesome collection of art—including fine paintings, sculptures, paintings, and archaeological treasures that date back thousands of years. While in the museum, don't miss the Palace Salon, an impressive room that has been furnished in the elaborate style of the early 19th century.

Boat Trips: Lake Geneva (Lac Léman) has many quaint towns hugging its shoreline. You can drive to all of them, but one of the most romantic ways to visit is one of the sixteen boats that ply the lake. When you arrive in Geneva, go down to the pier and check the ferry schedules. It is a bit like a puzzle to plan your route so that you have the fun of hopping off and on at charming, small villages. It is especially challenging (and fun) to choose a picturesque village for lunch, and then check out when the appropriate boat will arrive to take you back to Geneva. If you miss the returning boat, there are buses and/or trains back to Geneva. There are also many boat excursions available in the summer season where everything is prearranged for you, such as the following examples.

Cruise along Geneva's Shores: a 55-minute cruise along the shores of Geneva, leaving from the Quay du Mont-Blanc or the Jardin Anglais.

Cruise of the Lower Lake: a 3½-hour cruise going to Nyon and Yvoire, leaving from the Quay des Eaux-Vives.

Tour of the Lake: an all-day tour of the lake, leaving from the Quay du Mont Blanc.

Lunch Cruise: a 1½-hour lunch cruise, leaving at 12:20 pm from the Jardin Anglais.

Evening Cruise: a 3½-hour cruise, leaving at 6:35pm from the Jardin Anglais.

SIGHTSEEING HIGHLIGHTS NEARBY GENEVA

Lake Geneva is in the shape of a quarter moon. The southern part of the lake forms the border with France. As you follow the northern shoreline from Geneva (positioned at the western tip of the lake) to Montreux (which is positioned at the eastern tip of the lake) the scenery is idyllic with steep hills covered with vineyards that terrace down to the water's edge. Snuggled next to the lake are appealing medieval villages and sophisticated towns that are fun to visit and conveniently close to Geneva. Most of these are accessible by boat, should this be your preferred means of transportation. If your time is limited, you can often go one direction by boat, and return to Geneva by a local bus or train. We have listed some of our favorite places to visit.

Vineyards along the shore of Lake Geneva

TOWNS TO VISIT ON THE SOUTH SHORE OF LAKE GENEVA:

Hermance: Just a short distance southeast of Geneva you come to the quaint medieval village of Hermance, which is tucked right on the edge of the lake. This is one of the last towns in Switzerland before you arrive in France. The town is accessible by bus, boat, or car. Many people from Geneva come here to dine at the very charming and exceptionally fine restaurant, Auberge d'Hermance, which also has a few guestrooms.

Yvoire: Although not in Switzerland, we cannot resist suggesting a visit to another medieval jewel, Yvoire—one of the most enchanting villages in France. Snuggled right on the lake, Yvoire is easily accessible to Geneva by boat or car (it is about a 32-kilometer drive from the city). This tiny walled, medieval town is an absolute jewel. Its fantastic setting, twisting cobbled streets leading down to the waterfront, colorful harbor, ancient castle, boundless displays of brilliant flowers, and quaint stone houses will win your heart. With its many restaurants in town, Yvoire makes an excellent place to stop for lunch. Our choice is the restaurant in the 200-year-old Hotel du Port, which has a terrace overlooking the lake.

TOWNS TO VISIT ON THE NORTH SHORE OF LAKE GENEVA (arranged in geographical order as you trace the shoreline east from Geneva to Montreux).

Note: If you prefer, you can stop to see some of the towns along the north shore when you leave Geneva and are en route to your next destination, Gruyères. However, since that is already a pretty full day, we recommend visiting the places that most appeal to you before leaving the city.

Coppet: Located about 12 kilometers from Geneva, Coppet is the first quaint lakeside town you come to after leaving the city. Picturesque, 16th-century, arcaded houses flank both sides of the road that runs through the middle of town. For sightseeing, visit the Castle of Coppet that was the home of Germaine de Staël. She was an outspoken young Swiss noblewoman living in Paris who unwisely criticized Napoleon and had to flee to the safety of her father's castle in Coppet. The lavishly furnished castle is open from mid-

April through September. If you want to take a boat excursion to Coppet for lunch or dinner, the Hôtel du Lac has a delightful restaurant with a lakefront terrace.

Rollet: The highlight of the small village of Rollet, which is beautifully situated on the waterfront in the center of the wine-growing region, is its handsome, 13th-century, moated castle that stretches to the edge of the lake. Built by the Duke of Savoy, the castle is very picturesque with a proper moat, turrets, and towers.

Morges: (Northeast of Geneva, on the north shore of Lake Geneva): Morges, a tranquil town snuggled on the edge of the lake is enveloped by beautifully manicured vineyards. Like so many of the towns that grew up along the lake, it has its own fortification, a dramatic walled castle accented by ramparts and towers. Within the castle you find a museum that will delight boys of all ages: the Figurine Museum that features dioramas of lead soldiers in famous battles, ranging from Babylon to Mexico. Another museum in town is the Musée Alexis Forel, which is located in a 15th-century mansion. Sponsored by the famous engraver, Alexis Forel, the museum features rooms with antiques that span periods from the 15th to the 20th centuries. For little girls of all ages, one of the highlights of the museum is a large doll collection.

Tolochenaz: If you are an admirer of Audrey Hepburn, before leaving Morges, take a bus or car to Tolochenaz, which is just a couple of kilometers west of town. This was the home of Mrs. Hepburn, who lived here for the last thirty years of her life. She was much beloved by people throughout the world, including local volunteers who have set up the Audrey Hepburn Pavilion which displays many of the mementos and photographs of her life. In addition to being a much-admired actress, she devoted many years of her life traveling around the world to help children in need. Proceeds from the entrance fee go to her foundation, which perpetuates her dedication to orphans and young children.

Saint Sulpice: Just before you arrive in Lausanne, you come to the small medieval town of Saint Sulpice. A pretty promenade traces the edge of the lake, and just up the street from the boat dock, there is a pretty, unostentatious stone church that dates back to the 11th century. Originally built as a Benedictine priory, the church hosts many musical events.

Lausanne: Lausanne is a charming city that dates back to the 4th century when the Romans built a settlement here on the shore of the lake. In later years, the city moved away from the waterfront and to the top of the hill for better defense. This shift created a city that today is made of three sections: the lakeside area, the business area, and the Old City.

The part of Lausanne that stretches along the lake is called Ouchy. It used to be a small fishing hamlet, but today is quite posh with grand lakefront hotels, pretty parks, soaring fountains, lovely gardens, a beautiful promenade, and a boat harbor brimming with yachts of the rich and famous.

Vieille Ville, the oldest part of town with twisting narrow streets, stretches across the top of the hill. Many of Lausanne's prime sightseeing targets are here, such as the stunning 12th-century Cathedral of Notre Dame (considered by many to be Switzerland's most beautiful Gothic church), and the Château Saint Marie, a handsome yellow sandstone castle built in the 14th century for the bishops of Lausanne.

The newer, more mundane part of the Lausanne is its business area, which is sandwiched between Ouchy and the Vieille Ville.

Cully: One of the most peaceful places along Lake Geneva is the medieval village of Cully. Its setting is particularly appealing since the town is off the main road. The town is very attractive with picturesque old buildings and cobbled streets that lead down to the waterfront where a pretty park stretches in front of the lake.

Montreux: Montreux is a sophisticated town nestled along the shore of the eastern tip of Lake Geneva. Densely wooded hills rise steeply to the east, forming a protective screen behind the town and capturing the warmth of the sun. Montreux's view (out over the gorgeous blue waters of Lake Geneva and beyond to soaring mountains) is breathtaking. An old-fashioned promenade traces the waterfront, a favorite spot for a lazy stroll.

Because of its allure as a place to live, large apartments have been built in Montreux, but it still exudes an aura of old-world elegance with its grand hotels and exclusive mansions with lawns stretching to the water's edge. Artists and musicians too have long been drawn to the beauty of Montreux. For those who enjoy gambling, Montreux has a casino, but one of the main attractions is the romantic Castle of Chillon, perched on a tiny peninsula 3 kilometers south of town.

Clarens: Just a short distance from the center of Montreux you come to a very upscale suburb called Clarens. This jewel has a glorious setting with panoramic views across the lake to the snow-clad French Alps. For many years Clarens has been a favorite vacation spot for the rich and famous from all over the world—many of whom stayed to build beautiful villas.

Glion: For the most spectacular view in the area of Montreux, take the small funicular that climbs the steep hill from the ferry landing at Territet (about 1 kilometer south of Montreux) to Glion, a small town perched high above Montreux. The best vantage point is the charming Hotel Victoria (a fine place to have lunch or dinner).

FROM GENEVA TO GRUYÈRES

On your way to Gruyères we suggest a leisurely route that includes sightseeing highlights, three mountain passes, and superb scenery.

Leaving Geneva, follow the route along the north shore of Lake Geneva. As you leave the city, there are two choices: either take the fast expressway A1, or the slower country road that follows the lakeshore, meandering through the quaint towns lining the waterfront. Assuming you have already visited some of the towns along the lake, we suggest you take the expressway, which runs high on the hillside above the lake. The scenery is lovely with tenderly cared for vineyards terracing gracefully down to lake.

When you come to Lausanne, don't take the road into town, but instead bypass the city by going north for 3 kilometers and when you come to the junction, take the A9 toward Montreux. Just a few minutes beyond Montreux, take the exit marked to the Castle of Chillon (Château de Chillon).

Castle of Chillon: The origins of the Castle of Chillon date back to the 11th century (and probably much earlier since Roman coins have been excavated on the site). In the 12th century the castle was taken over by the Counts of Savoy, who for the next several centuries continued to expand and enhance it. Real fame came in the 19th century when writers such as Shelly, Cumas and Victor Hugo told the world about Chillon's singular beauty. But, it was Lord Byron's "The Prisoner of Chillon," the poem about François de Bonivard's imprisonment in the castle that made it so famous. The setting is a photographer's dream—it wouldn't be more picture perfect. Perched on a tiny island jutting into Lake Geneva, the castle looks

Castle of Chillon

more like a Disneyland creation than the real thing—a genuine fortified castle. A quaint covered bridge (which used to be a drawbridge) links the mainland to the castle which is encircled by a thick stone wall interspersed with round, turreted towers. Once inside, there is much to see including the chapel, Bonivard's underground prison, and various grand halls with medieval furnishings.

Castle of Aigle: After your visit to the Castle of Chillon, return to the A9 and continue south. Very shortly you come to the exit marked to Aigle. Leave the expressway here and drive into town and following the signs to Aigle Castle. This is an absolutely stunning castle—a real jewel whose fairy-tale quality is further enhanced by its lovely setting on a gentle knoll wrapped by endless fields of manicured vineyards. The wines produced here are acclaimed as some of the best in Switzerland.

The castle, which was built in the early part of the 13ᵗʰ century as a stronghold for the Counts of Savoy, would alone be worth a visit just because it is so picturesque, but it also features two museums and an exceptionally attractive restaurant.

Aigle Castle

You cannot drive up to Aigle Castle so park your car below and walk up the road to it. The first museum is not in the castle, but rather housed in La Maison de La Dîme (Tithe House), positioned just across the street from the castle gate. As you enter *La Maison de La Dîme*, there is a charming restaurant, which makes a great lunch stop, particularly if it is a sunny day since it has a splendid outdoor terrace. Upstairs from the restaurant is the

Wine Label Museum that displays wine labels from over 52 countries, dating from the early 19th century to the mid-20th century. It won't take long to go through this museum since it is quite small. Don't tarry because you need to allow plenty of time for the castle.

Walk across the road from La Maison de La Dîme to the castle. As you enter into the courtyard there is a ticket office. One ticket suffices for entry both into the Wine Label Museum and the Castle. It is fun to begin your tour by a walk around the ramparts before exploring the many rooms of the castle. Your tour is self-guided and the rooms are all numbered, corresponding with those on the leaflet given to you as you enter that explains what you are seeing. There are 17 rooms in total, including the wine cellar, private living quarters, an art gallery, and a reconstruction of an 18th-century tavern.

Leaving Aigle, continue south on the small back road toward Ollon, at which point you leave the lower Valais and take a narrow road in the direction of Villas-sur-Ollon. The first part of the road gently weaves up through beautiful vineyards and grassy meadows and then becomes more fractious as it climbs higher up into the mountains. When you come to Villars, a well-known ski resort in winter and a haven for hiking in summer, follow signs to Les Diablerets and Gstaad (do not turn off on the road that goes to Gryon and Bex). As you leave Villars you traverse the Col de Croix, a pass which offers excellent views: on the left are beautiful alpine meadows and on the right, impressive mountain peaks.

The Col de Croix drops down to the town of Les Diablerets where you turn right toward Gstaad, going over another pass, the Col du Pillon, which presents a different type of scenery; the mountains, soaring over 3000 meters, are more precipitous and covered with glaciers. You will gasp in amazement when you see gondolas suspended by cables that seem to be thousands of meters in the air, using far-spaced towers for support. The cable cars literally get lost in the clouds. There are many photo opportunities along the way: herds of cows adorned with bells, green meadows dotted with alpine huts, glaciers, and mighty mastiffs.

When the road flattens and you arrive in the quaint village of Gsteig, look to your left where there is a richly decorated, Oberland-style chalet that oozes old world charm with

its darkened wood façade, brilliant red geraniums, and tables on the terrace with red and white checkered tablecloths. Behind the chalet (now the Bären hotel) there is charming church with a tall spire stretching into the sky; the two buildings together make a stunning photograph.

After Gsteig, you come to Feutersoey. Although the town is not special, if you want to buy a cowbell, this is a good place. On the left side of the road is an antique shop, the Antiquitäten Romang, where you can find a large selection of wonderful old bells.

Gsteig

From Feutersoey, it is only about fifteen minutes or so until you arrive in Gstaad. In spite of the fact that Gstaad has an international reputation as a very chic ski resort catering to the wealthy jet-set, the town retains much of its old-world, charming simplicity. The setting of Gstaad is magnificent, with rugged mountain peaks rising steeply on each side of the valley. In summer the hiking and mountain climbing is excellent, while in winter Gstaad offers one of the most famous networks of ski trails in Switzerland. The center of town is pedestrian-only. There are excellent hotels, many boutiques, and colorful restaurants in Gstaad, making it an exceptionally good choice as a place to spend the night, if you have time to extend this itinerary. In spite of its sophisticated exterior, at its heart, Gstaad is still a simple farm town. In the early morning you can frequently hear the melody of cowbells as the cows are walked through the streets on their way to pasture.

From Gstaad continue north for 4 kilometers to Saanen where you turn east (on road 11) and continue for about 22 kilometers to Reidenbach. Turn left at Reidenbach and continue west in the direction of Bulle and Gruyères. As the narrow road climbs up from the Simmental Valley, it first goes through green meadows and gentle hills. As you approach the Jaun Pass, the road begins to make many more turns and rises sharply upward. The scenery here is nothing short of spectacular with stunning views of distant valleys and mountains whose deeply cut escarpments (favorites for rock climbers) are reminiscent of the Tetons or the Dolomites. After cresting the Jaun Pass, the scenery is once again gentler as you drop down into the beautiful Pont du Javroz Valley. On your left, you will see a pretty vista of Lac de Montsalvens. When you arrive in Broc, follow signs to Gruyères.

Gruyères: Although considered by some to be a bit touristy, Gruyères remains one of our favorite places in Switzerland—a toy-like, medieval jewel crowning the top of a small hill, visible from afar as you approach. This is such a special place that it is considered a national monument and is protected by the Swiss government. Cars are not allowed into the village, which is pedestrian-only. However, you can drive briefly into town to leave your luggage at your hotel before parking your car in one of the designated areas below the entrance into town. This postcard-perfect village attracts busloads of visitors who crowd the small main street

Gruyères

during the day. Happily, most of the tourists come only for a few hours and in the evening the village regains its fairy-tale quality. Plan your sightseeing excursions to avoid the bustle of the midday influx of tourists and return in the late afternoon to this idyllic Swiss village which is then yours to enjoy in peace and quiet. Sit on the terrace of your hotel and have a drink, listening to the tinkling of cowbells as the sun fades.

Within the town there is just one main street, prettily faced by enchanting farmhouses that have been converted into restaurants, hotels, and boutiques. The one cobbled street that traverses the town dead-ends at the Castle of Gruyères, a marvelous fortress. A visit to the castle, which is built around a courtyard, is highly recommended. In addition to an art gallery (where exhibits change from time to time) there are numerous rooms that are handsomely furnished in antiques, including a huge dining room, bedrooms, and a kitchen with a huge fireplace that used to be where all the food was cooked. The castle is open daily April to October from 9 am to 6 pm, November to March from 10 am to 4:30 pm.

Gruyères is a convenient town to use as a base for sightseeing. If you are lucky, you might even have the chance to listen to some of the horn blowers, dressed in the regional costume, blow their impossibly long horns. The town is surrounded by rolling hills that flow gently up to magnificent mountains. In summer the incredibly green, lush meadows are dotted by contented black-and-white spotted cows with bells that tinkle softly as they graze lazily in the pastures. Adding to the idyllic scene, wildflowers abound in the fields and window boxes overflow with bright geraniums.

After seeing so many cute cows nearby, it is not surprising to learn that Gruyères is in the center of one of Switzerland's famous dairy regions—the cheeses and creams are marvelous. While in Gruyères be sure to enjoy a delicious quiche, a crock of rich fondue, or, if in season, linger over a bowl of delicious fresh berries smothered in divinely rich, thick cream.

Cheese Museums: A highlight when in Gruyères is to discover how the delicious cheeses you have been enjoying are produced. We highly recommend you visit two museums—one very modern, one very old.

The closest cheese museum is La Maison du Gruyère, located at the bottom of the road as you come down from Gruyères, opposite the Pringy-Gruyère train station. Here you find, housed within a large modern building, the cheese factory, a museum, a restaurant, and a shop. The factory produces up to 48 huge wheels of Gruyère cheese a day. There is an excellent, self-guided tour of the factory. As you enter you receive a packet with samples of aged cheeses and pick up your headset. The dialog is in various languages including, of course, English. You follow a designated path passing by excellent displays that show the history of cheeses, and then on into the cheese-making factory where you look down from a high, glassed-in gallery to view the entire process of cheese making. The factory has four 4800-lire vats and a cellar where up to 7,000 wheels of cheese can be stored and aged. As you progress, all of the stations are marked—you just need to access your headset to hear a narration describing what you are seeing. The factory is open from 9 am to 11 am and from 1 pm to 2 pm or 3 pm depending on the time of year.

Moléson-sur-Gruyères, cheese making

In striking contrast to the modern factory in Gruyères, it is great fun to go to the tiny village of Moléson-sur-Gruyères to see cheese being made in the old traditional way. Moléson is nestled high in a mountain meadow where for hundreds of years farmers have been taking their cows in the summer to graze in the lush pastures, and while there, to make cheese. For this excursion, go down the hill from Gruyères, turn left and follow signs to Moléson, about an 8-kilometer drive. When you come into town, park your car where you see a sign to the Fromagerie d'Alpage and walk up the hill on a private road to the wonderful 17th-century, stucco and timbered farmhouse. Here you have a chance to see cheese being produced in the traditional way, just has it has been for hundreds of years. In the front part of the house there is a shop where all kinds of local products can be purchased. Just behind is the room where the cheese is produced. The tour starts with a video showing the manufacturing of regional products and continues with watching one of the local, expert cheesemakers stirring the fresh milk in a huge metal caldron over an open fire. Later, the cheeses are pressed into large round wooden boxes. Plan your day so that you can be at the old factory at lunchtime since one cozy room serves as a restaurant, where many cheese dishes are featured. If the day is warm, meals are served outside on the terrace. NOTE: You cannot just arrive and expect to take a tour of the Fromagerie d'Alpage since the number of visitors is strictly limited. Reservations are essential. Tours are given daily from mid-May to mid-October—the first one at 9:30 am. Be sure to call ahead (026) 921 10 44 or email: mail@fromagerie-alpage.com. The website is *www.fromagerie-alpage.ch*. If there is no answer, it is possible to make a reservation at the Gruyères Tourist Office: (026) 921 85 00 or email: info@moleson.ch.

Cailler-Nestlé Factory: If you are a devotee to the joys of chocolate, when planning your trip to Switzerland, include a visit Caillers-Nestlé factory located in the town of Broc (about 5 kilometers north of Gruyères). Its history dates back to 1897 when Alexandre Cailler, who was bicycling through the area, discovered the perfect spot to open his new chocolate factory. Milk is one of the most important ingredients in producing fine chocolate, so when he saw so many lush pastures dotted by plump cows, Mr. Cailler decided that Broc would be the ideal place to set up shop. The factory is a bit out of the heart of town, but strategically placed signs lead you to it. From the moment you park your car and start walking toward the factory, you will immediately become aware of the fragrance of chocolate. The 45-minute tour begins with a video giving the history of chocolate. Then a guide leads you through various rooms with displays featuring its history, starting with the Aztecs who were the first to discover and use the cocoa bean from which they made a bitter drink. The Conquistadors brought this exotic bean back home and the cocoa drink became a favorite of the Spanish court. Later, the Swiss learned to further process the bean, combining it with rich cream, creating the wonderful chocolate we know today. Don't leave before the end of the tour; it finishes in a tasting room where large tables are set with trays laden with samples of every imaginable kind of chocolate candy cut into small squares. You can nibble to your heart's content—all included in the tour price. The factory is open for visitors from Monday afternoon through Friday from May 2 to the end of October (closed on holidays). The tours, which are limited in number of participants, are offered at 9:00 am, 11:00 am, 1:30 pm, and 4:00 pm. Tel: (026) 921 51 51.

GRUYÈRES TO ZÜRICH—WITH A STOP EN ROUTE

If your time is limited, you can drive directly from Gruyères to Zürich in just a few hours. However, we recommend you break your journey and spend at least a night in one of the towns described below. The suggested route to Zürich includes more sightseeing than is possible to squeeze into in two days. Although you won't have time to do it all, our suggestions will provide an idea of the possibilities.

Fribourg: From Gruyères, follow signs to the freeway A12, and continue north for 25 kilometers to Fribourg, a beautifully preserved medieval city, most of which is on a bluff wrapped by a bend of the Sarine River. The splendid 13th-century Saint Nicolas Cathedral, famous for its life-sized statues, dominates the town. Within walking distance is the impressive 16th-century Hôtel de Ville (town hall) adorned with an impressive clock tower, the Musée d'Art et Histoire (Museum of Art and History), the 18th-century Basilique of Notre-Dame, and the splendid 13th-century Franciscan church, Église des Cordeliers. The upper part of part Fribourg is interesting, but my favorite section is the lower part of the city which is even older. You can reach it by walking down a steep road to the river and crossing over the Pont de Saint Jean, and then you are in the ancient part of the city with its maze of quaint streets, historic houses, pretty squares, and renaissance fountains. You can cross back over the river by means of the Pont de Berne, a delightful old covered bridge.

Murten: From Fribourg, it is about 15 kilometers on a small back road through the countryside to Murten, a jewel of a walled medieval village nestled on the banks of Lake Murten. You cannot drive into the heart of town, but there is a large, underground garage near the main gate. You enter Murten through a gate in the medieval wall that completely surrounds this fairy-tale village with its cobbled streets, quaint houses, flower boxes, brightly painted fountains, and charming squares. Before exploring the town, climb up to the ramparts and walk the wall for a bird's-eye preview of what you are going to see. Murten is like an outdoor museum. Strolling through the town, you can study many of the 15th-century buildings and the walls that date from the 12th century. There is a castle at the western end of town built by Peter of Savoy in the 13th century. As you stroll, watch for the town hall, the French church, the German church, the Bern Gate (with one of the oldest clock towers in Switzerland), and the Historical Museum which displays weapons, banners, and uniforms from the Burgundian battles. Plan your day to allow time for a boat ride on Lake Murten. There is a schedule posted on the dock or the tourist office can give you the times.

Murten

Murten is the most charming town in the area, however if you want to do a bit more exploring, there are things to see nearby. One place of interest is Avenches. You can reach it by following signs to the A1 (just a couple of kilometers from Murten) and heading south toward Yverdon. After about 6 kilometers, take the Avenches exit. It is hard to believe as you look at this sleepy little hamlet of about 2,000 inhabitants that in the 1st and 2nd centuries it was a powerful Roman city boasting a population of over 20,000. You can grasp the mood of this "lost city" of the Romans when you visit the amphitheater built to seat 10,000. In a tower over the amphitheater's entrance is a museum displaying some of the artifacts found in the excavations and an interesting pottery collection.

Leaving Avenches, return to the A1 and continue south for 11 kilometers. Exit at Payerne and go into town to visit its famous 11th-century abbey. This Benedictine abbey is supposed to have been founded by the Empress Adelheid, wife of Emperor Otto I. The church is one of the finest examples of Romanesque architecture in Switzerland.

From Payerne, do not return to the expressway but instead take the small backroad west to Estavayer. Like Murten this is a medieval walled village; however, unlike Murten, it is not on Lake Murten, but sits on a hill overlooking the much larger Lake Neuchâtel. Estavayer is a quaint town, but not quite as fairy-tale perfect as Murten. After strolling through Estavayer, take the back roads north along the west side of the lake and circle back to Murten

Bern: Leaving Murten, return to the A1 and follow signs to Bern. Continue on the expressway as it loops around the north side of the city. Take the Bern Wankdorf exit and follow signs to the center of the city. The road leads to the Nydeggbrücke (Nydegg Bridge). If you are only going to be in Bern for a few hours, there are several parking areas before you cross over the bridge where you can leave your car for a short while and walk into town. On the left-hand corner as you face the bridge, there is a tourist office where you can pick up maps and brochures, plus watch a short video on Bern's history. Just in front of the tourist office is the Bäengraben (the bear pit) where you can say hello to the bears that have been a symbol of Bern for hundreds of years. The legend goes that the nobleman who founded the town decided to name it for the first animal shot on a hunting trip. As you have probably guessed, it was a bear; hence the name Bern. If you plan to spend the night in Bern, it is best to park your car in the center of town. To do this, cross over the Nydeggbrücke and, at the first street, turn right and follow signs on Postgasshalde that lead to an underground parking garage.

The River Aare and the Skyline of Bern

Bern, an enticing, well-preserved 16th-century walled city, sits on a plateau that is looped by the Aare River, at a point where its banks fall steeply to the river below. To further enhance the setting, the Alps rise in the background. The setting alone would make Bern worth a stop, but the town is brimming with character—truly a 13th-century storybook wonderland. Bern is the only Swiss city that has been declared a world heritage landmark.

The main street in the old town is Marktgasse, which stretches from one end of town to the other. Along the street are many charming medieval buildings, arcaded sidewalks, intriguing shops, and brightly painted whimsical fountains. However, my favorite attraction in Bern is the clock tower, which until the 13th century served as the west gate of the city. Be in the square at four minutes before the hour when the "show" begins: as the bell peals, a succession of figures parade across the clock including the most popular of all—darling little bear cubs.

One place you must not miss during your exploration of Berne is its 15th-century church, Münster of Saint Vincent. It should be on your *must see* list, if for no other reason than to take a look at its stunning statues, wood carvings, and handcrafted stonework. There are over 232 statues alone of the Last Judgment. You can't help but notice the gorgeous stained-glass windows. For a breath-taking view, climb the 270 steps on the spiral staircase to the bell tower (the highest in all of Switzerland).

Solothurn: Leaving Bern, take the A1 north in the direction of Basel. After 45 kilometers turn off to Solothurn, one of the oldest Roman settlements in Switzerland. From the expressway, follow signs to the center of town. Although a modern industrial area has grown up in the outskirts of Solothurn, once you enter through the gates into the old town, you are magically transported back hundreds of years to a beautiful, Baroque walled city on the banks of the Aare River. It is fascinating to walk through the streets that exude the aura of bygone years with colorfully painted fountains, charming small

squares, whimsical clock towers, and 16th-century houses with brightly painted shutters. There are two churches you must not miss. The first to see is the beautiful Saint Ursen Cathedral that faces onto a small plaza leading down to Marktplatz. The interior is ornamented by elaborate stucco work and features a spectacular Baroque pulpit. Another church is the Jesuit Church—a real beauty enhanced by splendid frescoes and elaborate stucco designs. Solothurn also has several museums including the Arsenal Museum which displays weapons, suits of armor, and military uniforms going back to the Middle Ages. Another choice is the Kunstmuseum featuring paintings from Swiss and French masters.

Basel: From Bern, return to the A1 and continue north to Basel, a distance of about 100 kilometers. Because Basel has such a strategic location (on the banks of the Rhine River where the borders of Germany, France, and Switzerland join), it has flourished as a city of commerce since the medieval ages. The Rhine acts as the gateway to the North Sea, so Basel is also a very busy port.

The periphery of Basel is not particularly scenic, but when you arrive at the heart of the old town, you find a wonderful medieval city dotted with enchanting squares, marvelously preserved historic buildings, stunning cathedrals, bridges, brightly painted fountains and an endless assortment of museums. Be sure to visit the 12th-century cathedral and the market square (*Marktplatz*) which is host every morning to a flower and vegetable market. The town hall (*Rathaus*) dates from the 16th century and is beautifully decorated with frescos. There is an excellent Museum of Fine Arts (*Kunstmuseum*) displaying works of art from the 15th and 16th centuries. The Museum of Antique Art (*Antikenmuseum*) features sculptures and paintings dating from pre-Hellenic times. You can walk everywhere and should do so. This is the best way to capture the ambiance of this colorful city. Meander the heart of the old town, stopping for a bite to eat at one of the outdoor cafés before going on to one of the city's more than 30 museums.

Begin your sightseeing at the Mittlere Brücke, the colorful bridge in the historic heart of town. Its origins date back to the 13th century, at which time it was a simple wooden bridge, but one of great importance since it was the only way to cross the river anywhere in the region. In days of yore, criminals were tossed off the bridge; but in 1634, it was decreed that beheading was more efficient.

From the Mittlere Brücke it is just a short walk to the Basel's Marktplatz, a large, picturesque, market square dominated by a magnificently embellished town hall. It is also the starting point for five different, self-guided walking tours, each of which begins and ends at the Markplatz. Color-coded signs direct your way, each depicting a different historic figure. There is the Hans Holbein Walk (green-on-blue signs, about an hour-and-a-half walk), the Paracelsus Walk (green-on-blue signs, about an hour walk), Tomas Platter Walk (yellow-on-blue signs, about a 45-minute walk), the Jakob Bruckherdt Walk (light-blue-on-blue, about a 45-minute walk), and the Erasmus Walk (red-on-blue signs, about a half-an-hour walk).

For another Basel highlight, in summer it is possible to take boat trips along the Rhine, always a fun outing on a sunny day. These excursions offer a leisurely view of the city. This method of sightseeing is especially interesting because from the river you can view many of the marvelous old buildings and also cross under some of the bridges that span the Rhine River so colorfully.

When you leave Basel, go east on the A3 for about 16 kilometers and take the Stein exit. Go into Stein and cross over the bridge into Germany, then continue east on the road that traces the Rhine. The Rhine forms the border between Germany and Switzerland. At this part of the itinerary, the German side of the river is more picturesque than the Swiss side.

Continue along the scenic river route for 27 kilometers to Waldshut, then cross the bridge back into Switzerland, and take road 7 east. Just beyond the town of Glattfelden, turn left on 27 toward Schaffhausen. The road crosses the Rhine again at Eglisau, a sweet picturesque town where you might want to stop and take a photo.

Rheinfall: From Eglisau continue on toward Schaffhausen. About 4 kilometers before you arrive in Schaffhausen, you arrive in Neuhausen where you follow signs for the Rheinfall (Rhine Falls), the most dramatic waterfall in Europe. In days of yore, boat traffic was stalled at the waterfall as merchants had to unload their river cargo and carry it around the falls before continuing their journey.

When you arrive at the Rheinfall, park your car in one of the designated areas and follow the path to the bottom of the falls. There is an awesome view of the falls from the shoreline, but it is much more fun (although perhaps a tad damp) to buy a ticket and board one of the small excursion boats that maneuver to the middle of the river and slide up under the plunging masses of water. If you are so inclined, you can climb to the top of the rock, in the middle of the waterfall.

Rheinau: If you want to add another stunning picture to your Swiss photo album, visit the Island of Rheinau that sits on a loop of the Rhine, 6 kilometers south of the Rheinfall. What makes this island so exceptionally picturesque is its stunning Benedictine Monastery (highlighted by with twin bell towers). Because of its two fine organs, concerts are frequently hosted here. (Open April, May and October, Tuesday through Saturday, 2

Munot Fortress at Schaffhausen

pm to 4 pm; Sunday and holidays 1:30 pm to 5 pm. Open June through September, Tuesday through Saturday, 10 am to noon and 1 pm to 5 pm; Sundays and holidays, 10:30 am to noon and 1 pm to 6 pm.)

Schaffhausen: After visiting the Rheinfall and the island of Rheinau, continue north for just a short distance to Schaffhausen, a quaint medieval city that grew up along the banks of the Rhine just above the point where the river plummets to a lower level, forming the Rheinfall. It is fun to walk through the city's maze of alleys and discover hidden plazas, clock towers, statues, and painted houses. Its name originates from the "ship houses" where cargo was stored when ships had to be unloaded for their goods to be carried past the Rheinfall. Towering over the town is a handsome castle, the Munot Fortress. Ferryboats pull up to the dock in Schaffhausen where you can hop on board for a short river tour, or if time allows, a trip to Stein am Rhein, the next stop on this itinerary.

Stein am Rhein: From Schaffhausen, continue east for 20 kilometers to Stein am Rhein, a walled medieval town built along the banks of the Rhine. Busloads of tourist flock in for the day, but they can't spoil the cozy ambiance of one of Switzerland's most enchanting towns. After entering the main gates, you find yourself in a fairy-tale village with each building almost totally covered with fanciful paintings. The town is very small so it will not take long to explore. Settle under an umbrella at one of the riverside restaurants, or park on a bench with a refreshing *apfelsaft, bratwurst, und brot* and enjoy the constant passage of boats that ply the river. Stein am Rhein, with its streets winding up from the river to the heart of the old town, is charming to

Stein am Rhein

explore on foot. Hauptstrasse and the Town Hall Square are extremely picturesque with their fountains and flower-decked houses. There is a boat dock where you can board excursion boats that ply the river.

FINAL DESTINATION–ZÜRICH

Leaving Stein am Rhein follow road #13 east for a few kilometers. When you arrive at Eschenz, turn onto a small road heading south and follow signs to Frauenfeld. After about 18 kilometers, take the A7, which soon joins with the A1 and continues on into the center of the Zürich. If you have time to extend your holiday, the next itinerary *Swiss Highlights—The Best of the Best*, originates in Zürich and joins seamlessly with this one.

Note: Should you want to squeeze in one more jewel before this itinerary ends, visit the tiny hamlet of Regensberg, one of the most charming medieval walled towns in Switzerland. If you want to include Regensberg, bypass Zürich and continue west toward Basel. On the outskirts of Zürich, one of the first exits is Weiningen. Leave the expressway here and follow signs to Dielsdorf. When you come to the outskirts of town, watch for a road going to the left to Regensberg. This picturesque walled village crowns a small hill laced with vineyards. You might want stop for lunch or a cup of tea here. Or, should you prefer to stay in the countryside instead of the city, consider using Regensberg, (which has an outstanding small hotel, the Rote Rose) as your base of operation instead of Zürich.

Regensberg

Geneva to Zürich via Medieval Jewels

Swiss Highlights –
The Best of the Best

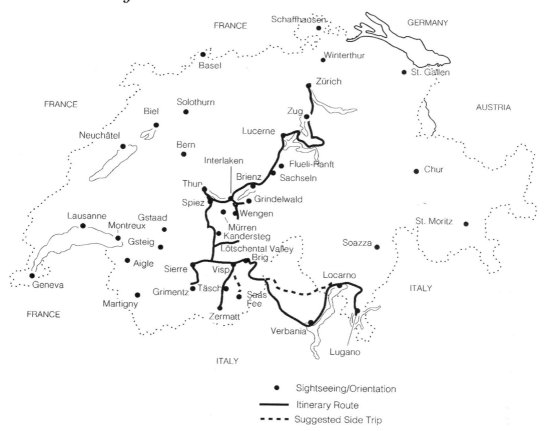

FRANCE

Schaffhausen

GERMANY

Winterthur

St. Gallen

FRANCE

Basel

Solothurn

Biel

Zürich

Zug

AUSTRIA

Neuchâtel

Bern

Lucerne

Chur

Interlaken

Flueli-Ranft

Brienz

Sachseln

Thun

Grindelwald

Spiez

Wengen

Lausanne

Gstaad

Montreux

Mürren

St. Moritz

Gsteig

Kandersteg

Soazza

Aigle

Lötschental Valley

Sierre

Visp

Brig

Grimentz

Täsch

Locarno

Martigny

Saas Fee

ITALY

FRANCE

Zermatt

Verbania

Geneva

Lugano

ITALY

●   Sightseeing/Orientation
── Itinerary Route
▬ ▬ Suggested Side Trip

83

Swiss Highlights—The Best of the Best

Kapellbrücke, Lucerne

If you want to see the most interesting and beautiful parts of Switzerland, including the picture-book-perfect scenery repeatedly seen on postcards, this is an ideal itinerary. The beauty throughout Switzerland is astounding, but unless you are planning a lengthy stay, it's impossible to see it all in one visit. This itinerary gives you Switzerland *in a nutshell*—a tantalizing taste of its beautiful towns, charming villages, lovely lakes, lush valleys, and astonishing mountains.

Choose either Zürich or Lucerne as your originating city. (We give sightseeing suggestions for both.) They are so close that we suggest you stay in one and take a train to visit the other. Even if you have a car, it is much easier (and quicker) to take a train between the two than to struggle with traffic and find a parking garage. Trains depart at least once an hour from 6 am to 11 pm and the trip takes about 50 minutes.

If this itinerary begins your Swiss holiday and you are flying into Zürich, don't pick up your car until the next leg of your trip. You can take a fast train directly from the airport to the city center of either Zürich or Lucerne. Not only is this practical, but also economical since you will save several days' cost of car rental. Within either city you can walk almost everywhere.

From Zürich or Lucerne this itinerary heads south to Interlaken and the stunning Jungfrau region, then on to see more splendid mountains (including the Matterhorn) in Zermatt, then continues south (almost to the Italian border) to the romantic lakes of southern Switzerland.

RECOMMENDED PACING: We recommend a minimum of ten nights for this itinerary. *This does not include the nights you choose to stay at the end of your trip in the Lake District.* As you read through the itinerary, you will note that we suggest places en route that are very special. If you want to include time at one of these locations, it will extend the total days, but you will be well rewarded. The following is a suggestion on how to plan your time:

FOUR NIGHTS in Zürich or Lucerne: Four nights will give you three full days: one day to enjoy wandering through the city, one day to take a boat ride on the lake, and one day to visit either Lucerne or Zürich (depending upon which you have chosen as your base of operations).

THREE NIGHTS in the Jungfrau region: Three nights in the Jungfrau region will give you two full days—one day for the Jungfraujoch excursion (an absolute *must see*) and another day to take a walk in the mountains, visit Interlaken, take a boat excursion, or visit the quaint town of Thun.

THREE NIGHTS in Zermatt: Three nights in Zermatt will give you two full days to stroll through the town, enjoy some of the beautiful walking paths, and take advantage of the available trams and railways up into the mountains.

THE ITINERARY ENDS in the Southern Lake District. If you are planning to extend your trip, the following itinerary, *Swiss Treasures off the Beaten Path*, dovetails seamlessly with this one.

ZÜRICH

Zürich is a splendid, cosmopolitan city with an idyllic, lakeside setting. Although very popular with travelers from around the world, Zürich does not have the feeling of a tourist center. Instead, as you walk the streets, you experience the bustle of a "real" city. Of course there are tourists, but shopping next to you in the little boutique will be the local housewife, hurrying down the promenade will be businessmen on their way to work, and a couple from Zürich will probably be sitting next to you at a sidewalk café. There is a bustling atmosphere in Zürich, a gaiety to the city.

The River Limmat, Zürich

Zürich is a great city for walking. Meander through the medieval section with its maze of tiny twisting streets, colorful squares, charming little shops, and tempting cafés. It is fun to walk down the promenade by the Limmat River (which runs through the center of the city) to the lakefront and cross over the Quaibrücke (bridge) to return by the opposite bank. When weary, cross back over one of the bridges that spans the river to complete your circle. From both sides of the river the old section of Zürich radiates out on little twisting streets like a spider web.

Spend some time along the lakefront with its pretty parks and gardens. From the piers there are a fascinating variety of boat excursions to little villages around the lake. On a sunny day take an excursion on one these. There is a schedule posted at each of the piers stating where the boats go and when they depart. During the summer there is frequent service and a wide selection to suit your mood and your timeframe.

Shopping in Zürich is a dream. The two most popular shopping streets are Bahnhofstrasse and Limmatquai, both with many top of the line boutiques. Even just window shopping is great fun. When it comes time to dine, you have your choice of more than 1,700 places to eat and drink.

For those of you who relish sightseeing, Zürich has a rich selection of things to see including over 50 museums and more than 100 art galleries. Below is a selection of some of the possibilities. Note: most of the museums in Zürich close on Monday.

SIGHTSEEING HIGHLIGHTS IN ZÜRICH

Walking Tour: Always one of the best ways to capture the ambiance of a town is by taking a walking tour with a local guide to explain what you are seeing and tell fun tales of the city that you might otherwise never hear. The tourist office in Zürich offers just such an excursion. Tickets are sold at, and the tour starts from, the tourist office which is located in at the Hauptbahnhof, Zürich's central train station. This adventure explores the charming Old Town. (May until November, weekdays, 2:30 pm; Saturday & Sunday, 10 am & 2:30 pm.) Note: when in the tourist office arranging for your walking tour, ask what special events are taking place during your visit. Zürich has a rich selection of cultural events.

Zunfthaus zur Meisen: Located directly on the Limmat River, the Zunfthaus zur Meisen is housed in a splendid 18th-century wine merchants' guild house. As indicated by the name, the museum features fine porcelain treasures from throughout Europe, including of course, the famous German town of Meissen. (Located on the west bank of the Limmat.)

Schweizerisches Landesmuseum: If you have time for only one museum in Zürich, choose the Schweizerisches Landesmuseum, which covers Switzerland's cultural heritage going back to 10,000 BC. The exhibits are marvelously presented, including such highlights as a 16th-century chapel (its stained-glass windows are fabulous) and a vast collection of coats of arms and banners from the 14th century. To catch a glimpse of life in the 17th century, rooms are set up and furnished as they would have been at that time. Boys of all ages will be captivated by the toy soldiers set up to depict a model of the Battle of Murten, which took place in 1476. Another *must see* in the museum is an 18th-century pharmacy that was brought here from the Benedictine Abbey in Muri and reassembled. (Located on the west bank of the Limmat.)

Fraumümuster: If you are a devotee of Chagall, be sure to visit the Fraumümuster to see its stained-glass windows designed by Chagall. The Fraumümuster dates back to the 9th century. It was first founded by the German King Ludwig who built an abbey here and installed his daughter, Hildegard, as headmistress. (Located on the west bank of the Limmat.)

Rathaus: Zürich's town hall (Rathaus) is built on piles hammered into the riverbed of the Limmat so the building actually stretches out over the water. An arcaded walkway adorns the front of the building. The origin of the town hall dates back to medieval times. (Located on the east bank of the Limmat.)

Kunsthaus: The Kunsthaus is reputed to be the most important art galley in Switzerland. Its paintings cover a wide span of time from medieval religious art to the 20th century. Its vast palette of artists include works by leading Swiss painters (including our favorite

Albert Ankor) along with a large selection of Impressionist painting including works by Renoir, Degas, Picasso, Chagall, and Renoir. (Located on the east bank of the Limmat.)

Grossmünster: Cathedral buffs won't want to miss the impressive and imposing 12th-century Grossmünster cathedral whose twin towers dominate the Zürich skyline. Supposedly the present day structure was built upon an 8th-century church founded by Charlemagne, whose stature adorns the crypt. (Located on the east bank of the Limmat.)

ZÜRICH TO LUCERNE

There is no expressway linking Zürich and Lucerne. However, it is possible to take four-lane roads some of the way. The fastest route is to take the A3 south from Zürich in the direction of Chur. Exit from the A3 at Horgen and go west in the direction of Baar and Lucerne. After about 6 kilometers, you arrive at the A4. Take this freeway for a few minutes and exit when you see the sign to Zug, which is about 5 kilometers to the south.

Zug: A visit to Zug introduces you to one of Switzerland's oldest cities whose origin dates back beyond the Middle Ages to the Neolithic era. By far the most attractive part of Zug is its medieval core, which is like a town within a town. One side faces onto the harbor of Lake Zug, from which a maze of streets stretches back to the old walls of the town, some of which are still intact. As you wander through the quaint old town you will see many colorfully painted, tall, narrow 16th-century houses with steep gabled roofs. In the center of town is the Kolinplatz, a square highlighted by a fountain adorned by a statue of Wolfgang Kolin, a Swiss knight who gained local fame for his many brave deeds. The highlight of this old part of Zug is the whimsical clock tower above the city gates. It is cute as can be with a steeply pitched, tiled roof in a blue and white herringbone design, topped by a bell tower and jaunty steeple.

From Zug, continue south following the lake to Doldau and join the A4 going south toward Brunnen. Get off the freeway here and continue on to Lucerne on the road that traces the north edge of the lake. This will take you through some of the sweetest villages along the lakefront.

Vitznau: Your first stop is Vitznau, which has a lovely lakefront setting that is further enhanced by the wooded hills that rise behind the town. From Vitznau you can take a 35-minute ride on Europe's oldest cog railway (built in 1871) that climbs to the Rigi-Kul summit, which affords a sensational panoramic view.

Weggis: A short drive beyond Vitznau brings you to Weggis, one of the prettiest resorts along Lake Lucerne and a favorite target for the ferryboats. Be sure to take a stroll along the lovely promenade that traces the water's edge and leads out to a small peninsula that juts into the lake.

Küssnacht am Rigi: The next stop along the way is Küssnacht am Rigi, a small village located on a northern finger of land that stretches into Lake Lucerne. What makes this town particularly attractive is that the highway bypasses it so there is no through traffic. The main street, lined by colorful 16th-century buildings, leads down to the lake, ending in a small square facing the waterfront. On the square is a handsome, Baroque town hall. Also facing the square is the Hôtel du Lac Seehof, an excellent place for lunch or dinner. It has a romantic, tree-shaded terrace on the edge of the lake, right by the boat dock. Küssnacht am Rigi also is famous for its folk hero, William Tell, who, at a site nearby, is said to have shot the Austrian governor with his mighty crossbow while leading his people in their battle to win freedom from Hapsburg rule. From Küssnacht it is a short drive into the heart of Lucerne.

LUCERNE

Lucerne is a charming medieval town with a fairy-tale setting located directly on the lake with a beautiful mountain backdrop. This is one of our favorite places in Switzerland, an exceptionally romantic city with the charm and intimacy of a small town. Hugging the edge of Lake Lucerne, the site is pure perfection. With its magical setting, Lucerne makes a delightful beginning for any itinerary, offering a tempting glimpse of what is to come—lakes, mountains, rivers, quaint bridges, historic buildings, masses of colorful flowers, and a selection of romantic excursions by boat.

Remnants of stone walls trace an outline around the old town of Lucerne. Although the ramparts that once encircled the city have deteriorated with time, the old section remains a marvelously preserved example of a medieval city—an exceptionally attractive one. Stately ancient buildings line the Reuss River, which rushes through the center of town. It

Lucerne

is lined by colorful buildings and spanned by charming bridges. The most famous of these is the Kapellbrücke (Chapel Bridge), which was built in the 14th century to accommodate the ever-increasing merchants coming over the Gotthard Pass as they traveled north into Germany. With its wooden roof, cute octagonal water tower, walls painted with murals, masses of bright geraniums, and a little chapel midway, this jewel of a bridge is one of the most photographed sites in Lucerne and a trademark of the city.

You can best enjoy all of Lucerne on foot; it is a wonderful town for lingering. Just strolling through the quaint streets and enjoying a snack in one of the small cafés overlooking the river can easily fill an afternoon. There are always many tourists in Lucerne since its enchantment is no secret. However, the bustle of activity and happy travelers adds a festive spirit to the city. When planning your activities, remember that most Swiss museums close on Mondays.

SIGHTSEEING HIGHLIGHTS IN LUCERNE

Walking Tour: The Lucerne Tourist Office offers an excursion called "A Walk Around Lucerne"—a walking tour that also includes a short ride on the city train. Along the way your guide will explain many interesting facts (and humorous stories) about the city's history, its churches, narrow streets, bridges, and quaint medieval squares. The two-hour tour takes place daily from May through October. November through April, the tour is on Wednesdays and Saturdays. The departure time is 9:45 am from the tourist information center at the train station. If you are with friends or family and there are five people in your party, private theme tours are available. Ask about these at the tourist office. This would be a fun way to have your own specialized excursion.

Museum of Transport and Communications: The Museum of Transport and Communications, one of Switzerland's finest museums, follows the development of transportation and communication up to the exploration of space.

Boat trips on Lake Lucerne: You must include at least one boat trip on Lake Lucerne while staying here. There are steamers constantly crisscrossing back and forth across the lovely lake, stopping at small villages along the way. Boat schedules are posted at each dock. Plan your day so that you arrive in one of the cute villages at midday to have lunch at a lakeside restaurant (Küssnacht is one of our favorite stops) and then return later to Lucerne. In addition to the regularly scheduled routes, there are many boats that offer specialty outings such as dinner cruises. For a truly relaxing day, sign up for the all-day (6-hour) circle cruise of the lake.

Rosengart Museum: This museum, which features the private collection of Sammlung Rosengart and his daughter Angela Rosengart, is one of our favorites. Along with modern art, it has an amazing selection of Impressionistic paintings including works by Picasso, Monet, Renoir, Matisse, Chagall, and Cézanne.

Picasso Museum: The same Rosengart family, whose art collection is exhibited in the Rosengart Museum, donated many paintings by Picasso to the city which are displayed in a 16th-century home. In the museum there are also many photographs of Picasso and his family, giving you a glimpse into this great artist's personal life.

Franziskanerkirche: This Franciscan church is Lucerne's most ancient building, dating back to the 13th century.

Historisches Museum: Housed in a 16th-century Renaissance building that connects via its gatehouse to Lucerne's historic covered bridge, the Spreuerbrück, the Historisches Museum depicts the history of Lucerne through its display of costumes, folk art, crafts, and weapons.

Museggmauer: Lucerne's medieval heritage is apparent in the remnants of its old city walls. Parts of this medieval fortification, with its nine towers, still stand on the north side of town running from the river to the lake.

Kuntsmuseum: The Kuntsmuseum is housed in Lucerne's Congress Center, an ultra modern, steel and glass building that was built in 2000 by the French architect, Jean Nouvel. The focus of the museum is on Swiss painters from the 18th to 20th century.

Mount Pilatus: Recommended for a sunny day is an outing from Lucerne to the highest mountain peak in the area, Mount Pilatus. The most enjoyable route for this excursion is to take the lake steamer to the town of Alpnachstad and then the electric cog railway up to the top of the mountain. From the rail terminal it is only about a ten-minute walk to the peak of the mountain where there is a spectacular panorama.

Einsiedeln: Another excursion from Lucerne is to the town of Einsiedeln to see the home of the famous Black Madonna. The Monastery of Einsiedeln was founded by Meinrad, a Benedictine monk, who built a small chapel for the Black Madonna (a statue of the Virgin Mary), which had been given to him by Zürich priests. Meinrad was later murdered by some men who mistakenly thought he had hidden treasures. Later, the Monastery of Einsiedeln was built over Meinrad's grave and another chapel was erected to house the Black Madonna. This site has become a pilgrimage, not only for Catholics, but also for tourists who are attracted to the Einsiedeln Abbey, an excellent example of Baroque architecture.

Richard Wagner Museum: If you are enchanted by the works of Wagner, visit the Richard Wagner Museum which is on the lake on the southern outskirts of Lucerne in a neighborhood called Tribschen. The museum is in the home where Wagner lived from 1866 to 1872, when he composed many of his masterpieces. It was in this villa that he married Cosima, the daughter of the Austrian composer, Franz Liszt. This charming lakefront villa where he lived has a wonderful collection of antique musical instruments. The museum is closed on Mondays and also from December to mid-March.

LUCERNE TO THE INTERLAKEN & JUNGFRAU REGIONS

When its time to move on, leave Lucerne on the A4, heading south toward Interlaken.

Flüeli-Ranft: Exit the A4 at Sachseln and follow signs to Flüeli-Ranft. This tiny village, nestled up in the hills, has great religious and political significance. It was here that Saint Nicholas of Flüe, a deeply religious person, was born in a simple peasant's cottage. He married and fathered ten children. He lived a normal life until, when in his 50s, he felt the irresistible call to live the life of solitude (with ten children, perhaps it is understandable). He went into the hills behind Flüeli-Ranft where he lived as a hermit and spent the rest of his life in meditation. Because of his reputation as a fair and peace-loving man of inspired wisdom, many priests and political leaders came to him for advice. When a war between the cantons seemed inevitable, Saint Nicolas negotiated a compromise and instead of going to battle, the cantons were united into confederation in 1481. One can visit the small home where Saint Nicholas of Flüe was born and hike to the hermitage where he lived in solitude for so many years.

Sachseln: From Flüeli-Ranft, take the small road marked to Sachseln, which like Flüeli-Ranft, is also a very holy pilgrimage for Catholics since Saint Nicholas of Flüe is buried in a beautiful church here.

From Sachseln, continue south, following signs to Brienz and Interlaken. The road leads downward from the Brunig Pass to the town of Brienz and beyond to Interlaken.

The scenery around Interlaken and the nearby Jungfrau region is breathtaking. Within the immediate area there are spectacular mountains, scenic lakes, and pretty villages with charming places to stay. From the following sightseeing suggestions, choose a hub to use as your base of operations. Stay in just one place. Don't move around since everything is within easy driving distance. We have broken down the sightseeing into three sections: Sightseeing Highlights in the Interlaken Region, Sightseeing Highlights in the Jungfrau Region, and the Jungfraujoch Excursion.

SIGHTSEEING HIGHLIGHTS IN THE INTERLAKEN REGION

Interlaken: Interlaken, which translates to "between the lakes," has a fabulous location on a spit of land connecting two splendid lakes, the Brienzer See to the east (Lake Brienz) and the Thuner See (Lake Thun) to the west. It is not surprising that this superbly-located town with incredible mountain views has been a popular resort for over a hundred years, as evidenced by its grand old Victorian-style hotels. Although its glamour has faded a bit, tourists from all over the world still come to shop, visit the casino, and make excursions into the mountains (especially the Jungfrau circle trip). There are also numerous steamers that in summer depart from Interlaken and ply the waters of both Lake Brienz and Lake Thun. Although both are beautiful, our favorite of the two is Lake Brienz, which is wrapped by mountains.

Thun: Thun is a picturesque medieval village nestled at the west end of Lake Thun. It has an intriguing shopping area with two levels. You walk along the top level built above the arcaded buildings below, and drop to the lower street to do your shopping. Crowning a hill above the town is a fabulous old castle, built in the 12th century by the Duke of Zähringen. Getting there by a covered staircase from the village is half the fun. From the turrets, which are open as a museum, there is a ravishing panoramic view of Thun, the lake, and mountains beyond.

Brienz: Nestled along the waterfront at the east end of the Brienzer See, the picturesque village of Brienz has a web of narrow streets shadowed by wooden chalet-style houses and shops. Brienz is a woodcarving center and most of the carvings available for purchase throughout Switzerland come from here. Brienz is also famous for its violin-making school. There are many excursions you can take from here, including a fun ride on a little red train, the Brienz Rothorn, which climbs to the mountain top for a breathtaking, panoramic view of the Bernese Alps and Lake Brienz. The train leaves from the heart of Brienz, across from the train station and boat dock. This wonderful old steam locomotive traverses some exceptionally beautiful scenery on its three-hour round trip journey to the 2,350-meter summit of the Rothorn. (*www.brienz-rothorn-bahn.ch*.)

Boat on Brienzer See

Ballenberg: Nearby Brienz, on the Syssensee, there is an outstanding open-air museum called Ballenberg, offering a delicious taste of the culture and architecture of the various Swiss cantons. More than seventy buildings have been brought to the park and reconstructed. Crafts and old ways of living and working are brought to life by people dressed in local costumes and the interiors of the houses are furnished with appropriate antiques. When it's lunchtime, purchase a bounty of bread from the baker and sausage or

Open-Air Museum at Ballenberg

cheese from the farmer and have a picnic—or settle in at the village inn for a meal. A path weaves through this park of over 80 hectares and travels a course that takes you through the various cantons of Switzerland. You can tour the park on foot or, for a fee, by horse and buggy. Due to the vastness of the park, even if you decide to selectively visit just a few cantons, plan on allocating at least a half day here. Bus service is available from Brienz to the park (*www.ballenberg.ch*).

Iseltwald: If you are exploring the towns around Lake Brienz, one of the cutest of all is the tiny village of Iseltwald, located on the south shore of the lake. This would make a good stop one day for lunch or a cup of tea.

SIGHTSEEING HIGHLIGHTS IN THE JUNGFRAU REGION

Grindelwald: If you want to take the Jungfraujoch excursion, Grindelwald is the closest mountain village along the route to which you can drive. The setting of this glacier village is spectacular, with views of three giant mountain peaks, the Eiger rising to 3,970 meters, the Wetterhorn to 3,701 meters, and the Mettenberg to 3,104 meters. From the little station in town the train departs for the dramatic Kleine Scheidegg and on to the Jungfraujoch. Not only is Grindelwald a convenient place to take a train ride up to the base of the Jungfrau, but it is also a haven for hikers and climbers.

Grindelwald is a draw for sport enthusiasts year round. In winter the focus is on the snow conditions, terrain, and the best adventures in downhill and cross-country skiing. In summer the same lifts that take skiers up the mountain give hikers a head start along trails that climb in the shadow of the Eiger. There are also trams that operate only in summer and make hikes to glaciers and high meadows feasible in the span of a day.

Wengen: Part of the charm of Wengen is that it can be reached only by train. You leave your car in the parking lot at the Lauterbrunnen station and take the train for the spectacular 20-minute ride up the mountain. As the train pulls up the steep incline, you catch glimpses through the trees of the magnificent valley below. When you reach Wengen, you will be entranced: it has one of the most glorious sites in the world—high on a mountain plateau overlooking the breathtaking Lauterbrunnen Valley, a valley enclosed with walls of granite graced with cascading waterfalls. A backdrop for the total picture is the awe-inspiring Jungfrau massif with its three famous peaks, the Jungfrau, the Mönch, and the Eiger. This is a center for outdoor enthusiasts and sportsmen, while tourists come from all over the world to soak up the spectacular Alpine beauty. Summer is my favorite time of year in Wengen when the marvelous walking paths beckon. Along these trails there are new vistas at every turn, each more beautiful than the last. If walking is too gentle for your spirit, you can take climbs into the Bernese Oberland. If you are going to do some serious climbing, you should hire a local guide to accompany you. In addition to being a Mecca for the mountain enthusiast, Wengen is also an excellent base for the excursion to the Jungfrau. This is a circle trip taken by a series of little trains to the summit of the Jungfraujoch. Dominated by the Jungfrau, this boasts the highest train station in Europe and from its vantage point you will marvel at the spectacular vistas of the surrounding, awe-inspiring peaks. Known the world over, this trip is probably the most famous mountain-sightseeing adventure in Switzerland—one you will not want to miss.

Kleine Scheidegg: Kleine Scheidegg is the jumping-off point for the final leg of the Jungfraujoch excursion. Located above the timberline, the town is just a cluster of buildings hugging the windswept plateau. The wide, sweeping vistas of the rugged peaks of the Eiger, the Mönch, and the Jungfrau are overpowering. If the day is sunny, it is great fun to sit out on the open terrace with a beer and a bratwurst while soaking in the splendor of the mountains and watching tourists set off on the tiny train that soon disappears as it tunnels into the glacier.

Mürren: Mürren is a village clinging to a ledge high above the Lauterbrunnen Valley, with a startlingly steep granite wall dropping straight down from the village to the valley far below. The only access is by cable car from Stechelberg, tram from Lauterbrunnen, or, of course, for the true outdoorsman—by foot. Across the valley the Jungfrau towers into the sky, incredibly close, incredibly powerful. The Jungfrau circle of towns (Grindelwald, Wengen, and Kleine Scheidegg) is on the opposite side of the valley. If you don't have time for the Jungfraujoch excursion, there is a thrilling mountain adventure right from Mürren. Just step again onto the cable car, which will whisk you ever upward (with a change from one cable car to another en route) and get off at the icy barrens at the top of the mountain, the Schilthorn. Here you are treated to an awesome view of some of the most incredible mountain peaks in the world, right at your fingertips. Plan to have lunch here. There is a dramatic revolving restaurant with walls of glass called the Piz Gloria, which slowly circles so that you can savor the view while you dine.

Lauterbrunnen & Trümmelbachfälle: Lauterbrunnen, a popular place to leave your car and climb aboard the train for the Jungfraujoch excursion, is nestled on the floor of the valley. Before parking in Lauterbrunnen for the train trip, drive south for a few more kilometers, watching for a sign on the left side of the road for the Trümmelbachfälle, one of the most unusual waterfalls in the world. Park you car at the designated area near the road. From there it is just a very short walk over to the entrance to the falls—yes, "entrance." In the side of the mountain a steel door opens to an elevator that ascends within the mountain. When you get out, follow the path that winds down the hillside, snaking in and out of the mountain en route. Along the way you see ten dramatic waterfalls, gigantic, powerful thrusts of water gushing down from the Eiger, Mönch, and Jungfrau glaciers through twisted fissures in the rock. As you walk along the roaring water, there are balconies at various levels, strategically placed for photos and viewing.

Lauterbrunnen Valley & Trümmelbachfälle

Swiss Highlights—The Best of the Best

In the darker recesses, the falls are illuminated, increasing even further the magic of the experience. The whole outing should not take more than about an hour. However, if you are in a hurry and there is a line waiting for the elevator, you can easily walk up the well-marked path for the same views.

JUNGFRAUJOCH EXCURSION

The Jungfraujoch excursion is a journey on a series of small trains, synchronized to provide you with a perfect prize—the Jungfraujoch, with the highest train station in Europe sitting 92 meters below the summit of the Jungfrau. The most popular starting points for this outing are any of the following train stations: Interlaken Ost, Lauterbrunnen, Grindelwald, or Wengen. Although the trip can be taken in segments or as a side trip from one of its starting points, most tourists prefer to squeeze the ultimate enjoyment from their outing by taking the complete circle trip from Interlaken.

The Jungfraujoch excursion is one of the highlights of Switzerland. Unless you have traveled the route, it sounds quite complicated, but it is not. We explain, step-by-step, how this fabulous mountain adventure is put together and then you can tailor the trip to suit your special needs, beginning and ending at the town you have chosen to spend the night. The diagram on the following page demonstrates how the journey and options coordinate.

The complete circle trip begins at Interlaken Ost (Interlaken East) train station. However, you can also climb aboard at any of the stations along the route, for example, Lauterbrunnen, Kleine Scheidegg, Wengen, or Grindelwald, and the fare adjusts accordingly. Assuming Interlaken as your departure point, it is a 25-minute train ride to Lauterbrunnen where you change trains for the 45-minute ride up the mountain to Kleine Scheidegg (stopping en route to pick up passengers at the little town of Wengen). You have to change trains again at Kleine Scheidegg for the final ascent to the Jungfraujoch. For last thrilling leg of your adventure, the train creeps up the steep mountain and disappears into a 6½-kilometer tunnel through the glacier—reappearing at the Jungfraubahn, the highest rail station in Europe. It is possible to take an elevator even higher through the mountain to a vista point from where, on a clear day, it seems you can see the whole of Switzerland. You will also find an ice palace carved into the glacier, dog-sled rides, shops, a post office, and restaurants. For this journey, be sure to take sturdy shoes for walking on the glacier, gloves, a warm sweater or jacket, sunscreen, and sunglasses. When you leave the Jungfraujoch, it is necessary to retrace your journey to Kleine Scheidegg. For scenic variety, many travelers prefer to return to Interlaken from Kleine Scheidegg by a circle route. To do this, board the train for Grindelwald where you connect with another train that takes you directly to Interlaken.

The Jungfraujoch is an expensive excursion, but a once-in-a-lifetime adventure, especially when the weather cooperates and blue skies color a magnificent backdrop for these majestic peaks. There are numerous daily train departures and tickets are available for purchase at hotels, campsites, tourist offices, train stations, or travel agencies.

Jungfraujoch Excursion

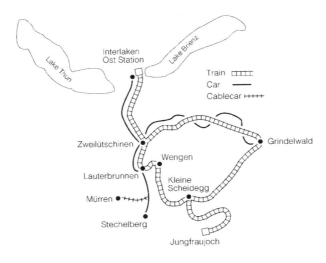

Swiss Highlights—The Best of the Best

FROM INTERLAKEN & THE JUNGFRAU REGION TO ZERMATT

Zermatt: As you travel from Interlaken to Zermatt, we suggest more places to see along the way than you could possibly accomplish in one day. We have squeezed in a wealth of exciting things to do en route to give you a platter from which to choose your favorites. A bit of your decision will probably be based upon the weather since we recommend two side-trips that involve twisting roads up narrow valleys, one of these is the Lötschental Valley and the other the Val d'Annivieres. If the sun is out both of these are unforgettable, but on a rainy day you might not be able to see a thing. So, study the itinerary, map out your personalized route, and let your final decision be governed by the weather.

Spiez

When it is time to continue on to Zermatt, take the road that runs along the southern shore of the Thuner See that goes from Interlaken toward Thun. Just before reaching the town of Spiez, turn south on a road leading to the Kandersteg Valley. Continue on this road to Frutigen. Where the road splits, follow signs going left to Kandersteg (not right to Adelboden). About 8 kilometers beyond Frutigen, watch for a sign for the Blausee (Blue Lake). Park your car near the main road and walk along a wooded path through a forest of twisted, mysterious trees. You begin to wonder where in the world you are going when suddenly you come upon a tiny, gorgeous lake—a photographer's dream. The incredibly blue, clear lake is set in the forest with a jagged Alpine horizon. There are usually many people here, as it is a favorite excursion of the Swiss who like to come to eat lunch lakeside in a little chalet-type restaurant. This is also a popular stop for families with children who enjoy taking one of the boat rides or just circling the lake on the twisting path through the gnarled forest. The effect is rather like a scene from *Hansel and Gretel*.

Kandersteg: From the Blausee, continue to Kandersteg, a small village tucked at the end of a box canyon where the only means of further transportation is to put your car onto one of the trains that tunnels through the mountain. Although this suggested itinerary goes on to Zermatt, if you have time to linger, Kandersteg is an idyllic place to spend a few days. There are some exceptionally charming hotels here, making a stay here even more enticing. Kandersteg nestles in a flower-strewn meadow dramatically embraced by towering Alpine peaks. This is a great destination from which to take walks or just sit and enjoy the breathtaking scenery. Nearby trails (with benches strategically placed so you can stop to enjoy the view) cater to all levels of athletic pursuit (from a leisurely stroll to a high-powered mountain ascent). If you stay longer in Kandersteg, there is a chairlift at the end of the valley that takes you up to Lake Oeschinen where rugged cliffs jut dramatically into the sky, forming a backdrop to the clear mountain lake. The lake lies below the terminal of the chairlift and is reached via a path through mountain meadows. On a clear day it is especially inviting to walk down the mountain rather than take the chairlift.

As you continue on your way to Zermatt, look for signs to the Kandersteg train station where agents will direct you where to buy your ticket and line up for the next train. When it arrives, you are instructed where to park "piggy-back" on the train. You stay in your car as the train rambles on through the dark tunnel and pops out once again into the light on the other side. The first stop on the other side of the tunnel is Goppenstein where you drive off the train and are on your way.

Kandersteg

Lötschental Valley: From Goppenstein, a very special mountain adventure awaits—the Lötschental Valley. Instead of continuing south toward the Rhône Valley, follow signs to the Lötschental Valley and the towns of Blatte and Fafleralp. Take the narrow road as it goes east along the side of the Lonza River and winds up through one of the most beautiful valleys imaginable. On a clear day, the views are unsurpassed. Along the way you pass through ancient little villages, untouched by time. One of the prettiest of these is the town of Blatten, where there are several simple (but very nice) hotels with spectacular views. If you have the luxury of a few extra days, this would make a wonderful place to spend some time. From Blatten the road continues on to where the valley dead-ends at the base of the majestic Breithorn, a 3785-meter-high mountain masterpiece. At the last town along the route called Fafleralp there is a small restaurant where you can get a snack or a cold drink.

From the Lötschental Valley, retrace your way back to Goppenstein and turn south. After 9 kilometers you come to the N9, that traverses the Rhône Valley. Turn west here and continue for approximately 15 kilometers to Sierre. Before you come into town, take the turnoff going south, marked to the Val d'Annivieres.

Val d'Annivieres: The scenery through the Val d'Annivieres is beautiful, but be forewarned that the road is narrow and twists and turns as it climbs higher into the mountains. Don't attempt this side trip in the winter, but in the summer, if the day is brilliant and you are not intimidated by mountain driving, Grimentz makes a fantastic detour. When you come to Vissoie, the road splits. At this junction, take the branch that goes to the right toward to your sightseeing goal, Grimentz, a fantastic Valais village clinging to a mountain ridge.

Grimentz: The small mountain village of Grimentz is an architectural gem—so special it is protected by the Swiss government. This very old village is filled with marvelously preserved Valais-style homes whose heavy slate roofs are weighted down by chunky rocks to protect them against the winter storms. Park your car at the entrance to the village and stroll down the tiny streets that are closed to all but foot traffic. The lanes are lined by simple wood houses whose rough-hewn, age-blackened exteriors contrast dramatically with masses of flowers cascading from every window box. It is hard to believe that the Grimentz of old could ever have been as picturesque as it is today, for each resident seems to vie with his neighbor for the most stunning display of brilliant red geraniums. The effect captivates the senses: brilliant blue sky (with a little luck), snow-capped mountains, green pastures, blackened-with-age wooden houses, flowers, flowers, and flowers. If the timing is right, after wandering through the village, stop and enjoy a cheese fondue lunch on the terrace of the Hotel de Moiry, located just at the entrance of the pedestrian-only zone.

After the side trip to Grimentz, return to the N9 and turn east. As you near Visp, take the well-marked turnoff south toward Zermatt. The only choice you have along the way is where the road splits: the left branch of the road leads to Saas-Fee and the right leads to Zermatt.

Zermatt: You cannot drive into Zermatt as no cars are allowed within the city limits. However, this is not a problem as there are car parks at each of the small neighboring towns. Täsch is as far as you can go by car, so park here, buy your ticket at the station, and board the train for the rest of your journey. After about a 15-minute ride, you arrive at the Zermatt terminal where you will notice a few horse-drawn carriages waiting in the plaza in front of the station. In winter, these convert to horse-drawn sleighs. In the past few years, electric golf-type carts have gradually replaced almost all of the horse drawn carriages and sleighs—only a few of the most posh hotels still offer this romantic means of transportation. During the height of the season, many of the hotels send their "carriage" to meet all the incoming trains—each hotel has its name on the cart or carriage or the porter's cap. If for some reason you do not see *your* porter, there is a large panel in the center of the station with the names of all the hotels, listed with a corresponding code to call the hotel directly so that they will send someone to fetch you. This service is usually free of charge.

Zermatt is a city in the sky, not the sleepy little mountain hamlet of yesteryear. Yet, in spite of the hoards of tourist, new shopping arcades, countless hotels, and newly built condominiums, Zermatt is still an enchanting destination. How can you resist its weathered farmhouses, quaint little streets, unbelievable displays of brilliant flowers, charming hotels, and cozy restaurants? Plus, you just can't go home without seeing the Matterhorn, one of the world's most glorious mountains.

While in Zermatt there are two especially popular sightseeing excursions: the Gornegrat and the Klein Matterhorn, neither of which should be taken if visibility is poor. The Gornegrat ascent entails a ride on a cog railway up to the Gornegrat Station, which is located on a rocky ridge looking over the town of Zermatt and beyond to the Matterhorn. From the Gornegrat Station a walk down to the next station gives you views of the

Zermatt

Matterhorn and the surrounding mountains. The Klein Matterhorn ascent involves a ride on a small cable car to a mid-station, then three or four rides on a large gondola/cable car. The station at the summit is at the highest altitude of any station in Europe (3,820 meters). The views are spectacular.

While in Zermatt you must take advantage of its well-marked footpaths and walks. You can follow one of the beautifully marked trails drifting out from the village core and suddenly find yourself in meadows of wildflowers, or take a chair lift, tram, or train up the mountain, from which point you can walk all or part of the way down. Numerous small cafés are scattered along the trails. It is truly the civilized way to hike when you can stop along the route for a glass of wine or cup of coffee and delicious pastry.

Saas Fee: If would like to experience another town in the same region as Zermatt, consider staying in Saas Fee. It is located at the end of the Saastal or Saas Valley, which branches off from the road to the much more famous resort of Zermatt. Ringed by more than a dozen mountains, Saas Fee perches on a shelf high above the valley. The town is closed to traffic—all cars must be left in the huge, modern, multi-story car park on the edge of town. If you are staying overnight, park in lot number one. Dial your hotel and tell them you have arrived and soon an electric cart will come to pick you up.

Saas Fee is primarily a ski town but is still bustling in summer with hikers and tourists. It has attractive shops (lots of watches, skiing and hiking equipment) and some delightful restaurants. Hiking opportunities abound, from gentle walks to "high routes" (challenging hikes in the mountains). Saas Fee offers some intriguing diversions, including rides on the underground metro to the Mittelallalin, site of the world's highest revolving restaurant. Even more fascinating is the Ice Pavilion, the world's largest ice cavern, where the exhibits include a crevasse within the Fee Glacier. If you are staying for several days, consider purchasing the seven-day Wander Pass, which covers fees for the Ice Pavilion, a day of skiing, Saas-Fee museums, buses, and cable cars along the Saas Valley.

FROM ZERMATT TO THE SOUTHERN LAKES

Leaving Zermatt, take the train back to the parking area in Täsch and retrieve your car. It is a long day's drive from Zermatt to the Swiss-Italian Lake District—so try for an early departure. Head north to Visp where you join the N9 freeway going east in the direction of Brig. After about 8 kilometers, take the turn off that heads south over the Simplon Pass. The first part of the drive is over a four-lane highway that gently loops up the hill, providing a dramatic view of the Rhône Valley far below. Soon the road becomes two lanes, but although there are many twists and turns, the road is beautifully banked and not particularly difficult. Before you know it, you are in Italy and the road begins to wind downward through the Val Divedro. The first small town across the border is Iselle. Before you come to Domodóssola, the four-lane highway begins again and continues south to Gravellona where you turn east on the SS34 to Verbana, a journey of about 12 kilometers. When you arrive in Verbana, continue north on SS34 toward Locarno. This is a scenic drive that hugs the edge of Lake Maggiore. On weekends and during the summer months when everyone is on holiday, this road can be distressingly slow due to heavy traffic. If you want to stop, the most charming town along the way is the beautiful medieval village of Cannero Riviera. The oldest part of town, located to the north, is where you want to be. The lanes leading down to the waterfront in the old part of town are so impossibly narrow, that it is best to park your car a bit away from the lake and walk to the waterfront. There is a romantic promenade along the lake with lovely parks. The best place to stop for a snack or lunch is at the Cannero Lakeside Hotel. This has a beautiful outdoor terrace, just near the ferry landing. Stoll just a bit north from the hotel and you will discover a tiny, ancient, fisherman's cove.

About 12 kilometers beyond Cannero Riviera, you cross once again into Switzerland and it is only about another 11 kilometers before arriving in Ascona on Lake Maggiore. If you choose Lake Lugano as your hub, continue on from Ascona to Locarno, and follow signs to Lugano. Note: see the following itinerary *Swiss Treasures off the Beaten Path* for more information on the Lake District.

Shortcut option: There is another option on your route between Zermatt and Lake Maggiore—a shortcut to the Swiss-Italian lakes on a truly a spectacular road that follows the Melezza River Gorge into the beautiful Centovalli. If it's foggy or raining, don't even think about this alternative. But, if it is a brilliant day and you are keen for back roads, you will be awestruck by the natural beauty along the way. For this shortcut, follow the itinerary as shown until you come over the Simplon Pass, the first town after crossing the border into Italy is Iselle. About 10 kilometers after Iselle, you come to Crevoladóssola, where you leave the highway and take a small road (S337) east to Locarno (a total of 43 kilometers). Just before you arrive in Locarno, take the road going south to Ascona.

FINAL DESTINATION–THE SOUTHERN LAKES:

This itinerary finishes in the romantic lake district of Southern Switzerland. If you want to extend your holiday, the following itinerary, *Swiss Treasures off the Beaten Path,* loops from the Lake District back to Zürich.

Swiss Treasures
off the Beaten Path

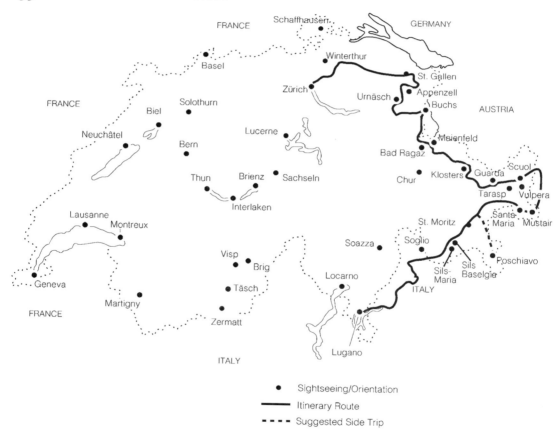

Sightseeing/Orientation
Itinerary Route
Suggested Side Trip

Swiss Treasures off the Beaten Path

Ascona on Lake Maggiore

The majority of tourists on their first trip to Switzerland visit one or more of its best-known tourist destinations, such as Geneva, Zürich, Lucerne, Interlaken, Bern, and Zermatt. All of these jewels are outstanding—well deserving their fame. However, we would like to introduce to you a selection of our favorite places, some of which you might never have heard of since they are a bit off the beaten path. This itinerary begins at your choice of either Lake Maggiore or Lake Lugano, both gorgeous lakes in the southern part of Switzerland, almost on the Italian border. It is stretching a bit to say these lakes are off the beaten path, but we introduce some very special villages around the lake that are not well known. From the Lake District, our route then cuts across a corner of Italy and continues north to the stunning hamlet of Soglio. Leaving Soglio, the road traces the Inn River to the upper reaches of the Engadine Valley, just before the Austrian border. Here you find mountain villages that seem forgotten in time, so beautiful you will never want to leave. The next suggested stop is in Appenzell, a moderate-sized town in an idyllic area enhanced by beautiful old farmhouses, lush meadows dotted with contented cows, and lovely villages. From Appenzell, the itinerary loops back to Zürich.

RECOMMENDED PACING: We recommend a minimum of nine nights for this itinerary. *This does not include the nights you choose to stay at the end of your trip in Zürich.*

THREE NIGHTS in the Southern Lake District: Three nights in the Lake District will give you two full days to explore this romantic part of Switzerland. You need sufficient time to take boat excursions on the gorgeous lakes, do a bit of sightseeing, and visit nearby quaint villages. Lake Maggiore and Lake Lugano are very close to each other, so select one or the other lake as your hub. If you choose Lake Maggiore, we suggest Ascona as a place to stay. If you choose Lake Lugano, we recommend Lugano, Morcote, or Castagnola.

TWO NIGHTS in Soglio: Two nights in Soglio will give you one full day to relax in this beautiful village, do a bit of sightseeing, and enjoy leisurely walks in this incredibly stunning part of Switzerland.

THREE NIGHTS in the Engadine Valley: Three nights in the glorious Engadine Valley is the bare minimum to enjoy all the wonders this beautiful area has to offer.

ONE NIGHT in Appenzeller Land: you can get by with just one night in Appenzell since the town is so small and much of the sightseeing will be en route.

ITINERARY ENDS in Zürich.

NOTE: You will not have time to include all of the sightseeing we suggest. We have described what we consider to be the most interesting places along the way, please choose those that seem most enticing to you.

LAKE MAGGIORE

Ascona: In days gone by, Ascona was a sleepy fishing village, but today tourists are its main source of activity and it is no wonder—Ascona is a jewel. The town is so exceptionally pretty that it attracts many artists from around the world. The town sits directly onto Lake Maggiore whose waves lap gently at the dock where boats are moored next to the picturesque, pedestrian-only square called Piazza Motta. This square looks onto the lake which is traced by a promenade shaded by trees and enhanced by colorful gardens. Facing the square, and beyond to the lake, is a row of pastel-colored buildings with heavy tiled roofs—a scene much more Italian than Swiss. These charming buildings are now hotels, cafes, and shops. It is fun to sit at one of the terrace cafes and sip a cup of coffee or glass of wine and watch the boats glide in and out of the harbor, picking up and letting off happy passengers. Behind the front row of houses, cobbled lanes spider-web back into the medieval village where there are many shops and boutiques. From Ascona, steamers ply Lake Maggiore, one of Switzerland's most romantic lakes. There is a good selection of boat excursions you can take. One of the most interesting is to Isole di Brissago, a tiny island where you can tour beautiful tropical gardens. There are frequent ferries that go to Locarno, which has a similar setting to Ascona but is a larger town and not as quaint. Visit the 15th-century Santi Pietro e Paolo church. Be sure to notice its stunning altar painted by Giovanni Serodine. Another church to visit is Santa Maria della Misericordia, which is famous for its 15th-century frescoes. For museum buffs, the Museo Comunale d'Arte Moderna, housed in a 16th-century palace, features local artists.

Ascona, protected from the northern cold by massive mountains, enjoys the sun from the south and is well known for its temperate climate. When the weather is cold and dreary in the northern part of Italy, it is a tempting option to head to the Swiss-Italian Lake District where the sun shines most of the year and flowers bloom all winter.

LAKE LUGANO

Lake Maggiore is beautiful. However, Lake Lugano is equally lovely. If you prefer to stay in Lake Lugano, follow signs east from Ascona to Locarno. Although the distance is short, there is usually lots of traffic so it might take longer than expected. Passing Locarno, continue toward Bellinzona. Before you arrive in Bellinzona, at the first opportunity, take the A4 south to Lugano. Stay on the A4 expressway until you come to the Lugano Sud exit and follow signs to the center of town. Choose a place to stay in one of the towns listed below. Each has its own personality and will make a good hub. They all are connected by the ferry system, although Lugano (being the more major city) has more frequent service.

Lugano: Lugano is an appealing medieval town hugging the northern shore of Lake Lugano. Its ambiance is more Italian than Swiss—not surprising since you are almost on the Italian border. The old section of town with its maze of narrow streets is a delight— what fun to browse through its boutiques and little shops. The splendid promenade that stretches along the lakefront is a superb place to stroll. Almost all of the sightseeing within the town is best done by foot, since many of the streets are closed to cars.

The Lugano Tourist Office offers free walking tours, which give a richer insight into the places you visit than if you were to walk alone. There are three different tours, each on a different day. The tours are offered from March 21 until October 17. Sometimes schedules change so be sure to check at the tourist office when you arrive in Lugano to double check the times and days of departures. The tours are listed below.

Classic Walking Tour: This free guided tour highlights the cultural aspects of Lugano, wandering through the pedestrian streets of its historic center and visiting its architectural monuments. (Mondays, 9:30 am departure from Chiesa degli Angioli in Piazza Luini, return 11:45 am.)

History Walking Tour: This free guided tour brings to life Lugano's history and personality through its buildings, churches, statues, and colorful squares. (Wednesdays, 9:30 am departure from the Tourist Office, Palazzo Civico, return 11:45 am.)

Lugano's Parks and Gardens Walking Tour: This free guided tour visits Lugano's parks and gardens. Due to the temperate climate, many kinds of plants, trees, and flowers thrive here. The first stop is the Church of Santa Maria degli Angioli. Then the tour proceeds to the Belvedere Garden, and ends up the Ciani Park. (Fridays, 9:30 am departure from the Tourist Office, Palazzo Civico, return 11:45 am.)

Cathedral of Saint Lawrence (Cattedrale San Lorenzo): Be sure to visit Lugano's grandest church, the Cathedral of Saint Lawrence. Its handsome renaissance façade and Baroque interior are well worth a visit.

Saint Mary of the Angels Church (Santa Maria degli Angioli): The 15th-century Santa Maria degli Angioli, whose façade is much less ornate than that of the Cathedral of Saint Lawrence, was originally built as a Franciscan monastery. However, its interior has a treasure: two 16th-century frescos by Bernardo Luini depicting the Crucifixion of Christ and the Last Supper. Their detail and rich colors are stunning.

Boat Excursions: For a special treat, hop aboard one of the ferries that are constantly gliding in and out of the pier that is located in the center of town. There is a posted schedule at the ferry ticket office that shows the destinations of the boats and their departure times. Some of the boats are for tours of the lake and make a round trip from Lugano. It is fun to study the schedule and plan a day of sightseeing on the lake, stopping at one of the colorful towns along the way for lunch. You can easily stretch your boat ride out to an all-day excursion or squeeze it into a couple of hours. A few towns accessible by boat that are especially pretty are described below.

Castagnola: Castagnola is a lakeside hamlet near Lugano that is made up of a strip of houses, restaurants, and hotels that stretch along a trail that runs along the lakefront. There is no road—the only approach is by boat or by foot along a pretty path. The isolation is part of the fun. There are a few hotels and restaurants. There is an especially pleasant walk from Castagnola to Gandria (see below).

Castagnola

Gandria: Gandria is a small medieval fishing village that clings to the hillside above the lake. The tiny town is just a little beyond Castagnola, with a path linking the two villages.

Morcote: If you only have time to include one village on your ferry excursion, choose Morcote—a picture-perfect village that clings to a hill that seems to rise straight up from Lake Lugano. The town is a jumble of painted houses with arcaded walkways. Leading off behind the front row of buildings is a maze of narrow alleyways. Although its setting is remarkably quaint, it is not easy to navigate Morcote by car, so it might be preferable to come by a ferry from Lugano instead of driving. If you aren't spending the night here, allow sufficient time to have lunch on the terrace of one of the open-air restaurants that hang out over the water. If you feel in tiptop shape, climb up the steep back alleys which will bring you to the Church of Santa Maria del Sasso, which contains some outstanding 16th-century frescos. Also in Morcote there is a beautiful private park where you will find plants artistically displayed in gardens overlooking the lake.

Morcote

THE LAKE DISTRICT TO SOGLIO

If Lake Maggiore was your base of operations while in the Lake District, when it's time to travel on, take the road from Ascona to Lugano, and then continue as described.

From Lugano, go east along the north shore of Lake Lugano in the direction of Menággio. In just 6 kilometers you pass the border into Italy. The road becomes very narrow and you need to squeeze your car through some of the tiny medieval villages. Our favorite stop along this part of the lake is Valsolda San Marmete, a tiny, picturesque village with one of our favorite hotels, the Stella d'Italia. If the timing is right, you might want to stop for refreshment on its romantic lakefront terrace. In a short while you arrive in Portezza, the town at the eastern tip of Lake Lugano. The road continues on to Menággio where you turn north on SS340, going through many tunnels along the way as the road follows the shoreline of Lake Como. In about 27 kilometers you come to the small town of Sórico. Just beyond the town, you cross a bridge and come to the junction of SS37 where you head north in the direction of Chiavenna and Saint Moritz. When you reach Chiavenna, the road begins to climb up into the mountains. At the town of Castasegna, you leave Italy and are once again in Switzerland. At this point, the highway number changes to 3. Very soon after crossing the border you come to a road on your left signposted to Soglio. Take this narrow road, which climbs the steep hill to Soglio.

Soglio: If you have accommodations at the Hotel Palazzo Salis, you can drive briefly into Soglio to drop off your luggage; however the one-way streets were never designed for cars and you need to hold your breath for fear of scraping your car on the buildings or encountering another car. It you are dauntless, brave the excursion into the village. Otherwise, leave your car in the parking lot just before the church and walk into town (hopefully your luggage is on wheels).

Soglio is one of the most stunning small towns in Switzerland—truly spectacular. Perched high on a sunny ledge above the splendid Bregaglia Valley, Soglio looks across to spectacular jagged mountain peaks. The village is tiny—no more than a few narrow alley-like streets lined with charming buildings, many of them rustic wooden farmhouses.

As you enter the lower part of the village, one of the first buildings you come to is the 14th-century San Lorenzo Church, a real beauty with a tall spire stretching into the sky, creating a striking silhouette of the town that can be seen from afar. Peek inside—the church is lovely. Then open the gate and wander into the adjacent cemetery and look out over the belvedere that encloses the rear garden.

The views from Soglio are breathtaking and constantly changing. As you look across the valley the moods are affected dramatically by the time of the day. Early-morning light leaves a sliver of gold on the snowy escarpment enhanced by shifting clouds caressing the mountain peaks. Soglio is not only a picturesque stopover but, in addition, a superb base for hiking along tranquil paths. Chestnut trees line some of these beautiful trails and cows munch lazily in the meadows. And, even though you are high above the valley, the walking is pleasantly undemanding.

Soglio

SOGLIO TO THE ENGADINE VALLEY

From Soglio twist back down the narrow road to the highway and continue north in the direction of Saint Moritz. This is a beautiful drive following the Maira River as it cuts a path through the mountains.

Stampa: Very soon after descending from Soglio, you come to the quaint rustic village of Stampa, the birthplace of the three famous artists—all members of the talented Giacometti family—Giovanni, Augusto, and Alberto. Ciäsa Granda, a museum in what used to be their family home, has a collection of some of their paintings and sculptures. The museum is open from 2 pm to 5 pm.

Cassaccia: Approximately 15 kilometers beyond Stampa, you come to the village of Cassaccia, which was in the medieval times an important town due to its strategic location at the foot of the Maloja Pass. Traders on horseback stopped here before going over the mountain. Ruins of a small church stand above the village. The church was dedicated to San Guadenzio, the patron saint of Bregaglia, who (according to legend) came here in the 4th century to convert the region to Christianity and was beheaded for his efforts

Leaving Cassaccia, the road goes over the Maloja Pass and drops down into the Engadine Valley which follows the Inn River (also called the En River, hence the name of the valley) north and loops into Austria. The southern part of the valley is called the Upper Engadine (*Ober Engadin*) and the more northern part of the valley near the Austrian border is called the Lower Engadine (*Unter Engadin*). Because this itinerary is highlighting places that are "off the beaten path," we suggest you continue north to the less well-known part of the valley, the Lower Engadine, and make this your base of operations.

If you have the luxury of time, stop for a few days on your way to the Lower Engadine Valley in one of the many enticing towns (described in the following pages).

Another option for extending your holiday (or as a side excursion on your way to the Lower Engadin) is a trip over the Bernina Pass to the medieval town of Poschiavo (described below).

At the bottom of the Maloja Pass you come to a beautiful lake, the Silser See and immediately afterward, to a second lake, the Silvaplaner See. These two lakes are divided by a thread of land that acts as a natural bridge between them. On this bit of land there are two "sister" towns, Sils-Baselgia and Sils-Maria. Although they have separate names, the streets of one town actually continue on into the other. The towns merge in a pedestrian zone, so if you are driving, each town must be accessed by a separate road. This is a very popular resort and in summer horse drawn carriages are waiting in the heart of the village to take you for a ride.

Sils-Baselgia & Sils-Maria: the Sils area is a paradise for cross-country skiing in the winter and for hiking, boating, biking, fishing, sail surfing, and swimming in the summer. The scenery is stunning and the variety of marvelous walks is staggering. You can take one of the many trails up into the mountains or enjoy gentle walks along the paths that circle the lakes. A favorite outing is a boat ride on the Silser See to the lovely hamlet of Isola where you can enjoy lunch before returning on a footpath along the lake to Sils.

If you are interested in the life of the 19th-century philosopher, Friedrich Nietzsche, his summer home in Sils-Maria is open as a museum, which contains memorabilia of his life. The museum, Nietzsche House, is open daily except Monday from 3 pm to 6 pm.

The two lakes, the Silser See and the Silvaplaner See, form a figure 8 in a sunny meadow that is wrapped by mountains. What a beautiful sight!

Saint Moritz: Approximately 15 kilometers after leaving Sils-Baselgia and Sils-Maria, you arrive in Saint Moritz. Known to the jet-set elite throughout the world as *the* place to be seen in the ski season, Saint Moritz is also popular as a summer resort. The town backs right up to the mountain so it is just a short walk to the funicular to go skiing. From its terraced position on the side of the hill, Saint Moritz looks down to a pretty tree-rimmed lake. In winter, horse races cross the frozen expanse and, in summer, a path skirts its edge. In town, the streets are lined with chic designer boutiques selling exquisite merchandise. Saint Moritz has not grown with the same purity of architecture as some other ski areas such as Gstaad and Zermatt, but it is much less "concrete high-rise" than its sister ski area, Davos.

Celerina: Located about 5 kilometers north of Saint Moritz, Celerina is famous for its jazz festival. This is a particularly picturesque Engadin village with many wonderful old houses that nestle in a meadow. The Inn River flows through the center of town, further enhancing its charm. Though so very close to Saint Moritz, Celerina has the charming ambiance of a small country village rather than a sophisticated ski resort.

Optional Side Trip–Postchiavo: Taking the main road 27 north from Saint Moritz, in 7 kilometers you come to a junction. Turn right here on road 29 going south toward Poschiavo and Tirano. In a few minutes you pass through the upscale resort of Pontresina (famous as a skiing and climbing center) where there are many large hotels on the hillside with fine views of the surrounding mountains. Leaving Pontresina, you travel through the Val Bernina and then the road climbs the mountains to the Bernina Pass. At first the scenery is quite barren with views of the massive Morteratsch Glacier. From the summit, the road descends through pristine fir forests, then around some more hairpin turns, and drops down into the Poschiavo Valley. The road continues on into Italy to the town of Tirano, which is just across the border. However, your target is the charming village of Poschiavo, nestled in a pocket surrounded by wooded mountains. This off-the-beaten-path jewel looks and feel much more Italian than Swiss.

Poschiavo is quite small, only 3,300 people live here. However, it has always been a town of great importance since it is on one of the main trade routes between Italy and Switzerland. The climate here is particularly favorable since the town is protected by high mountains from the harsh weather from the north and exposed to the Mediterranean influence of warmer weather from the south. Surprisingly, palm and cypress trees thrive in the mild climate.

Because the center of town is pedestrian only, you need to leave your car on the outskirts in a parking lot (you can drive into town temporarily to leave your luggage if you are staying overnight here). The heart of Poschiavo is a maze of medieval streets. The main square (the Piazza Communale) is particularly picturesque. Within a few blocks there are two churches (including the especially lovely 16th-century Church of San Vittore), handsome palaces in the Italianate style, the Casa Torre (a Romanesque tower), and many handsome, pastel-colored houses.

Just 10 kilometers south of Poschiavo you come to Lake Poschiavo, a popular resort area. The town at the north end of the lake is called Le Prese, which used to be a spa town until its sulphur springs dried up. Now Le Prese is popular as a center for hiking, fishing, and water sports.

Continue south along Lake Poschiavo and when you come to its southern tip, take a turnoff on the left to Miralago, a cute hamlet snuggled on a slope that rises from the water's edge. It has a splendid view out over the lake to the towering mountains beyond. Although the town is so tiny, it has a 17th-century Baroque church, consecrated to Saint Gottardo.

After your visit to Poschiavo, retrace your way over the Bernina Pass, through Pontresina and on to Samedan where you rejoin the itinerary continuing north on highway 27 along the Engadin Valley.

You will pass through Zuoz, a small medieval village, and then on to Zernez where you turn east on 28. The road travels through the heavily forested Swiss National Park, over the Ofenpass, and then down into the unspoiled rural beauty of the Müstair Valley.

Müstair Valley: Stretched along the sweep of the Müstair Valley are several unspoiled hamlets. As you descend over the Ofenpass, you come to Santa Maria (a tiny town with Grisons-style buildings and a very attractive church) and then Müstair (the last town before the Italian border). Müstair is a pretty little village of thick-walled houses dating back to the 13th century whose character seems more Italian than Swiss—it's as if the border line has slipped back in favor of Italy. Very few people speak English here. The ambiance is one of an authentic old European town, untouched by commercialism. The dialect is decidedly Italian and the locals' salutation is *arrevoir*.

When it is time to leave Müstair, drive east for one kilometer to where the Müstair Valley flows into Italy. After crossing the Italian border the route heads through the Monastero Valley for 6 kilometers to where you take a turnoff that joins a road heading north to Résia and Nauders. Just beyond Résia Pass, you cross into Austria. Four kilometers after entering Austria (just before the town of Nauders) turn west on 185 which drops you once again into Switzerland and the Engadin Valley. This route might seem a bit confusing, but when you study your Swiss map, the puzzle will fall into place.

LOWER ENGADINE VALLEY (UNTER ENGADIN)

The northern part of the Engadine Valley is one of our favorite places in Switzerland. The scenery here is positively dazzling. This narrow glacial valley, which follows the Inn River, is enclosed by stunning mountain peaks. This valley is not a destination filled with museums and formal sightseeing, but rather offers the sheer joy of nature at its finest. As you wander through the valley you discover spa towns tucked along the riverbank, villages perched on high mountain shelves, and incredibly beautiful hamlets nestled in lush mountain meadows. Another bonus is hiking in the Swiss National Park, a nature preserve in the mountains that frames the valley to the south.

Choose one of the towns below, and make it your hub from which to go out each day exploring. All of the described towns have wonderful places to stay.

Guarda: You definitely must visit the adorable town of Guarda—probably the most picturesque village in the valley and one that is well worth a detour to visit. This tiny town has a breathtaking site—perched high on a mountain ledge overlooking the Engadine Valley and beyond to incredibly beautiful mountains peaks. Its setting is similar to that of Soglio which you visited earlier on the itinerary. The town consists of just a few steep narrow cobbled streets enhanced by fountains and faced by some beautiful 17th-century houses that display fine examples of the style of architecture found in this part of the Engadine Valley. These houses are painted in various pastel colors and enhanced by an art form called *sgraffiti* (from which our word "graffiti" probably originates). This style of artwork involves a technique in which the top layer of plaster on a building is scraped away, revealing intricate patterns that have been worked into the plaster below. Some of the artwork is geometric designs, but frequently they are wonderfully whimsical pictures. Just a short distance east from Guarda (perched on the same mountain shelf), you come Ardez, another Engadine town rich in *sgraffiti*. It is worth the short detour to see its artwork—don't miss the house with the intricate design depicting Adam and Eve under the apple tree.

Tarasp: Along with Guarda, Tarasp is one of the highlights of the Lower Engadine Valley. It must not be missed. Of all the sites in this guide, none is more beautiful. From Vulpera, a small road leads up into a wide, lush meadow enclosed by mountain peaks. A tranquil little lake nestles next to the lower part of the town. The oldest part of Tarasp sits on a gentle knoll where a few, centuries-old, charming farmhouses cluster around a fountain. As if all this were not enough, a stunning, 12th-century castle is perched on a spur of rock, overlooking the town. Well-marked trails spider web in all directions from

Tarasp Castle

Tarasp, leading up into the mountains. The urge to pick up your walking stick and stride off across the meadows with the other happy hikers is almost irresistible.

Scuol: Scuol (sometimes spelled Schuls) is an old spa town that rises from the banks of the rushing Inn River. A covered bridge at the foot of the village crosses the river. Due to its thermal waters, Scuol grew in popularity in the late 19th century as a spa. Some of the buildings in town are modern, but, happily, at its core Scuol remains a charming medieval village with colorfully painted houses, cobbled squares, many flowers, statues, fountains, and a picturesque white church topped by a tall steeple.

S-Charl: From Scuol a small, single-lane, somewhat intimidating, road (part of which is unpaved) twists up into the mountains, dead-ending in S-Charl, a hamlet that lies in a splendid meadow adjacent to the Swiss National Park, a totally protected, natural paradise. There are but a cluster of buildings here, including a few restaurants and a hotel. Most people come to enjoy the pristine majesty of the mountains and to hike in the beautiful park.

Vulpera: Vulpera is located to the south side of the Inn River and climbs up a gentle hill toward the mountains. Like Scuol, Vulpera grew in popularity in the 19th century as a spa and as a result, grand Victorian-style hotels were built here. This old-fashioned glamour still lingers a bit although nowadays many of the hotels and buildings are modern.

ENGADINE VALLEY TO APPENZELL

Leaving the Engadine Valley, drive west on 27 to Susch where you take the 28 toward Davos. The road runs through the Susasca Valley for a short distance and then climbs over the Flüla Pass whose summit displays a barren, stark beauty. After a number of hairpin turns the road drops down and flattens out as you approach Davos. Unless you are a skier there is no reason to stop since the town isn't very special. At Davos, turn north and in about 10 kilometers you come to Klosters.

Klosters: Klosters backs up to the same mountains as Davos and the two ski areas interconnect like a giant spider web. Like Davos, much of Klosters is newly constructed but (in contrast to Davos) it has grown with a gracious style encompassing the Swiss chalet motif. There are many lovely boutiques and restaurants. The town is very well situated for hiking in the summer or skiing in the winter. The train station is the terminus for a cable lift that rises high above the village to the marvelous ski runs. Also popular in winter are tobogganing, cross-country skiing, curling, and ice skating. However, my favorite time for Klosters is the summer when the fields are vibrant with wildflowers, with the majestic mountains standing guard.

From Klosters it is an exceptionally lovely drive following the Landquart River to Landquart, at which point, you join the A13 going north.

Maienfeld: If as a child you were enchanted by Johanna Spyri's book, *Heidi*, stop in Maienfeld to visit the re-creation of what was supposedly Heidi's village, located in the scenic mountain area that inspired the story. If you choose to squeeze in this side excursion, exit the A13 at Maienfeld/Bad Ragas and follow signs to Maienfeld. The closest place to park is the Heidihof Hotel, which (with its contemporary architecture) doesn't blend in at all with what you would expect as part of Heidi's world. From the hotel, a five-minute walk brings you up to the house that has been designated as "Heidi's." It is open as a museum from April to November from 10 am to 5 pm. Oberrofels is the tiny hamlet above Maienfeld that has been renamed "Heididorf" (Heidi's town). The area is very beautiful and you can follow a scenic path from Heididorf up into the high mountain pastures leading to places featured in the book. All is a bit contrived, but fun.

If visiting Heidi's village isn't high on your priority list, don't exit at Bad Ragas, but instead stay on the A13 to Buchs where you exit and travel west on 16. You soon come to Gams where the road begins a gentle climb. The scenery is extraordinarily beautiful with majestic mountains framing the view to your left, and to your right, lush farmland. The road continues through woodland and over a mild pass, dropping down into another valley. Just after Nesslau, turn right at the village of Neu Saint Johann and continue in the direction of Rietbad and Saint Gallen. You go by the very old, very quaint village of Ennetbühl and continue on to Urnäsch.

Urnäsch: When you come to the main square of Urnäsch, park your car and walk to the Appenzell Folk Art Museum, a four-story house with shutters and window boxes, located on the left side of the square as you drive into town. The museum is closed until 1:30 pm, but if you are in Urnäsch in the afternoon, this is a dandy little museum. Its purpose is to show the customs, traditions, and life in the Appenzell region in olden days. It is fun to visit the rustic, reconstructed farmhouse interiors where the rooms are furnished as they were long ago and to see the collection of hats and costumes. Children will like the collection of toys and dollhouses. When finished sightseeing, follow signs from Urnäsch to Appenzell, about an 11-kilometer drive.

Appenzell: Appenzell is a picture-book village, popular with tourists who flock to see the fanciful paintings on the façades of the buildings, a colorful variety of artwork—landscapes, folk art, flowers, abstract designs, animals, and people. Appenzell is also well known for exquisite embroidery and delicious cheeses. Politically, it is famous for its demonstration of real democracy: on the last Sunday in April, the citizens, usually wearing their colorful traditional costumes, gather in the village square to elect representatives to their local canton with a show of hands. Another appealing aspect of Appenzell is the tranquil countryside that surrounds it. This area of Switzerland (often called Appenzeller Land) is lush with rolling, gentle green fields dotted with plump cows lazily munching grass to the rhythm of their cow bells. Snuggled in these lovely pastures are large farmhouses adorned with masses of flowers. The family home is attached to the barn so that the animals are easily accessible during winter snows.

APPENZELL TO ZÜRICH

From Appenzell drive to Hundwil (about 10 kilometers from Appenzell) and then turn to Stein (not to be confused with Stein-am-Rhein described in the earlier itinerary, *Geneva to Zürich via Medieval Jewels*).

Stein: It's fun to stop in Stein to visit its Folklore Museum (*Appenzeller-Volkskunde Museum*) which, like the museum mentioned earlier in Urnäsch, shares the life-style and customs of the people in this lovely part of Switzerland. Featured are some of the local crafts such as carpentry, weaving, and belt making. One exceptionally interesting exhibit shows 19th-century handiwork by the local farmers who painted furniture in their homes, as well as decorating their day-to-day utensils such as milk pails and farm instruments. One part of the museum is devoted to paintings by local farmers who depicted scenes from their everyday life on pieces of wood. As you have been traveling through the area around Appenzell you have undoubtedly seen many examples of this wonderfully engaging, almost child-like style of art. Johannes Müller, a clockmaker who was born in and lived in Stein until he died at the age of 91, was the most famous of these painters. You can quickly recognize his work because the picture is always similar—a line of cows, accompanied by their shepherds and children dressed in colorful traditional costume, zigzagging up lush green meadows on their way to the high alp.

From Stein, follow signs to Saint Gallen, a city between Appenzeller Land and Lake Constance, which is located just a short distance to the north.

Saint Gallen: The name of Saint Gallen harks back to the 7th century when an Irish monk named Gallas arrived here and laid the foundation (supposedly with the help of a bear) to what was to become a famous Benedictine Monastery. As the years progressed, a prosperous town (famous for textiles and embroidery) grew up around the abbey.

As you approach the city, its modern outskirts seem quite a contrast to the tranquil, pastoral beauty of Appenzeller Land. But, continue on to its historic center which is well worth a visit—if for no other reason than to visit its stunning cathedral and adjacent Abbey Library. The lavishly embellished library is the star attraction. It houses a staggering collection of 2,000 ancient manuscripts and 100,000 books. To protect the library's precious inlaid wood floor, felt slippers are loaned to visitors to slip over their shoes.

FINAL DESTINATION–ZÜRICH:

Leaving Saint Gallen, follow signs to the expressway and take the A1 west. It bypasses Winterthur and continues on to the center of Zürich.

Swiss Train, Boat & Bus Adventures

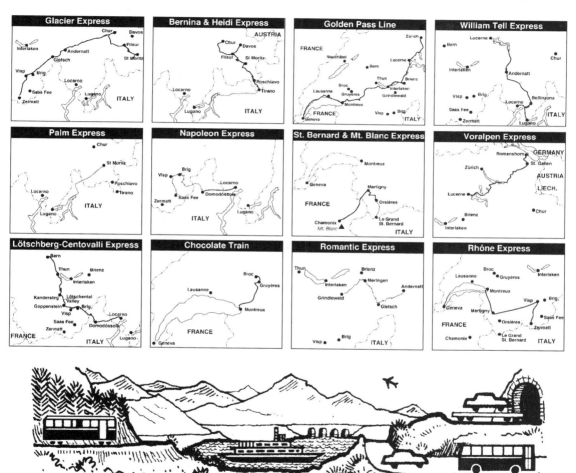

Swiss Train, Boat & Bus Adventures

Switzerland has an unbelievable network of trains, boats, and buses. You can travel to even the tiniest hamlet tucked in a remote mountain valley by public transportation. What makes this means of travel all the more enticing is the efficiency of the Swiss—everything works like a finely-tuned clock. The schedules are so splendidly coordinated that when you step off a train, a bus or boat is waiting to whisk you to your next destination. Or, as your boat pulls up to the dock, a bus or train is merely steps away. Although you might need to make numerous connections, you could follow any itinerary featured in this guide by taking advantage of the outstanding public transportation system. However, to make this style of travel even more hassle-free, the Swiss offer many tours that that follow incredibly scenic routes to a selection of the most popular destinations in the country. Some of these tours (such as the Glacier Express) are by private train, but the majority take advantage of the Swiss pubic transportation service.

Even if you prefer the freedom of traveling by car, consider enhancing the driving portion of your vacation by adding one or more of the following twelve special excursions by train, boat, and bus onto your itinerary. There are a few prerequisites to this style of travel. First, it is essential that you travel lightly. If you feel there is no way you could possibly pack everything you need into one moderately-sized suitcase, forget the idea of public transportation. Cumbersome bags become a burden when trying to make quick connections and diminish some of the joy of travel. Secondly, it is highly recommended that you purchase one of the Swiss passes mentioned in the introduction. A few trains are not covered by a rail pass, and many of those that do, charge a supplement for mandatory seat reservations. But, all in all, these passes are a very good value and extremely convenient. When you make your reservations, ask the agent what type of pass is best for your chosen itinerary. Also, be sure find out if advance seat reservations are needed. Likewise, inquire if dining car reservations are necessary. Also, be sure to verify all the time tables since schedules change—and, as you now know, if you are a minute late, your train, bus, or boat will have left without you!

Switzerland's awesome transportation network features more than 2,000 kilometers of public routes, over 50,000 kilometers of well-marked hiking trails, 9 national bike routes, 700 scenic bus routes, and 20 lakes with ferry service. Adding to these statistics, almost every significant mountain has a gondola, aerial cableway, cogwheel train, gondola, or funicular. The possibilities are endless. Note: if you want to learn more about the history of travel in Switzerland, when you are in Lucerne visit the Swiss Transport Museum.

For the sake of simplicity, we describe travel in one direction in the following twelve itineraries. However, most of the itineraries can be run in reverse.

GLACIER EXPRESS: Travel by Train
Route: Zermatt to Saint Moritz

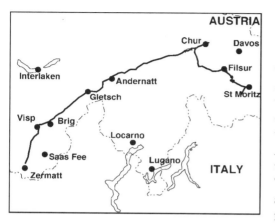

To ride the *Glacier Express* between Zermatt and Saint Moritz is truly a dream come true for any train buff. Before this privately owned train was inaugurated, one had to hip-hop across Switzerland, switching trains several times along the way. Fortunately, this all changed when a Swiss entrepreneur connected the two resorts via the fabulous *Glacier Express*, which operates all year. In 2005, the train proudly celebrated its 75th anniversary. Traveling at an average speed of 30 kilometers an hour, this attractive red train is merrily marketed as being the "Slowest Fast Train in the World." It is no wonder that the 8-hour journey is not a quicker one. Along the way the train goes through 91 tunnels, crosses 291 bridges, chugs over three passes (the Furka Pass, the Abula Pass, and the Oberalp Pass), traverses glaciers, meanders through mountain meadows, passes by rushing rivers, and weaves through canyons—all while you relax in comfort while soaking in the awesome beauty from your picture window. There is even more to the adventure if you plan ahead and make a luncheon reservation when you book the train. If so, you have the pleasure of dining in an old-fashioned dining car brimming with nostalgia—the walls are elegantly paneled in wood and the romantic ambiance is further enhanced by bronze fixtures, soft lighting, and tables set with crisp linens and fresh flowers. What a memorable adventure to climb aboard the train in Zermatt, settle down in your cheerful, bright compartment, enjoy a gourmet meal in the Victorian dining car, chat and laugh with fellow passengers, and arrive relaxed and happy in Saint Moritz. If you prefer to end your trip in Chur (a walled city that is on the direct train route to Zürich) instead of going to Saint Moritz, this is an option. Just let the agent know when you make your reservation.

BERNINA EXPRESS & HEIDI EXPRESS: Travel by Train & Postal Bus
Route: Chur or Saint Moritz or Davos to Lugano

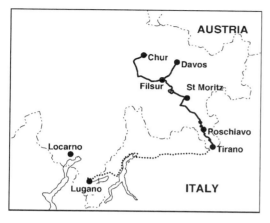

The *Bernina Express* travels through some of the most glorious scenery in Switzerland. As an added bonus, you may customize the journey to what suites you best. The train originates in the medieval town of Chur, a convenient starting point since it is an important terminal with frequent service from Zürich and other major cities. Or, you may prefer to board the train in Saint Moritz rather than in Chur. Another option is to begin your trip in the famous ski resort of Davos (the train that originates in Davos is called the *Heidi Express*). The best option of all is to continue by bus from Tirano, Italy, ending your trip on the shores of Lake Lugano. If you so desire, you can connect by train from Lugano to Locarno, which is located on lake Maggiore. The *Bernina Express* operates all year between Chur to Tirano, but the bus between Tirano and Lugano only runs in the summer months. Starting in the high alps, the *Bernina Express* winds its way through mountains and valleys from north to south, ending just across the Italian border in Tirano. Along the way the train goes through the beautiful Engadine valley, climbs up one of the highest rail routes in Switzerland, chugs over the Bernina Pass (without the use of cogwheels) and through the glorious Poschiavo Valley to Tirano. After lunch in Tirano, it's on to Lugano by bus. This route is all the more special because of the contrasts of scenery and climate. What fun it is to leave the glacier-clad mountains in the north and pop into sun-drenched Lake Lugano where palms and oleanders thrive. In summer, the train offers open coaches that allow you to breathe in the fresh mountain air and puts the scenery at your finger tips. Note: Remember your passport since the *Bernina Express* goes into Italy.

GOLDEN PASS LINE: Travel by Train
Route: Lucerne to Montreux

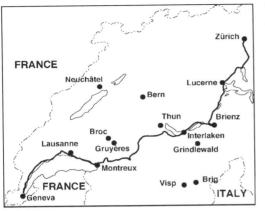

The *Golden Pass Line* features premier trains that cross the heart of Switzerland, linking two of its most precious jewels: Lucerne and Montreux. If you prefer, you can begin your trip in Zürich instead of Lucerne, and extend your journey beyond Montreux by continuing on to Geneva. This popular route travels across the center of the country in regal style, passing along the way mountains, rivers, lakes, picturesque villages, and lush pastures dotted with happy cows. There are three trains a day that make the journey—all of which involve a change of trains in Interlaken. Since you need to switch trains anyway, you might opt for a layover in Interlaken. This would give you time to stroll this once-grand resort town that still reflects a bit of its Victorian heritage. Another option from Interlaken would be to hop on one of the ferries for a boat excursion on Lake Brienz or Lake Thun. Best yet, if the day is sunny, there is no more dazzling adventure in Switzerland than a side trip by train from Interlaken to the Jungfrau. After you leave Interlaken, another recommended place to stop and catch a later train, is the quaint village of Gstaad, a really picturesque resort with many boutiques. When making reservations, ask about the various options of places to stop and the types of trains available. If you yearn for the days of yore when travel was a romantic journey, by all means ask about the "Golden Classic," which first came into use in May 2005. This delightful train, refurbished in the grand nostalgic style of the Orient Express, exudes romance and comfort with its wood paneled walls and Victorian décor. You will also be thrilled with either of the two "Panoramic Trains" that travel this route. Both of these have huge windows that reach to the top of the car, affording stunning views.

WILLIAM TELL EXPRESS: Travel by Boat & Train
Route: Lucerne to Lugano or Locarno

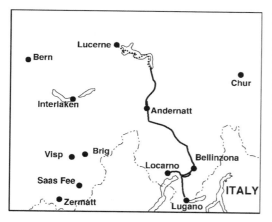

For the pure joy of travel, the *William Tell Express* is unsurpassed. This excursion (available from May to October) originates in Lucerne, one of the most charming cities in Switzerland. The trip ends in the stunning Southern Lake District, where you can choose between two romantic jewels as your final destination: Locarno (on Lake Maggiore) or Lugano (on Lake Lugano). The fun begins from the moment you catch your first glimpse of the delightfully old-fashioned paddle steamer at the Lucerne dock and realize it is "yours"—the ferry you will be taking for the first leg of your journey. The boat trip from Lucerne (located at the western tip of Lake Lucerne) to Flüelen (located at the opposite end of the lake) takes a leisurely three hours. Along the way you can relax in total comfort as you enjoy the enchanting scenery of one of Switzerland's most beautiful lakes, with views of wooded hills dotted with chalets, high mountain peaks, lush green pastures, and picturesque villages tucked along the shoreline. There is a commentary on board that explains what you are seeing en route, including stories of William Tell, the Swiss hero for whom the excursion is named. When you arrive in Flüelen, your air conditioned train with panoramic windows will be waiting. Once you hop on board, the route follows along side the Reuss River as it heads south, cutting its way through the mountains. The train goes by steep cliffs and deep ravines, and then begins to climb up from the valley and plunges into the 15-kilometer-long Gotthard Tunnel. After emerging once again into sunlight, the train drops down into the Leventina Valley and continues to Bellinzona. If you are going on to Locarno, you stay on the same train. If your destination is Lugano, you need to change trains in Bellinzona.

PALM EXPRESS: Travel by Postal Bus
Route: Saint Moritz to Lugano

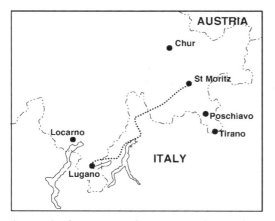

In summertime there is a wonderful bus excursion, called the *Palm Express*, which leaves daily from Saint Moritz and goes to Lugano, on Lake Lugano (about a 4-hour journey). This adventure is enticing as it blends two remarkably beautiful regions that are totally different in scenery, ambiance, and climate, yet equally lovely. You climb aboard the bright yellow postal bus in Saint Moritz where snow still caps the mountain peaks, and end your journey in balmy Lake Lugano where palm trees and tropical plants abound. The only way to travel this itinerary is by bus (or car) since no train route exists. The scenery is so outstanding along the way that you will be happy you opted for the bus so that no one will have to be at the wheel of the car and miss the ever-changing vistas. Your first part of the journey takes you south from Saint Moritz through the scenic Engadine Valley and past the pristine twin lakes of Silvaplana and Silser. Then the road climbs over the Maloja Pass and drops down into the narrow Bregaglia Valley, which is embraced by high mountains. As the bus continues south, ancient villages perched on mountain ledges come into view. Soon you cross the border into Italy where the road traces the shoreline of beautiful Lake Como and then cuts west to Lake Lugano. The bus drivers display admirable skill as they drive along the narrow roads and inch through the tiny streets of medieval villages, which were never designed for cars or buses. All too soon you are in Lugano, which has a remarkably romantic setting on the edge of the shimmering Lake Lugano. The train station (where the bus arrives) is on a shelf above the town. There is a funicular near the station that takes you down to the colorful historic center of the city. Note: Remember to take your passport since you will be going through Italy.

NAPOLEON EXPRESS: Travel by Postal Bus & Train
Route: Sass Fee to Locarno

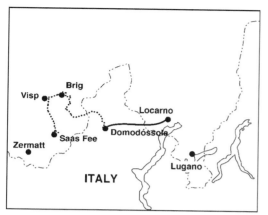

Zermatt, towered over by the dazzling Matterhorn, is a well known destination to all mountain lovers. However, not everyone is aware that Saas Fee, a town located just over the mountain from Zermatt, offers an alternate choice for a mountain holiday. Although the town is not as quaint as Zermatt, because of its splendid setting on a ledge of the mountain, the views are fabulous. Trains do not service Saas Fee, but postal buses make it easily accessible. A particularly popular bus route is called the *Napoleon Express*, which leaves Saas Fee and travels north through the beautiful Saastal Valley to the Rhône Valley and then heads east to Brig. At Brig you change buses for the next leg of your trip that takes you over the Simplon Pass. There is a tunnel through the mountain, but this is only for trains. By far the more dramatic option is to take the superbly engineered road that goes over the pass. Since the 17th century, traders have trudged up the pass with their heavily laden mule trains, but it was Napoleon who made the path a proper road in order to have an efficient way to transport supplies for his military campaigns. The road, which first opened in 1805, is not intimidating. At first the incline is gentle, but soon the bus begins to make large loops as it climbs the road up the mountain to its 2005-meter-high summit, the Simplon Kulm. The bus then descends downward, crosses the Italian border, and scoots along the Divedro Valley to Domodóssola. Upon arrival in Domodóssola climb aboard one of the blue and white cars of the Centovalli Railway for an amazing 55-kilometer journey that crosses over 83 bridges and slithers through 31 tunnels as it follows the Melezza River to Locarno, a lovely town located on the romantic shores of Lake Maggiore. Note: Remember your passport as you will be going into Italy.

MONT BLANC EXPRESS: Train, Martigny to Mount Blanc
SAINT BERNARD EXPRESS: Train & Postal Bus, Martigny to St. Bernard

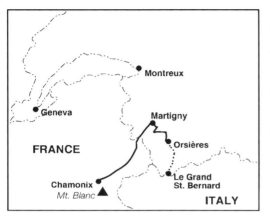

Switzerland offers two marvelous rail and bus tours (the *Mont Blanc Express* and the *Saint Bernard Express*), both of which offer adventure and glorious scenery. The tours originate in Martigny, an old Roman town at the west end of the Rhône Valley—22 kilometers from the French border. The *Mont Blanc Express* is an all-by-train excursion. Departing from Martigny, it climbs over the Col de la Forclaz, through the Trient Gorge, crosses the border into France, and wiggles in and out of tunnels as it descends to Chamonix, where the views of Mount Blanc (the highest mountain in Europe) are absolutely breathtaking. On a clear day there is no mountain in the world more beautiful. The *Saint Bernard Express* (which operates only in summer) combines transportation by both train and bus. The first leg of the trip is by train. It leaves Martigny and heads east along the Drance River before turning south through the Entremont Valley and on to Orsières. Here the rail line ends and you hop on a bus for the last leg of your journey to the Grand Saint Bernard Hospice, founded by Saint Bernard in the 17th century. With its bleak, wind-swept, forlorn setting, you would think this would be the last place in the world the monks would want settle, but it was perfect for their mission to rescue stranded travelers going over the pass. The monks trained gentle Saint Bernard dogs to assist them in their mountain rescue. Although times have changed and helicopters have assumed job once done by these brave dogs, they are still bred here for the sake of tradition and maintaining the breed. You can visit a museum, the kennels, and a 17th-century church. Note: Remember your passport for the *Mont Blanc Express* excursion as you will be going into France.

VORALPEN EXPRESS: Travel by Train
Route: Romanshorn to Lucerne

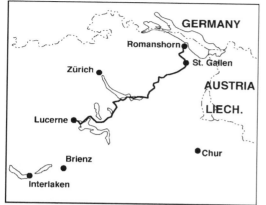

The *Voralpen Express* (sometimes called the Prealpen-Express) begins its journey in the charming city of Lucerne and heads northeast, ending the trip in Romanshorn. This is not a spine-tingling adventure where the train zigzags over high mountain passes, but rather it is a gentle, three-hour journey of great scenic beauty. The train has panoramic windows so that you can relax in your comfortable seat and soak in the lovely landscape as it glides by. If you want a snack, there is a bistro and a mini-bar on the train. This is a very popular route—trains leave almost every hour. If you zip directly between the two cities, the trip takes a bit less than three hours. However, there are many interesting places to visit along the way where you can get off for sightseeing and hop back on a later train, or make connections to another destination of your choice. One stop you might enjoy is Rapperswil, a town on the north shore of Lake Zürich that is overlooked by a mighty 13th-century castle. The nickname of the town is "City of Roses" and during the season, you will enjoy seeing roses throughout the town, including an outstanding garden in the Capuchin Monastery. As the train continues north from Rapperswil, the scenery changes as you approach the region called Appenzeller Land, an exceptionally picturesque area with pretty rolling hills, high mountain peaks, lush pastures dotted with cows, and charming villages. You might want to make another stop in Saint Gallen where you can visit the its imposing Saint Gallen Cathedral, and, of special interest, its amazing Baroque library in the Benedictine Abbey. Then, the train rolls on to Romanshorn, where the trip ends on Lake Constance (also called the Bodensee). From Romanshorn, you can continue your adventures in Switzerland, or take the ferry across the lake to Germany.

LÖTSCHBERG–CENTOVALLI EXPRESS: Travel by Train
Route: Bern to Locarno

The *Lötschberg–Centovalli Express* links two jewels, Bern, a medieval city that oozes old world charm, and Locarno, a resort located on the stunningly beautiful Lake Maggiore. Trains leave Bern frequently during the day and reservations are not needed. The train soon arrives at Lake Thun, where it briefly follows the shoreline and then goes south, following the Kander River as it cuts through the mountains. The route ends in the town of Kandersteg before being blocked by imposing mountains. From here, the train enters a 15-kilometer-long Lötschberg tunnel, emerging once again into the daylight at Goppenstein. If you have the time, get off the train here and board a bus that heads east up the remote Lötschental Valley and dead-ends at some of the most dazzling mountains in Switzerland. Along the way the scenery is spectacular as you pass through villages lost in time with clusters of wooden houses clinging to the sides of the steep valley walls. After enjoying the incredible mountain views and glaciers, return to Goppenstein by bus and continue on your way by train south to the Rhône Valley, where the train turns east to Brig. At Brig, the train heads south and begins the gentle ascent to the Simplon tunnel, emerging on the other side in Italy. In a very short time the train arrives in Domodóssola, where you change to one of the blue and white cars of the Centovalli Railroad for the final leg of your trip to Lake Maggiore. The scenery along the way is awesome as the train squeezes through narrow gorges with rushing waterfalls, hillsides lined with vineyards, woodlands with chestnut trees, and remote medieval villages. All too soon, you arrive in Locarno. Note: Remember your passport as you will be going into Italy.

SWISS CHOCOLATE TRAIN: Travel by Train
Route: Round trip from Montreux

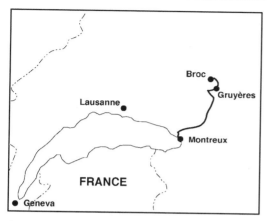

If the mere thought of chocolate makes your mouth water, you will not want to miss this delicious, all-day, round-trip tour from Montreux. However, this excursion isn't just for chocolate aficionados—if you don't even like sweets, you will have a wonderful time. Every Monday and Wednesday, from June through October, the Chocolate Train pulls out of the Montreux station at about 9:25 am. As the train heads north through lush valleys and gentle hills laced with vineyards, you are served complimentary coffee and croissants. In a little over an hour, the train pulls up to the Gruyères train station, and stops across from the Gruyères cheese factory. Time is allowed to visit this modern factory which incorporates a museum showing how the delicious Gruyères cheese is produced. As you begin the interesting tour, you are given samples of various aged cheeses and don headphones that present an audio narrative which follows with what you see along the way. After the cheese tour, a bus is waiting to take you up to Gruyères, a fairy-tale walled village perched on the top of a small mountain. The cobbled main street, lined by adorable houses, cute shops, and restaurants, leads to a picturesque castle that is open as a museum. After your time in Gruyères, the bus takes you back to the train and for the short ride to Broc, where you visit the Cailler-Nestlé chocolate factory. As you walk from the parking lot, the scent of chocolate fills the air. The tour begins with a short video presentation and then a guide takes you to the various displays, explains how chocolate is made, and how it has evolved from the bitter bean that Cortez brought back to Spain to the delectable chocolate we know today. The tour ends in a large room where trays are set out, loaded with a stunning variety of samples of candy cut into little squares for tasting. After the chocolate factory, it's back to the train, and you arrive back in Montreux about 5:40 pm.

ROMANTIC ROUTE EXPRESS: Travel by Postal Bus
Route: Andermatt to Grindelwald

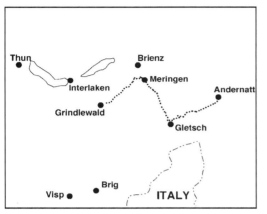

The *Romantic Route Express* is a fascinating bus adventure (available only in the summer months) that captures some of Switzerland's most extraordinary, rugged, high Alpine scenery. The trip begins in Andermatt, a mountain resort famous for skiing and hiking. As the yellow postal bus leaves town heading west, it ascends the awesome Furka Pass to its 2,341-meter-high, barren, windswept summit where you have a panoramic view of majestic mountain peaks and glaciers. From the summit, the road twists down to Gletsch where the bus turns north and climbs once again into the mountains, tackling more curves as it makes its way up the rugged Grimsel Pass—along the same route used hundreds of years ago by merchants who trudged wearily over the mountains by mule train. The road passes a few remote mountain hamlets as it heads to Meiringen. From Meiringen the bus turns southwest to Grindelwald, the final and most exciting part of the journey. For those passionate about discovering places off the beaten path, this part of the trip will be memorable. Even travelers who take pride in knowing most of the remote byways in Switzerland are often surprised to learn there is a back road to Grindelwald, a village in the stunning Jungfrau region. However, cars are only allowed to drive as far as the Schwarzwaldalp, which is just beyond the hamlet of Rosenlaui. Only buses are allowed as the road continues on, over the incredibly narrow road that makes many hairpin turns as it makes it way up and over the Grand Scheidegg pass and on to Grindelwald. You can end your journey at one of the lovely hotels in Grindelwald, or continue on by train to one of the other charming small towns in the gorgeous Jungfrau Region, such as Wengen or Mürren.

RHÔNE EXPRESS: Travel by Boat and Train
Route: Geneva to Montreux to Zermatt

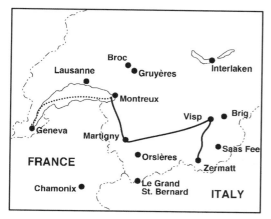

Like the Golden Pass Line, the *Rhône Express* (which operates from June through September) is one of the most popular train routes in Switzerland since it links two very popular destinations, the elegantly beautiful city of Geneva and the famous mountain resort of Zermatt, home to the majestic Matterhorn. The fun begins from the moment you step aboard the nostalgic, beautifully refurbished paddle steamer that dates from the turn of the last century. The trip begins at 9 am. If you book the whole tour, you can savor a three-course lunch (included in the price) enjoying the scenery as the boat glides in and out of charming lakefront towns wrapped by vineyard-laced hills. The southern shore of Lake Geneva lies in France where the peaks of the Savoy Alps soar into the sky. On a clear day, the dazzling Mount Blanc rises above all of the other mountains, adding a touch of perfection. A little less than five hours later, the boat maneuvers along side the Montreux dock. The next leg of your journey is by train from Montreux. A few minutes after the train pulls out of the station and goes south along the edge of the lake, look out the window to your right so that you won't miss the incredibly romantic Castle of Chillon, sitting on a little island just off the shore. At Martigny the train turns east and follows the Rhône Valley, one of Switzerland's main wine producing regions, and continues on to Visp. Here you change to the local train that heads south, following a gorgeous, narrow, mountain valley. A little less than nine hours after your adventure began in Geneva, the train chugs into the station at Zermatt. The line can go no further since the valley is blocked by huge mountains, including the spectacular, justifiably famous, Matterhorn.

DESIGN YOUR OWN TRAIN, BOAT & BUS ITINERARIES

The preceding twelve tours, using a combination of train, boat and bus travel, are excellent. You can enjoy them just as they are or use them as a foundation to customize your own holiday. By linking some of the itineraries together, your trip can include every place you dreamed of seeing. Using this "car-less" means of travel offers a great reward—no one misses the sensational scenery because he (or she) is at the wheel.

Remember when planning your customized trip that you don't have to complete any leg of the itinerary in one day—you can break your journey along the route and catch a later train, bus, or boat. Relax and enjoy the adventure of travel—your transportation becomes part of the fun. To give you an idea of how the various Swiss tours can be linked and customized, we have outlined a suggested train, boat and bus tour below that joins six of the tours together. You can select part or all of what most catches your fancy.

Here's how it works: After spending a few days in the charming city of Lucerne, take *The William Tell Express.* The tour begins on a paddle steamer from Lucerne to Flüelen, and from there, by train to Lugano. After a few days in the romantic Lake District, take *The Palm Express* postal bus from Lugano to Saint Moritz. Enjoy a few days hiking in the mountains and then board *The Glacier Express* from Saint Moritz to Zermatt. Relax a few days enjoying the beauty of the Matterhorn and then take *The Rhône Express* from Zermatt to Montreux, and from there, the ferry to Geneva. Do some sightseeing and shopping in Geneva and then take *The Golden Pass Line* train from Geneva to Interlaken. Spend a few days in the Interlaken region so that you will have time to experience one of Switzerland's most dramatic and beautiful adventures—the Jungfraujoch excursion. You can stay at a hotel in Interlaken, or, if you want to be right up in the mountains, take the local train to either Wengen or Grindelwald. After a few days in Interlaken, continue by train on *The Golden Pass Line* back to Lucerne, thus completing your "circle." If you want a bit more train adventure, from Lucerne, take *The Voralpen Express* from Lucerne to Romanshorn, a city on the shores of Lake Constance. From Romanshorn, you can continue by train to other destinations in Switzerland, or take a ferry to Germany.

Swiss Train, Boat & Bus Adventures

Hotel Descriptions

On my first visit to the Hotel Stern and Post my heart was won by Faro, an enormous Bernese farm dog napping in the middle of the lobby. Faro was such a fixture that postcards of this gentle "puppy" were sent to his many admirers. Unfortunately Faro has died, but Duke, an equally lovable Bernese farm dog is now winning the hearts of guests. The Stern and Post has been in the Tresch family for several hundred years. Elisabeth Tresch, who graduated from Cornell University Hotel School in New York, oversees the hotel with an unparalleled professionalism and warmly welcomes guests from all over the world. Her family heirlooms adorn the cozy, antique-adorned public areas and a wonderful story can be told about each—ask about the veterinary cabinet or the lock-up cabinet for the hotel silver, necessary in days of old when the employees were not to be trusted. Right on the main thoroughfare of Amsteg, the oldest part of the house dates back to 1789 when the inn was built to provide shelter to weary travelers. Today the Stern and Post is the only remaining coaching station along the Saint Gotthard Pass road. About a third of the simple guestrooms have antique furnishings, others have a modern decor. Ask for one of the bedrooms in the back overlooking the gushing stream. *Directions:* Take the Amsteg exit from the A2. The hotel is at the center of the village, approximately 500 meters from the exit.

HOTEL STERN AND POST
Owner: Elisabeth A. Tresch
Gotthardstrasse 88
CH-6474 Amsteg, Switzerland
Tel: (041) 883 14 40, Fax: (041) 883 02 61
24 Rooms, Double: CHF 150–CHF 220
Open: all year, Credit cards: all major
14 km S of Altdorf, Train: 6.5 km
Canton: Uri

The attractive town of Appenzell with its cobbled streets and bounty of shops is at the heart of the canton that bears the same name. At the edge of the pedestrian district on the historic Landgemeindeplatz, the Hotel Appenzell benefits from the expertise and warmth of the Sutter family who owns it. Margrit is often present to greet guests at the front desk, while Leo is responsible for the restaurant's fine offerings. The hotel has 16 lovely guestrooms, all non-smoking with private bathroom and either tub or shower. The hallways leading to the guestrooms are uncluttered and attractive with a few well-placed antiques. The rooms, whose doors are adorned with lovely stenciling, are similar in their decor and differ only in their color scheme—a soft yellow for the first-floor rooms and a soft rose for the second-floor accommodations. The guestrooms are new, tasteful, and comfortably appointed with internet access. The non-smoking restaurant is always bustling either with lunch or dinner guests or with those tempted by pastries from the adjacent bakery. A standard dinner menu offers traditional Swiss fare at a reasonable price. A breakfast buffet for hotel guests is offered in the intimate Dr Hildebrand Suite. *Directions:* Traveling from Zürich, take the Winkeln/Appenzellerland exit. Follow signposts for Herisau/Appenzell. At the roundabout, turn right. After 400 meters you'll find the Landgemeindeplatz, where you can park briefly in front or back of the hotel.

HOTEL APPENZELL
Owners: Margrit & Leo Sutter
Am Landgemeindeplatz
CH-9050 Appenzell, Switzerland
Tel: (071) 788 15 15, Fax: (071) 788 15 51
15 Rooms, Double: CHF 200–CHF 220
1 Suite: CHF 220–CHF 240
Restaurant & bakery closed Tue mornings
Closed: Nov, Credit cards: all major
20 km S of St. Gallen, Train: 400 meters
Canton: Appenzell, Interior Rhodes

The façade of the Romantik Hotel Säntis, located on the central square in the picturesque village of Appenzell, has been gaily painted a rust-red with yellow and black scrolling. The terrace in front is a favorite place for a cool drink on a warm day. Guestrooms are decorated either in attractive modern or reproduction country-style wooden furniture. The price for the room depends mostly upon its size. My favorite guestrooms are in the original part of the main house, although those in the newer wing are also very pleasant. The decor of each bedroom in the new wing is the same except for the color scheme. The public rooms seem geared to the influx of tourists who drop in for a midday meal, and the lobby offers a country welcome; however, the hotel has wisely insulated a quiet, peaceful lounge just for guests. A wing opened in 1997 houses a sauna, wellness bar, seminar center, and five additional large bedrooms. The gracious Stefan and his delightful Scottish wife, Catriona, are the fourth generation of the Heeb family to run the hotel. The family's pride and dedication as owners are very apparent, from the friendliness of the front-desk receptionist to the smile of the chambermaid. *Directions:* Traveling from Zürich, take the Winkeln/Appenzellerland exit. Follow signposts for Herisau/Appenzell. At the roundabout, turn right. After 400 meters you'll find the Landgemeindeplazt, where you can park briefly in front of the hotel.

ROMANTIK HOTEL SÄNTIS
Owners: Stefan A. & Catriona Heeb Family
CH-9050 Appenzell, Switzerland
Tel: (071) 788 11 11, Fax: (071) 788 11 10
30 Rooms, Double: CHF 230–CHF 270
6 Suites: CHF 270–CHF 310
Open: Feb to Dec, Credit cards: all major
20 km S of St. Gallen, Train: 400 meters
Romantik Hotels
Canton: Appenzell, Interior Rhodes

One of Switzerland's most deluxe hotels and a member of Relais & Châteaux, the Castello del Sole is a complete resort set in such a spectacular estate, with so many things to do, that you will be tempted not to leave the grounds. If you can afford to stay in one of the Pavilion suites, you may never leave your room—both breakfast and dinner can be served in your suite or on your balcony overlooking the estate. If your budget precludes you from selecting the most expensive accommodation, do not worry, for all the rooms are lovely. While the hotel has an à-la-carte dining room, I suggest that you opt for either half board (lots of choices in each dinner course) or full board, which includes a wonderful luncheon buffet either in the garden, or in the restaurant when the weather is inclement. Get your exercise in the indoor/outdoor heated pool or on one of the six tennis courts. Pamper yourself with facials and massages, enjoy the sauna, whirlpool, steam, and weight rooms, or simply stroll in the acres of grounds, perhaps taking the path down to the lake or visiting the hotel's vineyard. Practice on the putting green and enjoy a game at the adjacent golf course. A shuttle bus takes you into Ascona or you can borrow one of the hotel's bicycles. *Directions:* Arriving in Ascona, head for the town center, but do not enter the pedestrian zone: continue until you see the signs directing you to the estate.

CASTELLO DEL SOLE
Manager: Simon V. Jenny
Via Muraccio, 142
CH-6612 Ascona, Switzerland
Tel: (091) 791 02 02, Fax: (091) 792 11 18
43 Rooms, Double: CHF 600–CHF 760
38 Suites: CHF 860–CHF 3500
Open: Apr to Oct, Credit cards: all major
3 km SW of Locarno, Train to Locarno: 6 km
Relais & Châteaux
Canton: Ticino

The Romantik Hotel Castello enjoys an imposing position at one end of Ascona's lakeside promenade. This 13th-century castle has been extended over the years but still keeps its fortress look with thick walls and stone stairways. Guestrooms with handsome wood doors are decorated with a mix of modern and traditional furnishings. All guestooms are nonsmoking. The most impressive room is the tower room with its thick walls, high ceilings, and incredible frescoes. Guests who elect to stay on a demi-pension basis are offered an enticing menu served in a special dining room just for hotel guests. An à-la-carte restaurant, the Locanda de'Ghiriglioni, is also available for guests not opting for demi-pension and for non-residents. Tucked in the cellar, an attractive wine bar is a cozy place to enjoy a drink. Behind the castle is a secluded swimming pool and two wings of more contemporary bedrooms. Just across the road is an appealing, tree-shaded, lakeside garden where guests can relax while watching the colorful parade of people strolling along the promenade. *Directions:* Arriving in Ascona, follow signs for the town center and follow signs for lake parking. As you come to the lake, the Hotel Castello is on your right. Pull into the driveway to unload then park in the hotel's underground car park.

ROMANTIK HOTEL CASTELLO-SEESCHLOSS
Owner: Werner Ris
Lakeside Promenade
CH-6612 Ascona, Switzerland
Tel: (091) 791 01 61, Fax: (091) 791 18 04
45 Rooms, Double: CHF 248–CHF 588
Open: Mar to Nov, Credit cards: all major
3 km SW of Locarno, Train to Locarno: 6 km
Romantik Hotels
Canton: Ticino

Facing Lake Maggiore, Hotel Tamaro, a Ticino-style patrician house, is smartly attired in soft yellow with crisp-white shutters. Its tables and chairs spill out onto the lakeside promenade, creating a pleasing picture. Strollers settle here and enjoy a cup of coffee or an ice cream while leisurely watching the little ferryboats glide in and out. You may well be welcomed by Evelyn, the charming daughter of Annetta and Paolo Witzig, owners of the Tamaro. The hotel's inner courtyard (crowned by a glass ceiling for protection against inclement weather) has tables set gaily among many potted plants, giving the feeling that you are dining in a garden. The guestrooms are situated on various levels, and it's almost a game to find your room. Each bedroom varies greatly in style of decor, views, and size. I particularly enjoyed room 6, a standard corner room with windows facing both up the promenade and to the lake. The rooms are all decorated attractively with a charming, home-like ambiance throughout. Request a lake view—some even have a small balcony overlooking the promenade. *Directions:* In Ascona follow signs for the town center and as you see the pedestrian zone on the lakeside follow the waterfront to the hotel. You may drive up to the hotel to check in.

HOTEL TAMARO
Owners: Annetta & Paolo Witzig
Piazza G. Motta 35
CH-6612 Ascona, Switzerland
Tel: (091) 785 48 48, Fax: (091) 791 29 28
51 Rooms, Double: CHF 195–CHF 290
Open: Mar to mid-Nov, Credit cards: all major
3 km SW of Locarno, Train to Locarno: 6 km
Canton: Ticino

The Krafft, a modest hotel with an air of faded glamour, is located in a once-grand mansion that faces the Rhine River. As you enter, an intimate parlor to the left has a massive crystal chandelier, an ornate gilt mirror, high ceiling, and arched windows facing the street. The finest room in the hotel is a beautiful restaurant with tall casement windows that capture a splendid view of the river. From the reception, a handsome staircase with a wrought-iron and wood banister winds up to the guestrooms, all of which are different—both in décor and size. They are simply decorated, but the simple décor is reflected in the moderate room rate. Although the furnishings are basic, most of the bedrooms are spacious and all have private bathrooms. Ask for a room overlooking the river: these are definitely worth the additional cost. In 2005 the hotel a full renovation was completed without losing the charm of the past. In 2008 the hotel added 12 rooms in a renovated building across the street. The Krafft Hotel offers character, excellent location, pretty views, and low price. *Directions:* On the right bank of the Rhine, near Mittlere bridge (Mittlere Rheinbrucke).

KRAFFT HOTEL
Manager: Franz-Xaver Leonhardt
CH-4058 Basel, Switzerland
Tel: (061) 690 91 30, Fax: (061) 690 91 31
56 Rooms, Double: CHF 230–CHF 620
Open: all year, Credit cards: all major
100 km N of Bern, Train: 1 km
Schlosshotels & Herrenhauser
Canton: Basel-Stadt

If you are a fan of art nouveau, the Hotel Belle Époque, a boutique city hotel at the heart of this medieval city, is tailor-made for you. The hotel was renovated and refurnished in spring 2000 with a stylish and contemporary backdrop, done by one of Switzerland's finest interior decorators. Art nouveau (belle époque) furnishings and art from the early 1900s set the theme for the hotel—from the large paintings and murals in the cozy breakfast room and delightful bar, to the paintings hung in each of the bedrooms. The bedrooms are priced based on size. All have different color schemes that complement the artwork and lovely old furniture. Rooms with a view face the busy street while those at the back offer peace and quiet. Light refreshments are served in the bar and at the tables that form a terrace on the sidewalk under Bern's famous arcade—a delightful place to people watch. For dinner you can dine at the elegant in-house restaurant Le Chariot or have the friendly staff direct you to a restaurant in town. *Directions:* To find the hotel it is important that you exit the autobahn at Bern-Wankdorf and follow signs for "zentrum." When you see the old town across the river turn over the bridge and the hotel is on your right after 50 meters. Unload in front of the hotel and you will be directed to parking.

HOTEL BELLE ÉPOQUE
Owners: Jürg & Bice Musfeld-Brugnoli
Gerechtigkeitsgasse 18
CH-3011 Bern, Switzerland
Tel: (031) 311 43 36, Fax: (031) 311 39 36
17 Rooms, Double: CHF 290–CHF 600*
*Breakfast not included: CHF 19
Restaurant open Tue to Sat
Open: all year, Credit cards: all major
In the old section of Bern, Train: 2 km
Canton: Bern

The Romantik Hotel Chesa Salis, a 16th-century, Engadine patrician mansion nestled in a pretty hamlet, is a gem. It has a pastoral setting, splendid antique furniture, an outstanding restaurant, lovely bedrooms, and quality in every detail. Best of all, the hospitality of the Degiacomi family and their staff is superb. The hotel, built in 1590, was originally a farmhouse owned by the Moeli family, wealthy merchants from Italy. Later, the home was bought by the aristocratic von Salis family. The noble heritage of the building is witnessed today by its meter-thick walls, handsome craftsmanship, beautiful wood paneling, outstanding paintings, handsome beamed ceilings, intricate plaster etching on the exterior walls, frescoed ceilings, and colorful ceramic fireplaces. When you enter the reception area, there is an eclectic mix of old and new with handsome antiques blending with black leather sofas, and a contemporary glass counter highlighted by a modern painting. In contrast, most of the furnishings are definitely traditional in style. All of the guestrooms are lovely. Room 26 is a particularly spacious, beautiful room with large windows looking out to the garden. The most stunning room of all, room number 35, is tucked up under the eaves. Its white-washed paneled walls and low ceiling are exquisitely painted with antique, floral designs. *Directions:* Exit highway 27 at Bever. At the church, turn right to the hotel.

ROMANTIK HOTEL CHESA SALIS
Owners: Sibylla & Jürg Degiacomi
Bügl Suot 2
CH-7520 Bever-St. Moritz, Switzerland
Tel: (081) 851 16 16, Fax: (081) 851 16 00
18 Rooms, Double: CHF 200–CHF 370
Closed: mid-Oct to mid-Dec & mid-Apr to mid-Jun
Credit cards: all major
10 km N of St. Moritz, Train: 7 min. walk
Romantik Hotels, Swiss Historic Hotels
Canton: Graubunden

When your delightful hosts, Jacqueline and John Wegink, arrived in Belalp (high on a mountain meadow above Blatten) it was a foggy night. Their hotel had linoleum floors, ugly fluorescent lighting, and dismal décor. However, the next morning when they opened their curtains, the sky had cleared, and when they saw the dazzling panorama of mountain peaks, they agreed Belalp had to be one of most beautiful places in the world. The end of the story is like a fairytale. They returned home to Holland, but their hearts kept going back to the glorious mountain beauty in Belalp. They decided life is precious and happiness not judged by monetary success; so they called the tiny hotel in Belalp, asked the owner if he would sell, bought the inn, and moved to Switzerland. They totally renovated the hotel, mostly with their own labor and reopened it in 2004. The hotel is unpretentious, but endearing in its simplicity. The heart of the inn is its cozy lounge where comfy chairs are grouped around the fireplace and the adjacent dining room/bar where rustic log walls, terracotta floor, red checked fabric, fresh flowers, wood carvings, and crystal chandeliers set a scene of rustic simplicity and charm. The bedrooms are simple but very comfortable, and all have private bathrooms and internet connection. *Directions:* From Brig follow signs to Blatten where you take cable car to Belalp.

HAMILTON LODGE
Owners: Jacqueline & John Wegink
Blatten bei Naters
CH-3914 Belalp, Switzerland
Tel: (027) 923 20 43, Fax: (027) 924 45 45
14 Rooms, Double: CHF 150–CHF 200
Open: Jun to Oct & mid-Dec to mid-Apr
Credit cards: all major
40 km S of Kandersteg
Train to Cable Car: 5 min. walk
Canton: Valais

On a sunny day, one of the most breathtaking drives in Switzerland is through the spectacular Lötschental Valley that ends at the hamlet of Fafleralp, at the foot of Breithorn glacier. Along the way you pass through the picturesque hillside village of Blatten. The Hotel Edelweiss is right in the center of town with a glorious position overlooking the valley and up to mountains. The exterior of the hotel is very appealing: a three-story chalet-style house with a dark wood façade, balconies, and window boxes with cascading red geraniums. Although the front of the hotel is attractive, it is not until you walk onto the huge terrace in the back that the true glory of the hotel is revealed. Enjoy an unsurpassed, unobstructed view of the valley and stunning mountains beyond. Tables and chairs shaded by umbrellas dot the terrace, the heart of the hotel where everyone gathers on sunny days. In cold weather, there is pleasant indoor dining room. The guestrooms (most with balconies) have light wood-paneled walls, plump down comforters, and large windows that let in lots of sunlight. The Edelweiss is a small, simple, family-run hotel offering guests genuine hospitality, great food, very comfortable accommodations, and a superb base from which to take hikes. The Hotel Edelweiss has been a family operation for many years and Lukas Kalbermatten is the third generation to own the hotel.

HOTEL EDELWEISS
Owners: Charlotte & Lukas Kalbermatten
Lötschental Valley
CH-3919 Blatten im Lötschental, Switzerland
Tel: (027) 939 13 63, Fax: (027) 939 10 53
24 Rooms, Double: CHF 150–CHF 210
Open: all year, Credit cards: all major
208 km SE of Bern, Train: 5 km
Canton: Valais

For the Swiss living in the Bernese Alps, a popular family outing is to the Blausee, a tiny, deep blue, crystal-clear lake set in a 20-hectare nature park. After boating on the lake or walking through the densely-wooded forest, many stop to dine on the shores of the lake at the Blausee Restaurant, located in the hotel of the same name. On sunny days, the favorite place to have lunch or supper is on the spacious outdoor terrace. As might be expected, fresh trout is usually featured on the menu. There is also an indoor restaurant for chilly days housed in an attractive, two-story, building that looks a bit like an old-fashioned, English home. Coming to the Blausee has been fashionable since the 19th century and the restaurant has been serving guests for over 125 years. However, it wasn't until recently that guest rooms were added in a newly built section that unobtrusively stretches out behind the restaurant. It is really fun to stay on after the hoards of day trippers leave and enjoy the tranquil beauty of the lake. I expected the guestrooms to be quite simple, but they are amazingly nice. Those on the lower floor are modern in décor. My favorites are those tucked under the eves. These rooms are individually decorated with antique furniture and are very attractive. My favorite, #11, has windows overlooking the lake and a handsome antique headboard. *Directions:* Blausee is located 10 km north of Kandersteg, in Blausee Park.

HOTEL BLAUSEE
Manager: Baillods Family
Naturpark
CH-3717 Blausee, Switzerland
Tel: (033) 672 33 33, Fax: (033) 672 33 30
17 Rooms, Double: CHF 246–CHF 284
Closed: 3 weeks in Jan, Credit cards: all major
4 km south of Kandersteg
Canton: Bern

The Hotel Lindenhof has an absolutely gorgeous setting above Brienz on an expanse of grounds and beautiful gardens. Housed in five separate buildings, guestrooms vary dramatically—from standard to "adventure" rooms. Adventure rooms are a bit more eccentric in decor, the Heustock and Touristorama being two fun examples. The Heustock (Haystack) room has pine beds covered with red-check comforters and enjoys a view across a private terrace to the surrounding greenery. A loft is filled with hay for a sense of adventure. Referred to by the staff as the "James Bond Room" the Touristorama (#33) has a mattress set in a round frame that turns with the flick of a switch. Its bath is also very dramatic, closed off by plate glass and visible from the bedroom, while the shower is set in a rock and cascading waterfall. Family units housed in a nondescript building—less desirable in terms of setting and decor but very practical—are the only four without a view. Standard rooms are a bit smaller with no terrace. The reception is in the main building, and the stubli/bar makes a cozy spot to settle in front of the fire. The more formal restaurant has windows looking out to the terrace where tables are set in warmer weather. Your sense of adventure in dining can be indulged in the Adventure Restaurant, a cave-like room set under a ceiling of stars and moons. *Directions:* Arriving in Brienz, drive up the hill 100 meters after the station.

HOTEL LINDENHOF
Manager: Hansjörg Imhoff
Lindenhofweg, Haus im Grünen
CH-3855 Brienz, Switzerland
Tel: (033) 952 20 30, Fax: (033) 952 20 40
40 Rooms, Double: CHF 160–CHF 290
Open: mid-Mar to Jan, Credit cards: all major
18 km W of Interlaken, Train: 100 meters
Canton: Bern

When we first visited the Elvezia al Lago over 18 years ago, it was a sweet, modest little hotel. In spite of its simplicity we were captivated by its fabulous waterfront location and its blissful seclusion—it can be reached only by boat or by walking along a footpath along the edge of the lake. Today the romantic setting and seclusion remain unchanged, but the hotel's facilities have vastly improved over the years and there are now eight nicely furnished guestrooms, all with hairdryers, direct-dial phones, good bathrooms, televisions, and mini-bars. Best of all, all but one of the bedrooms has a view. My personal favorites are the three rooms on the top floor, especially number 5, which is on the corner with windows on two sides to capture the vista. Another bonus is Elvezia al Lago's restaurant. Although there is a cozy dining room inside, usually guests eat out on a terrace that extends over the water. There is a boat dock in front where the ferry regularly pulls up with restaurant guests and there is also a waterfront garden with lounge chairs where guests can relax and enjoy a dip in the lake. *Directions:* You can take a ferry from Lugano to Grotto Elvezia, or drive along the lake from Lugano toward Castagnola and leave your car in the parking area where the small road Via Cortivo ends. Then either walk to the hotel (about eight minutes) or call the hotel for a boat to pick you up.

ELVEZIA AL LAGO
Owners: Jean-Claude & Diana Zuber
Sentiero di Gandria 21
Castagnola
6976 Lugano, Switzerland
Tel: (091) 971 44 51, Fax: (091) 972 78 40
8 Rooms, Double: CHF 170–CHF 240
Open: Apr to Nov, Credit cards: all major
3 km E of Lugano, Train: 3 km
Canton: Ticino

The Chesa Rosatsch is a delightful hotel located about 5 kilometers north of St. Moritz in a pretty village, Celerina, that still retains its charming old world character over the glamour and glitz of its world famous neighbor. It is positioned in the Upper Engadin Valley, right next to the River Inn where the locals are often seen standing on the banks fishing. Within easy walking distance of the hotel is the beautiful San Gian Church, plus shops and restaurants. Chesa Rosatsch is made up of four connecting houses, the oldest dating back 360 years. You can quickly distinguish where one house ends and another begins since each is painted a different color: white, pink, rose, or light tan. Together they create a pretty picture reflecting in the river. The interior of the house exudes a "sophisticated" country style, with predominantly light pine furniture throughout. The restaurant, where breakfast and simple meals are served, is quite contemporary with a flood of sunlight streaming through large arched windows and Danish-modern chairs and tables. In contrast, the Stüva, a gourmet restaurant, is cozy with beautiful, antique wood paneling, wrought-iron chandeliers, beamed ceiling, and carved wood chairs. The guestrooms are very attractive, all with a similar look with light pine furnishings. *Directions:* Located right on the banks of the River Inn, next to the bridge.

CHESA ROSATSCH
Manager: Ueli Knobel-Rüegg
CH-7505 Celerina, Switzerland
Tel: (081) 837 01 01, Fax: (081) 837 01 00
36 Rooms, Double: CHF 190–CHF 360
1 Suite: CHF 390–CHF 660
Closed: mid-Apr to Jun, Credit cards: MC, VS
3 km NE of St. Moritz, Train: 3km
Canton: Graubunden

La Coudre is an elegant, small bed & breakfast tucked up in the gentle hills above Lake Geneva, a convenient location for exploring this beautiful region of Switzerland. Before your gracious hosts, Vivien and Marcel, decided to convert it into a tiny hotel, the lovely property was the home of Vivien's parents. You will fall in love at first sight with this exceptionally appealing manor. It's a pretty, three-story white house accented by green shutters and romantically laced with ivy. The interior is also outstanding—each room is decorator perfect, displaying the warmth and charm of a private home. The lounge (with a cute bar tucked at one end of the room) is pretty as can be with dark red walls setting off a pair of leather sofas set in front of an open fireplace. A full English breakfast is served each morning in a wonderful dining room with a magnificent parquet floor and tall French windows, accented by handsome floral draperies which overlook the garden. In warm weather, most guests prefer to enjoy breakfast at small tables set in the garden. Another appealing hideaway for a cup of tea is the glass-enclosed sunroom with pretty, white-wicker chairs. A handsome staircase winds up to the very attractive, individually decorated guestrooms (all with free internet access). My favorite has twin beds highlighted by stunning antique, hand-painted headboards and matching armoire. *Directions:* Located near the Coppet exit from the A1. Ask for exact directions.

LA COUDRE BED & BREAKFAST
Owners: Marcel Ackermann & Vivien Pestalozzi
200 Route des Coudres
CH-1298 Céligny, Switzerland
Tel: (022) 960 83 60, Fax: (022) 960 83 61
9 Rooms, Double: CHF 240–CHF 280
1 Suite: CHF 380–CHF 400
Open: all year, Credit cards: all major
17 km NE of Geneva, Train: 5 km
Canton: Geneva

The Hostellerie Bon Accueil is an outstanding little inn, brimming with old-world charm. The weathered wood chalet accented by green shutters and window boxes overflowing with geraniums dates back almost 300 years and still reflects the warmth and character of its farmhouse origins. Conveniently close to the famous ski resort of Gstaad, the inn hugs a sunny hillside overlooking Château d'Oex, a village famous for the production of cheese. Many chalet-style hotels look extremely appealing from the outside but most, disappointingly, seem to revert to a more sterile, modern ambiance once you enter the front door. Such is definitely not the case at the Hostellerie Bon Accueil. The owners have lovingly maintained a romantic, cozy appeal inside as well as out. The beautifully maintained hotel is endearing throughout with low, beamed ceilings, soft lights, mellow wood paneling, and an abundance of country-style antiques. The guestrooms are as sweet as they can be, with pretty floral fabrics and cute white embroidered curtains accenting the windows. The food is excellent and the restaurant is lovely with candlelit dining. In summer, however, the large terrace is the favorite spot to enjoy a meal with a view of the mountains to whet the appetite. *Directions:* From Château d'Oex, cross the railroad tracks and follow signs up the hill to the hotel.

HOSTELLERIE BON ACCUEIL
Manager: Marianne Bon
CH-1660 Château d'Oex, Switzerland
Tel: (026) 924 63 20, Fax: (026) 924 51 26
17 Rooms, Double: CHF 145–CHF 235
Closed: mid-Oct to mid-Dec, Credit cards: all major
15 km W of Gstaad, Train: 2km
Swiss Historic Hotels
Canton: Vaud

Chur, the oldest city in Switzerland, has at its heart a medieval section enhanced by hidden squares, fabulous churches, colorful fountains, remains of ancient walls, and an enticing network of cobbled streets. The Romantik Hotel Stern is perfectly situated in the center of the charming old part of the city. Pink, with white-shuttered windows, the building sits right on the street, with a pretty garden terrace to the side. From the moment you step into the foyer, an appealing, old world, ambiance prevails with fine country antiques and gleaming wood paneling adding to the cozy ambiance. It is obvious that great care has been taken to maintain the rich heritage of the building. The meticulously-kept guestrooms (most of which have been recently refurbished) have light knotty-pine furniture typical of the Grisons region, fluffy down duvets, fine linens, and modern bathrooms. The building is 300 years old and has many nooks and crannies reached through a maze of hallways. The food here is excellent and there are many cute dining rooms with age-mellowed pine paneling and rustic-style chairs. Because Chur is on the main rail line, it makes a convenient hub for exploring Switzerland. In recent years, Adrian Müller has taken over the hotel and his extraordinary warmth of welcome and eye for perfection has made this always popular hotel exceptionally outstanding. *Directions:* Follow signs to the city center where you will see signs to the hotel.

ROMANTIK HOTEL STERN
Owner: Adrian K. Müller
Reichgasse 11
CH-7000 Chur, Switzerland
Tel: (081) 258 57 57, Fax: (081) 258 57 58
65 Rooms, Double: CHF 200–CHF 295
3 Suites: CHF 300
Open: all year, Credit cards: all major
120 km SE of Zürich
Train: 500 meters, free pickup
Romantik Hotels, Canton: Graubunden

The Hotel du Lac is located on Lake Geneva only about 12 kilometers east of Geneva. Although the hotel is on a busy road, behind the hotel is a pretty garden with a lawn stretching down to a private pier on the lake. The Hotel du Lac carries the air of an elegant home rather than that of a hotel. It does not appear very old, but it is. In fact, in 1626 the hotel was granted the exclusive right to receive and lodge people arriving by coach or horseback. At that time travelers on foot were excluded as guests of the inn because, as a memorandum dated 1768 decreed, "The titled man of wealth riding in his own coach and four must not be housed with the peasant, the knife-sharpener, the chimney-sweep—the latter would feel too ill at ease." The Hotel du Lac has been carefully restored and now you, too, can dream you are one of the guests arriving by "coach and four." The hotel has retained many of its old beams, stone walls, and lovely antique furniture and artifacts. All the bedrooms are attractive: some have kitchenettes, five suites have balconies with lake views, and some have a small terrace squeezed into the jumble of tiled rooftops. For those who want to be away from the city, the Hotel du Lac offers an appealing choice for visitors to Geneva. *Directions:* Between Geneva and Lausanne, by the Route du Lac. The hotel is located on the main street, by the lake.

HOTEL DU LAC
Owner: Oswald Schnyder
CH-1296 Coppet, Switzerland
Tel: (022) 960 80 00, Fax: (022) 960 80 10
12 Rooms, Double: CHF 275–CHF 335*
4 Suites: CHF 480–CHF 590*
3 Apartments: CHF 580 daily
*Breakfast not included: CHF 26
Open: all year, Credit cards: all major
12 km E of Geneva, Train: 1 km, Boat: 2 blocks
Canton: Vaud

Le Vieux Chalet has a spectacular location high in the Jaunbach Pass, looking out across Lake Montsalvens over green pastures and forests to the distant castle of Gruyères and beyond to the towering, rugged mountains dominated by the dramatic peak of Moleson. The traditional chalet-style inn exudes an old-world charm with dark timbers, white stucco, deep overhanging eaves, and balconies heavily laden with flowers. The inside is just as appealing as the outside, with a most attractive, informal, pine-paneled dining room and a cozy, typically Alpine café where hikers often gather for lunch in summer. If the weather is fine, everyone drinks and eats on the spacious terrace where you can enjoy a panoramic Alpine view and excellent food. The five snug little bedrooms (three doubles, two singles) are pine-paneled and each has a small shower room. All have views but I especially like rooms 4, 5, and 6, which afford spectacular nighttime views of distant Gruyères when the castle is illuminated. Le Vieux Chalet has two large function rooms below it that are often used for summertime weddings. Crésuz-en-Gruyère is a convenient base for day trips to the charming hilltown of Gruyères or the beautiful city of Fribourg to the north. *Directions:* Leave the autobahn at Bulle and follow the signs for Gruyères. Take a left at the signpost for Charmey and follow this road for 6 km to Crésuz-en-Gruyère where you find Le Vieux Chalet to your left high above the road.

LE VIEUX CHALET
Owners: Monika & Victor Agugliaro
CH-1653 Crésuz-en-Gruyère, Switzerland
Tel: (026) 927 12 86, Fax: (026) 927 22 86
6 Rooms, Double: CHF 190
Restaurant closed Tue
Open: all year, Credit cards: all major
29 km S of Fribourg, 20 min by bus from Bulle
Canton: Fribourg

The Auberge du Raisin is located in Cully, a sleepy, quaint, wine-growing village hugging the shore of Lake Geneva. A few minutes' walk from the hotel leads you down the hill to a beautiful, tree-shaded park stretching along the waterfront—a perfect place to stroll while waiting for one of the lake steamers that pull into the dock. The fame of the Auberge du Raisin is based on its reputation for serving outstanding food accompanied by an extensive wine list featuring the finest wines from around the world. The chef, Adolfo Blokbergen, creates exceptional gourmet cuisine, attracting visitors from far and wide to his enchanting restaurant. The dining rooms, decorated with antique furnishings and highlighted by handsome old master paintings, exude a gentle, refined elegance that sets a romantic scene for the fine meals. The bedrooms too are outstanding. Individual in their decor, size, and arrangement, each is beautifully furnished in color-coordinated fabrics and maintained to perfection. Antiques are lavished throughout and are complemented by lovely, bountiful flower arrangements. This elegant, small Swiss inn, dating back to the 16th century, is a delightful place to stay while you explore one of Switzerland's most charming wine regions. *Directions:* Cully is a small town right on Lake Geneva, just 10 km southeast of Lausanne.

AUBERGE DU RAISIN
Managers: Mr & Mrs A. Blokbergen
1, Place de l'Hotel-de-Ville
CH-1096 Cully, Switzerland
Tel: (021) 799 21 31, Fax: (021) 799 25 01
10 Rooms, Double: CHF 350–CHF 590
Open: all year, Credit cards: all major
70 km E of Geneva, Train: walking distance
Canton: Vaud

At the heart of one of Switzerland's finest wine-producing regions, Cully is wrapped by terraced fields of grapes on three sides and fronted by Lake Geneva. It is one of the most picturesque of the charming villages that dot the shores of the lake. Many ferryboats stop at Cully's small pier across from a grassy park. Facing the park and the lake is the superbly positioned Hotel Major Davel, a pink-stucco building with gray-green shutters and a mansard roof. Many diners come by boat and stop in Cully to enjoy lunch in the hotel's glass-enclosed terrace restaurant with a view of the lake. Rolf Messmer, the hotelier, is also the chef and the food is excellent. Those looking for a reasonably priced place to spend the night will find that the Hotel Major Davel offers, in addition to the restaurant, good accommodation. Upstairs (there is no elevator), the guestrooms are not deluxe, but certainly adequate. Rooms 5 and 10 are corner rooms with the advantage of having windows on two sides. With just 13 rooms, the owners pride themselves on the personalized service that they are able to offer their guests—and guests show their appreciation by repeated visits. Rolf and Bernadette are a young couple who bring a new enthusiasm and warmth to this wonderful country hotel. *Directions:* Cully is a small town on the shore of Lake Geneva, just 10 km southeast of Lausanne. The hotel is right on the waterfront.

HOTEL MAJOR DAVEL
Owners: Bernadette & Rolf Messmer
CH-1096 Cully, Switzerland
Tel: (021) 799 94 94, Fax: (021) 799 37 82
13 Rooms, Double: CHF 180
Open: Jan 23 to Dec 10, Credit cards: MC, VS
70 km E of Geneva, Steps from boat dock
Canton: Vaud

Dielsdorf is a small town north of Zürich, only about 20 minutes by car from the Zürich airport, or about 25 minutes from Zürich by train. The hotel is owned by Christa and Eugene Schäfer who also own the Rote Rose, a wonderful little inn only a few minutes away by car in the town of Regensberg. The Rote Rose is small, with only nine rooms, so it's nice to have this as a second choice. The Hotel Löwen, built in the 13th century, has been completely renovated. The outside is painted white with small gables and shuttered windows enhancing the country appeal. Floral paintings by Lotte Günthardt, Christa's mother, the world-renowned rose artist, adorn the walls throughout this small inn. The bedrooms are pleasantly decorated and the suite is an especially large, light, and airy room. If you are on a budget, a guestroom without a private bath is a good value. The most attractive feature of the hotel is the very cozy dining room where beamed ceilings, pretty linens, antique accents, and fresh-flower arrangements combine to create an inviting mood—and the food is excellent. *Directions:* Just to the north of Zürich, take the Zürich/Affoltern/Regensdorf exit from the A1 then take the main road to Dielsdorf/Koblenz. The hotel is in the center of the village.

HOTEL LÖWEN
Owners: Christa & Eugene Schäfer
Managers: Elizabeth & Louis Bourdon
Hinterdorfstrasse 21, CH-8157 Dielsdorf, Switzerland
Tel: (044) 855 61 61, Fax: (044) 855 61 62
35 Rooms, Double: CHF 110–CHF 175*
*Breakfast not included: CHF 15
Closed: Jul 26 to Aug 9, Restaurant closed Sun
Credit cards: all major
20 km N of Zürich airport, Train: 300 meters
Canton: Zurich

To reach Engelberg you leave the shores of Lake Lucerne and weave through a gorgeous narrow mountain valley. There is just one road in and at the end of the valley as it climbs a switchback passage to Engelberg, a town set in the shadow of towering peaks. It is a skiers' heaven in the winter and in summer the high mountain valleys offer inviting opportunities for walking, hiking, and parasailing. Unable to find a hotel with old-world charm, we found a hotel with the most convenient location, the best views, and good value. Sitting on a lawn just a garden's distance from the tram station for Titlis, the four-story Hotel Sonnwendhof is newly built of white stucco, trimmed in wood, and colored with geranium-filled flower boxes. There is no other building between it and the base of the mountain to obstruct Alpine views. Guestrooms are light and airy in their decor, with light pines used for the ceilings, window and door frames, and the furnishings. Beds are topped with plump down comforters and every room enjoys a comfortable sitting area. Rooms looking up to Titlis are premium, especially top-floor rooms set under vaulted ceilings. Guestrooms on the other side look up to the peaks of Brunni. Public areas include a small bar, an attractive, simply decorated restaurant, and a central garden courtyard terrace. *Directions:* Take the autobahn south from Lucerne and exit at Stans. From Stans travel 20 km on the 130 to Engelberg.

HOTEL SONNWENDHOF
Manager: Elfi Odermatt
Gerschniweg 1
CH-6390 Engelberg, Switzerland
Tel: (041) 637 45 75, Fax: (041) 637 42 38
28 Rooms, Double: CHF 170–CHF 260
Open: all year, Credit cards: all major
32 km SE of Lucerne, Train: 500 meters
Canton: Obwalden

If you like places off the beaten path, you will love the Hotel St. Petersinsel, a romantic inn built in a 12th-century monastery on an island in Lake Bienne. Many famous guests have visited here, including Jean Jacques Rousseau, Josephine Bonaparte, and Goethe. If you arrive on a sunny weekend, you might dispute that this hotel is "off the beaten path" because this bit of paradise is well-known to the Swiss who arrive by the hundreds by bicycle, foot, or boat to enjoy a delicious, home-cooked meal in the courtyard of the monastery. However, with only 13 guestrooms, the hotel cannot accommodate many guests, so in the evening, the island once again assumes its utter tranquility. There are no roads to the monastery. You can come on foot (about an hour's walk from Erlach) along a scenic path that meanders through low lying reeds—a nature reserve filled with all sorts of birds, deer, and fox. But, with luggage, your best bet is to take a boat from Erlach (when making reservations, ask for time schedules and details as to where to board the ferry). The romantic monastery sits in the middle of a meadow with paths beckoning you to explore the nearby forests. All the guestrooms are charming, some are decorated with antiques, and some with modern furniture. My favorite is the corner room with two canopy beds—it is a real winner. *Directions:* Ask hotel for directions.

HOTEL ST. PETERSINSEL
Manager: Heinz Kern
Ile Saint Pierre
CH-3235 Erlach, Switzerland
Tel: (032) 338 11 14, Fax: (032) 338 25 82
13 Rooms, Double: CHF 220–CHF 235
3 Suites: CHF 300–CHF 350
Open: Mar to end-Oct, Credit cards: MC, VS
8 km E of Erlach, Train: 10 km
Swiss Historic Hotels
Canton: Bern

As you drive up the gentle hill and spot the dramatic Hotel Paxmontana on the crest, you will be immediately enchanted. Built in 1896 in the grand old Victorian resort style, the Paxmontana is a sprawling four-story mansion topped by a mansard roof with gabled windows, perky turrets, a Swiss flag, green shutters, and wraparound balconies. Although larger than most of the hotels in our guide, the Paxmontana has nostalgic, old-world character, impeccable upkeep, outstanding gardens, and the genuine hospitality of an intimate, family-run hotel. The lounges are spacious and attractively decorated. Stretching across the front is a delightful restaurant in a glass-enclosed porch where every table faces the window with an unobstructed view. A second, more formal, dining room has a charming forest view. The simple guestrooms are moderately sized and the bathrooms somewhat dated, but the upkeep is perfect and the decor is sweet and cheerful. Most guestrooms have a balcony, and all have a beautiful vista—those in front, a sweeping view of valley and mountains, and those in back, the pretty forested hills. Intentionally, no televisions or radios are in the rooms since most guests come for the joy of being close to nature and for long walks along the many wooded paths. Many guests come to visit the birthplace of the renowned Saint Nicholas, born in the 15th century in a nearby cottage. *Directions:* From Sacheln, follow the road up the hill to Flüeli Ranft.

HOTEL PAXMONTANA
Owner: Küttel Family
CH-6073 Flüeli Ranft, Switzerland
Tel: (041) 660 22 33, Fax: (041) 660 61 42
100 Rooms, Double: CHF 190–CHF 290
Closed: Oct 20 to Apr, Credit cards: all major
40 km SE of Lucerne, Train: 1 km
Swiss Historic Hotels
Canton: Obwalden

Hotel & Kurhaus Flühli derived its name from the early 1900s when tourists came to Flühli to drink the waters, which had the reputation of curative powers. Today, travelers come to the area for hiking and to enjoy nature. In 2004, this simple, old-fashioned hotel celebrated its 100th anniversary, and it looks much the same today as it did then—Swiss chalet-style with a touch of art nouveau. Hotel & Kurhaus Flühli's greatest asset is its warmth of welcome. The hotel is owned by the gracious Rosmarie and Edy Maag who previously owned another hotel, but for years had dreamed of the Hotel Flühli. When it became available, they bought it. The hotel is very much a family operation. Their daughter, Jolanda, who oversees the guests, has three pretty daughters and they are very much a part of the hotel as evidenced by their toys, books, and backpacks. As you enter the hotel, there are two restaurants: to your left is a very pretty dining room with green walls and to your right, an informal, cozy, wood-paneled, stübli-style restaurant, which not only serves meals, but also is a meeting place for many of the town locals. There are two types of guestrooms. Those in the new wing are very basic. Those in the original building are cozy with wood paneling on the walls and ceiling, and the small bathrooms have linoleum walls and floors. Ask for room 106 (with a balcony) or room 108 (a bright corner room). *Directions:* The hotel is in the center of town, on the main road.

☕ 🏃 CREDIT ☎ 🛗 ⵟ P 🍴 🚭 🖼 🔔 🥾

HOTEL & KURHAUS FLÜHLI
Owners: Rosmarie & Edy Maag
Dorfstrasse 3
CH 6173 Flühli, Switzerland
Tel: (041) 488 11 66, Fax: (041) 488 23 53
14 Rooms, Double: CHF 160–CHF 180
Open: all year, Credit cards: MC, VS
47 km S of Lucerne, Train: 1 km
Swiss Historic Hotels
Canton: Lucerne

Fribourg is a colorful medieval city built on a loop of the River Sarine. With a fabulous cathedral, museums, 16th-century clock tower, Renaissance fountains, and quaint bridges, there are also many outstanding, historic houses in town, one of which is the Romantik Hotel du Sauvage. This extremely attractive hotel, one block from the river, has a marvelous corner location in Fribourg's "old town". The stone side of the house faces the street leading to the bridge, Pont de St-Jean. The other side, made of white stucco, looks onto the pretty square, Plaza du Petit St-Jean. In summer, flower boxes dress all the windows adding to the hotel's appeal. The restaurant at the Romantik Hotel du Sauvage is well known for its fine food. Meals are served in a beautiful dining room. When the weather is warm, guests can enjoy eating outside on a terrace facing the plaza at tables and chairs shaded by umbrellas. Resembling a private home, all of the individually decorated guestrooms, some with beamed ceilings, are charming and display excellent taste, top-notch quality, and beautiful fabrics. The bathrooms are all particularly attractive with ceramic tiles hand-painted by your gracious hostess, the very skilled Madame Buchi, who is personally involved in running this delightful hotel. From the hotel, you can walk to the many sightseeing possibilities. *Directions:* Half a block from Pont de St-Jean, facing Plaza du Petit St-Jean.

ROMANTIK HOTEL DU SAUVAGE
Owner: Christiane Buchi
Planche Supérieure 12
CH-1700 Fribourg, Switzerland
Tel: (026) 347 30 60, Fax: (026) 347 30 61
17 Rooms, Double: CHF 240–CHF 350
Restaurant closed Sun & Mon and 2 weeks in July
Open: all year, Credit cards: all major
34 km SW of Bern, Train: 1 km
Romantik Hotels
Canton: Fribourg

Geneva is known for its wonderful lakeside hotels, but an appealing hotel exists in that quaint old section of the city—the Hotel les Armures, converted from a private residence dating from the 17th century. The mood and ambiance is intimate. There are no signs of tour groups, only guests sitting in a small lounge, talking quietly or reading—using the hotel as they would their homes. All the guestrooms have handsome wood doors and are decorated with traditional pieces and antiques. The standard room I occupied on my visit had a queen-sized bed, a small round table, antique-style high-backed armchairs, bedside tables with lamps, a small refrigerator, and a very nice bathroom with a hairdryer. The room was quite small but cozy, with a beamed ceiling and wood-framed windows looking over a quiet, shaded square and old fountain. Junior suites offer more spacious accommodation than the standard rooms. Personal favorites in the category of standard room are 201 with its beautiful 17th-century hand-painted beams and courtyard overlook and 401 with its lovely antique furnishings. Set against the exposed stone walls, rooms 407 and 409 are especially charming junior suites. When making a reservation, request detailed directions as the hotel is a bit difficult to find. Also request a room overlooking the square. The hotel has a restaurant, staggered over two levels. *Directions:* Located in the old town at the foot of Saint Peter's Cathedral.

HOTEL LES ARMURES
Owner: Nicole Borgeat
1, Rue du Puits St. Pierre
CH-1204 Geneva, Switzerland
Tel: (022) 310 91 72, Fax: (022) 310 98 46
27 Rooms, Double: CHF 625–CHF 650
5 Suites: CHF 650–CHF 950
Open: all year, Credit cards: all major
At the heart of old town, Train: 2 km
Canton: Geneva

Well located just off the Quai General Guisan, a block or so from the heart of the old pedestrian quarter of Geneva as well as convenient to the lake, the Hotel de la Cigogne offers the ultimate in personalized service and luxurious accommodation. The atmosphere reminds me of an exclusive club. It is gorgeous. Furnishings throughout the hotel are elegant and ornate. The sitting room off the lobby has painted murals and the intimate and beautifully paneled restaurant has a stained-glass ceiling. Guestrooms are individual in their decor, from the one modern room whose walls have been created to resemble a grotto, to the other 51 rooms, all beautifully appointed and decorated with fine antiques from an assortment of periods and styles. Even the so-called standard rooms are comfortable in size, but the junior suites afford the spaciousness of an additional sitting area. The majority of the master suites are on two levels and enjoy the added luxury of two bathrooms, one off the bedroom and one off the living room or salon. All guestrooms have private bathrooms, all with bathtubs—there are no showers at this hotel. Air conditioning is by ice-cool circulating water, which gives many health and comfort benefits. *Directions:* From the airport keep to Centre Ville after the Mont Blanc Bridge. Drive approximately 150 meters and do not turn left or right. The hotel is easy to spot with its orange awnings and ornamental gold stork, La Cigogne.

HOTEL DE LA CIGOGNE
Owner: Favre Family
17, Place Longemalle
CH-1204 Geneva, Switzerland
Tel: (022) 818 40 40, Fax: (022) 818 40 50
52 Rooms, Double: CHF 495–CHF 620
6 Suites: CHF 870–CHF 970
Open: all year, Credit cards: all major
At the heart of old town, Train: 1 km
Relais & Châteaux
Canton: Geneva

This lovely hotel, while three-star in rating, shares the same four-star attitude in terms of service as its regal neighbor, Hotel de la Cigogne. The location on the tranquil Place Longemalle is peaceful and the entry is dramatic with a hand-painted imported bar serving as the reception. The decor of the hotel is influenced by the owner's appreciation and use of color. Fifty-eight guestrooms are distributed over six floors, each floor sporting a different color theme. I was able to see a full range of rooms: 609 is a lovely corner room under angled ceilings that profits from windows on two sides overlooking the myriad of rooftops; 602 is a superior suite, cozy under heavy beams, and enjoys a lovely sitting area; and the manager's favorite, 607, staggered over three floors, enjoys a separate sitting area, a bedroom, a loft, and a spectacular private rooftop terrace boasting the best views in Geneva. Breakfast is a lavish buffet offered in a gorgeous room with pine floors and views out through an expanse of floor-to-ceiling arched windows. Running the length of the room is an outdoor terrace where chairs are nestled up against a wrought-iron railing and window boxes overflowing with red geraniums. *Directions:* Just after crossing the Mont Blanc Bridge, follow directions to Centre Ville and you come to Place Longemalle.

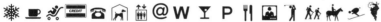

HOTEL LONGEMALLE
Owner: Favre Family
Manager: Philippe Vuillemin
13, Place Longemalle
CH-1204 Geneva, Switzerland
Tel: (022) 818 62 62, Fax: (022) 818 62 61
58 Rooms, Double: CHF 300–CHF 600
Open: all year, Credit cards: all major
At the heart of the old town, Train: 2 km
Canton: Geneva

The Grandhotel Giessbach, dating from 1874, is a picturesque Victorian-style, grand hotel—a sprawling, five-story building with towers, turrets, balconies, and flower boxes. Nestled high in a wooded forest, the setting is sublime. One side looks down to beautiful Lake Brienze and the other side has a spectacular view of the Giessbach waterfalls, right by the hotel. This irreplaceable jewel was to be demolished by land developers who planned to build a new jumbo, concrete hotel—ending forever an era. Thankfully, Franz Weber, miraculously saved the day by forming a foundation to raise money to bring the Grandhotel Giessbach back to its former splendor. The interior is stunning with gorgeous antique furniture throughout. Each of the guestrooms is individually decorated with fine furnishings. There is a splendid gourmet restaurant called Chez Florent, where the food is incredible, and the more casual Orangerie restaurant. When the weather is warm, guests dine outside on the terrace with views in every direction. You can drive up a winding narrow lane to the hotel, but it is more fun is to leave your car at the Interlaken-Ost parking lot and take the boat to Griessbach pier where a cute little red funicular (Giesserbachbahn) is waiting to chug 1000 meters up the steep mountain and deliver you to the hotel. *Directions:* Traveling the N8 between Interlaken and Brienz, exit at Brienz-Giessbach and follow signs to Axalp. The hotel is across from the Giessbach falls.

GRANDHOTEL GIESSBACH
Director: Matthias Kögl
Am Brienzersee
Giessbach
CH-3855 Brienz, Switzerland
Tel: (033) 952 25 25, Fax: (033) 952 25 30
70 Rooms, Double: CHF 240–CHF 600
Open: Apr 21 to Oct 21, Credit cards: all major
18 km E of Interlaken on Lake Brienz, Train: 5 km
Canton: Bern

Perched high in the hills above Montreux, the Hotel Victoria (a member of the Relais & Châteaux group) is a handsome hotel with a mansard roof. From the hotel, the pool, and the perfectly manicured gardens terraced below, there is a truly breathtaking panorama of Lake Geneva backed by jagged mountain peaks. From the moment you walk inside this beautiful inn, there is an old-world ambiance enhanced by handsome antique furniture. There are many niches in the various lounges where guests can relax—one of my favorites is the cheerful, bright, garden "sun room"—a delightful spot to enjoy a good book or afternoon tea. The bar area is inviting, with dark paneling enhanced by old paintings. There are two elegantly decorated dining rooms serving superb meals. The owner, Mr Mittermair, mingles throughout the dining room at dinner to make sure that his guests are well cared for. The guestrooms have been completely renovated and glamorous new suites added, with views so spectacular that you will never want to leave your room. Although this is a grand hotel, it is run with such warmth and fine management, you will feel like a guest in a private home. Compared to what you would pay to stay at a hotel in Geneva, the Victoria is a great value. *Directions:* Located 90 km from Geneva Cointrin airport, on the Montreux Rochers de Naye railway line, 10 minutes from the Montreux or Villeneuve motorway exits.

HOTEL VICTORIA
Owner: Toni Mittermair
Glion
CH-1823 Montreux, Switzerland
Tel: (021) 962 82 82, Fax: (021) 962 82 92
55 Rooms, Double: CHF 250–CHF 600
10 Suites: CHF 480–CHF 600
Open: all year, Credit cards: all major
90 km E of Geneva, Train: 200 meters
Relais & Châteaux
Canton: Vaud

The setting of the Hotel Krone is idyllic. Just across the street from the hotel, the River Rhine flows by and narrows on its course from Lake Constance. The Krone has an outdoor terrace on the banks of the river, with a cluster of small tables where meals are served in warm weather. When I first stayed at the Hotel Krone, I fell in love with this beautiful small inn, so well managed by the gracious Schraner-Michaeli family, who personally pamper each guest. The guestrooms have all been totally redone, each individual in decor and each lovely. My favorites were those decorated in a French style with beautiful rose-patterned fabrics. There are only two rooms that actually overlook the water, rooms 220 and 222. The intimate dining room remains, as always, an elegant, paneled room with tables exquisitely set with crisp linens and fresh flowers. Best yet, the food is exceptional. The Hotel Krone makes an excellent base for exploring the northern region of Switzerland and just steps from the door you can board the ferry that will take you along the Rhine. On a day's boat excursion you can visit the delightful village of Stein am Rhein with its wonderfully painted buildings or the medieval town of Schaffhausen. *Directions:* Gottlieben is located on the Untersee approximately 5 km to the west of Konstanz and the Bodensee. It is a small town and the Krone is right on the waterfront.

ROMANTIK HOTEL KRONE
Owner: Georg Schraner
Seestrasse 11
CH-8274 Gottlieben, Switzerland
Tel: (071) 666 80 60, Fax: (071) 666 80 69
25 Rooms, Double: CHF 180–CHF 330
Closed: mid-Jan to mid-Feb, Credit cards: all major
5 km W of Constance, Rhine ferry across from hotel
Romantik Hotels
Canton: Thurgau

It was love at first sight when I came to Grimentz, a tumble of storybook, dark-timbered chalets accented with colorful flowers, sitting high in the Anniviers Valley. How fortunate that at the entrance to the old village is the delightful, family-run Hotel de Moiry, a whitewashed inn with handsome wood shutters. Even if you are unable to spend several nights here, this is an excellent place to enjoy even just a meal, as we did on our first visit to Grimentz, a hearty lunch of fondue, salad, and crusty dark bread, leaving just enough room for a slice of strudel. On warm days you eat outside on the terrace or, if the weather is inclement, in the cozy, traditional dining room before a blazing fire kept lit to make raclette. How fortunate that we were able to return to spend the night and enjoy a traditional raclette dinner of grilled cheese, potatoes, gherkins, and little onions, in the convivial company of a group of hikers spending a week walking in the mountains. There is nothing fancy about the hotel—it is genuine, old-time Swiss. Upstairs, the simple bedrooms have crisp-white walls and pine paneling and each is accompanied by a shower room. *Directions:* From Lausanne take the A9 autobahn to Sierre where you follow signs for Val d'Anniviers, which winds you up the mountains for the 30-km drive to Grimentz.

HOTEL DE MOIRY
Owners: Andrea & Aurel Salamin-Walker
CH-3961 Grimentz, Switzerland
Tel: (027) 475 11 44, Fax: (027) 475 28 23
17 Rooms, Double: CHF 140–CHF 190
Open: Dec 18 to Apr 15 & Jun 1 to Oct 28
Credit cards: MC, VS
55 km SW of Brig
Train to Sierre, 1 hr by postal bus
Canton: Valais

The Gletschergarten, built in 1899, sits in a meadow of wildflowers, overlooking a glacier. Originally a large family home, the house gradually evolved into a small hotel. While helping her parents, Elsbeth met Finn Breitenstein, a member of the Danish ski team housed at the Gletschergarten. On the last day of the competition, Finn had an accident that delayed his departure—the rest is history. Elsbeth and Finn fell in love and today they are the third generation to operate the Chalet Gletschergarten, continuing the tradition of outstanding hospitality. (The Breitenstein family celebrated their 100th anniversary of innkeeping in 1999.) The hotel is filled with old-world charm, with pine-paneled walls, antique accents, original oil paintings by Elsbeth's father, and Oriental carpets. The cozily paneled dining room serves excellent food (be sure to take demi-pension). The bedrooms are attractive, all opening onto flower-laden balconies that wrap completely around each floor of the hotel. The rooms in front overlook the mountains, but I fell in love with our accommodation (room 21), a quiet room in the back with a pretty view of green hills. There is a motto on the front of this delightful inn that truly reflects its spirit and hospitality: "Gladness to the ones that arrive. Freedom to the ones that stay here. Blessing to the ones that move on." *Directions:* One km up the main street from the station immediately after the town church.

CHALET-HOTEL GLETSCHERGARTEN
Owners: Elsbeth & Finn Breitenstein
CH-3818 Grindelwald, Switzerland
Tel: (033) 853 17 21, Fax: (033) 853 29 57
26 Rooms, Double: CHF 220–CHF 300
Open: Dec to Mar & Jun to Oct
Credit cards: all major
20 km SE of Interlaken, Train: 1 km
Canton: Bern

You cannot help but fall in love with the Romantik Hotel Schweizerhof. It is an outstanding, deluxe hotel with fantastic views of the mountains and radiating a nostalgic old-world charm. The exterior is exceptionally attractive: a large chalet-style building with dark wood siding prettily set off by bright red shutters, a series of peaked roofs, many balconies, white curtains peeking through casement windows, and boxes of colorful geraniums. When you step inside, a cheerful, home-like ambiance prevails with pastel colors, light wood paneling, fine fabrics, antique accents, a really cute bar, a tiny library, and wonderful little cozy nooks to settle down with a good book or chat with friends. There are two beautiful dining rooms; but in warm weather most guests choose to dine on the sunny terrace in front of the hotel. The guestrooms in the newer wing of the hotel are splendidly decorated. Those in the older part of the building are more dated but a renovation is planned to bring all up to the same standard. What makes the Schweizerhof so truly special is the genuine hospitality of everyone who works there. A high standard of kindliness is set by your gracious hosts, Anneliese and Otto Hauser, who greet everyone staying at the Schweizerhof like friends of the family. They are frequently seen in the dining room speaking personally to each guest. *Directions:* As you drive into Grindelwald, turn left at a sign for the hotel.

ROMANTIK HOTEL SCHWEIZERHOF
Owners: Anneliese & Otto Hauser
CH-3818 Grindelwald, Switzerland
Tel: (033) 854 58 58, Fax: (033) 854 58 59
23 Rooms, Double: CHF 330–CHF 530*
16 Suites: CHF 420–CHF 760*
*Includes breakfast & dinner
Closed: Oct to Dec 18, Apr to end-May
Credit cards: MC, VS
20 km SE of Interlaken, Train: 1 km
Romantik Hotels, Canton: Bern

The Hostellerie de Saint Georges is a delightful hotel in the heart of the beautiful hilltop, walled, medieval village of Gruyères. The hotel is named for old Saint George himself—you will see our mighty hero slaying the dragon on the brightly colored emblem proudly displayed over the front door, and again on a carving hung over an antique chest in the main hallway. Each bedroom door displays a motif from the era of Saint George. On the door of one room there is a whimsical knight with sword raised high, on another a musician playing an instrument similar to a bagpipe, while yet another has a witch-like character riding a broom. The most expensive rooms (2 and 3) are spacious and lovely, with stunning views across the ramparts to the mountains. By comparison, the rest of the rooms are snug and simply decorated. If you are not able to reserve a room with a view, do not worry for you can enjoy the same view from the enclosed terrace where lunch and dinner are served. The menu naturally features local specialties made from Gruyères cheese. The quiche is so incomparably light, with such a delicate pastry, that it is tempting to order it at every meal. Another dining room specializes in food cooked to order on the open grill. *Directions:* Leave the autobahn at Bulle and follow the signs for Gruyères through Bulle. Drive into the village to unload and you will be directed to parking.

HOSTELLERIE DE SAINT GEORGES
Owners: Pascale & Frédéric Nédigue
CH-1663 Gruyères, Switzerland
Tel: (026) 921 83 00, Fax: (026) 921 83 39
14 Rooms, Double: CHF 180–CHF 280
Restaurant closed Mon, Jan & Feb
Closed: Nov, Dec & Jan, Credit cards: all major
33 km S of Fribourg, Train: 1 km
Canton: Fribourg

The Hostellerie des Chevaliers, a member of the Relais du Silence group, is located just outside the walls of the medieval village of Gruyères, just beyond parking area number 1. The hotel is found in two buildings: the main one houses the bedrooms and the breakfast room and is connected by a tunnel to the adjacent chalet containing the seminar rooms. Guestrooms are found on each of three floors. All but room 24 (the largest room with drapes and walls in a floral decor) are simply decorated and each has a small bathroom. Rooms under the eaves are more spacious, often able to accommodate up to four persons. If possible, request one of the rooms with a balcony overlooking the valley. These back rooms have wonderful, unobstructed views of the walled village of Gruyères and across the rolling hills grazed by sheep and cows to high mountains. *Directions:* Leave the motorway at Bulle and follow the signs for Gruyères through Bulle. Try to park in car park 1 but if you cannot, park in 2 or 3 and walk up to the hotel where you can often receive permission to park beside the hotel in its car park.

HOSTELLERIE DES CHEVALIERS
Manager: Pierre Bovay
Ruelle des Chevaliers 7
CH-1663 Gruyères, Switzerland
Tel: (026) 921 19 33, Fax: (026) 921 25 52
34 Rooms, Double: CHF 160–CHF 220
Closed: Jan & Feb, Credit cards: all major
35 km S of Fribourg
Train: 1 km (in Gruyères/Pringy)
Canton: Fribourg

Travelers idealize Switzerland and hope to discover their dream—a storybook land of sweet chalets, window boxes adorned with geraniums, balconies overlooking lush meadows, the gentle melody of cow bells, cozy furnishings, adorable villages, soaring mountains, and great food. All expectations are fulfilled at Le Grand Chalet. The hotel, built in 1989, mimics the chalet style seen in the quaint old farmhouses that dot the landscape. A small road winds up the hill from Gstaad (an exceptionally picturesque small village) to the beautifully positioned Grand Chalet. There is a light and airy look, fresh and pretty, filled with charm. The walls are white, the beams and paneling of blond wood, the Alpine-style furniture upholstered with pretty, country fabric, and frilly white curtains peek from beneath blue draperies. The living room, bar, and dining room flow together into a spacious room highlighted by a superb, old-world fireplace that warms all the rooms. Large windows in the dining room look over a splendid vista of green valley and beyond to the soaring mountains. This same picture-perfect view is captured from the balconies of the deluxe guestrooms. The owners of this intimate hotel, Josette and Franz Rosskogler, are gracious, caring hosts who ensure every detail is perfect and welcome guests as friends. *Directions:* From the north, turn left before the pedestrian section of Gstaad, following signs to the hotel.

LE GRAND CHALET
Managers: Pedro Ferreira & Steve Willié
CH-3780 Gstaad, Switzerland
Tel: (033) 748 76 76, Fax: (033) 748 76 77
20 Rooms, Double: CHF 260–CHF 550
3 Suites: CHF 440–CHF 800
Open: Jun to mid-Oct & Dec to Apr
Credit cards: all major
88 km E of Geneva, Train: 1 km
Canton: Bern

Hotel Descriptions   189

The Hotel Olden, a tradition for those in the know who visit Gstaad, is a chalet-style, cream-colored inn embellished with flowers, cheerful green shutters, and window boxes of red geraniums. This charming inn is a favorite of everyone, including the rich and famous who come in winter to ski. After a day on the slopes, guests gather in the bar for après-ski relaxation. In summer, dining outside on the terrace is a popular alternative to the lovely candlelit dining room where the live background music gives a romantic, supper-club atmosphere. In winter, dinner in the intimate cellar restaurant is a must. Bedrooms are found in the main building—delightful, luxuriously appointed traditional rooms—and in the chalet connected to the hotel by a rooftop terrace. With their luxurious, traditional decor, these chalet rooms are a must if you are under 6 feet tall (the height of the ceilings). Guests come back year after year in appreciation of the inviting rooms and outstanding food. *Directions:* Arriving in Gstaad, follow signs for Ober-Gstaad then the signpost to the hotel. Parking is either behind the hotel or in its private garage.

HOTEL OLDEN
Manager: Ermes Elsener
CH-3780 Gstaad, Switzerland
Tel: (033) 748 49 50, Fax: (033) 748 49 59
16 Rooms, Double: CHF 300–CHF 800
Closed: Apr & Nov, Credit cards: all major
88 km E of Geneva, Train: 3-minute walk
Canton: Bern

The Post Hotel Rössli has been in Ruedi Widmer's family since 1922. Ruedi was in his youth an ardent Alpine climber and skier. He still retains his qualifications but nowadays confines himself to taking guests on organized mountain walks, offering a program where he and several other guides lead excursions of climbing, walking, and generally enjoying the exquisite beauty of the area. It's refreshing to stay here at a traditional family hotel in a chic resort and experience old-style Swiss hospitality. The Alpine-style café bar is a gathering place for locals and guests alike—an excellent casual dining spot—though in summer it would be a shame not to eat outside in the garden opposite the hotel. As an alternative to the café there is a very nice restaurant specializing in traditional Swiss fare. Upstairs, you find reception, the bedrooms, and an eclectically decorated sitting room with old photos of the town on the walls alongside Ruedi's first hunting trophies. The pine-paneled bedrooms vary from light pine to mellow old pine. Standard rooms come with very snug shower rooms while the superior have more spacious bathrooms. *Directions:* Arriving in Gstaad, follows signs for the hotel, unload your luggage, and you will be directed to nearby parking.

POST HOTEL RÖSSLI
Owner: Ruedi Widmer
CH-3780 Gstaad, Switzerland
Tel: (033) 748 42 42, Fax: (033) 748 42 43
18 Rooms, Double: CHF 186–CHF 326
Restaurant closed Wed & Thur off season
Closed: May, Credit cards: all major
88 km E of Geneva, Train: 5-minute walk
Canton: Bern

Guarda, a cluster of old, intricately painted farmhouses with flowers at every window, nestles on a mountain shelf high above the Engadine Valley—one of the most picturesque hideaways in Switzerland. Happily, there is a gem of a hotel to match the perfection of the village. The Hotel Meisser is beautifully situated overlooking the expanse of green valley below, with a terrace where guests can enjoy refreshments served by waitresses in local costume. The hotel, a typical Engadine farmhouse, dates back to the 17th century. Throughout the hotel there is an old-world ambiance achieved through the use of antique chests, pieces of old copper, oil paintings, and baskets of fresh flowers everywhere. The main house offers simple accommodation, and two front corner rooms (15 and 16) afford memorable views and enjoy their own balconies. Across the street the converted farmhouse, Chasa Pepina, houses La Charpenna, a spectacular penthouse suite with pine beams and unobstructed hillside views, and the Stuva Veglia with its beautiful wood walls and floor—the accommodation is elegant and superbly appointed. The Meisser is truly a favorite for all its wealth of attributes and the wonderful family for which it is named. Settle in here for several days to appreciate one of Switzerland's most beautiful valleys and hotels. *Directions:* From the 27 between Susch and Scuol, exit at Giarsun on a small road that winds up to the village of Guarda.

HOTEL MEISSER
Owner: R. Meisser Family
CH-7545 Guarda, Switzerland
Tel: (081) 862 21 32, Fax: (081) 862 24 80
22 Rooms, Double: CHF 165–CHF 280
3 Suites: CHF 398–CHF 436
Open: Christmas to Easter, May to Oct
Credit cards: all major
81 km NE of St. Moritz
2.5 hrs from Zurich Airport
Canton: Graubunden

The village of Guarda, with its glorious setting overlooking the Engadin Valley, is one of our favorite destinations in Switzerland. Because the town is so popular, it is often difficult to secure accommodations, so we are glad to recommend the Pension Val Tuoi. It is immediately appealing—an endearing small house adorned with a flowery scroll design with two whimsical frolicking lions wrapping around the doorway. Inside, the country-style decor is appropriate to the building's origin in 1728 as a farmhouse. A pretty reception room opens to a comfy sitting room with antique paneling on the walls and ceiling. This is a perfect niche for chilly days: lots of books available, a game table, and a grouping of comfortable chairs. To complete the scene, there is a wonderful, very old, hand-painted dowry chest. The dining room is furnished with wooden tables and chairs with carved heart designs. Each bedroom is special in its own way. Room 14 is a large suite with a huge balcony—if you are staying a week or more, a door can be opened into a separate kitchen. Room 8 is lovely with a pretty balcony. However, my favorite room is 11, a spacious room in the oldest part of the house. Although it has no balcony, it has two large windows and is very cozy. Most of the bedrooms are located in the main house, but four (with kitchenettes) are in a pretty house across the street.

PENSION VAL TUOI
Owners: Maria-Louise & Werner Meiser
CH-7545 Guarda, Switzerland
Tel: (081) 862 24 70, Fax: (081) 862 24 07
17 Rooms, Double: CHF 108–CHF 180
Open: all year, Credit cards: MC, VS
81 km NE of St. Moritz
2.5 hrs from Zurich Airport
Canton: Graubunden

The medieval village of Hermance, located 15 minutes from Geneva's city center on the south shore of Lake Geneva, is the last community you come to before entering France. Easily accessible from Geneva by bus, car, or boat, the Auberge d'Hermance offers a nice alternative to city hotels. Located on a quiet side street about a block from the lake, the auberge is best known as an excellent countryside restaurant and guests come from far and near to dine. The centuries-old house has a terrace in front where tables are beautifully set in the "wintergarden" heated in winter for cozy, sunlit dining on chilly days. When it gets really cold, the indoor dining area enjoys a warm hearth. The specialty of the restaurant is "poulet ou loup de mer cuit en croûte de sel," which is comprised of either a chicken or a sea bass baked in a shell of large-grain salt so thick that it looks like a rock, which the waiter dramatically breaks open at the table with a wooden hammer. Most dinner guests never realize that upstairs from the restaurant there are six guestrooms available. The two that are least expensive are very good value, but also very small. If you want more luxury, splurge on one of the suites. *Directions:* Enter the city of Geneva and follow the sign to Le Lac, Evian. Drive along the lake for approximately 6 km until you reach Vesenaz. At the first crossroads, turn left in the direction of Hermance. Drive for 8 km in the countryside into Hermance.

ROMANTIK HOTEL AUBERGE D'HERMANCE
Manager: Antonio Manteigas
12, Rue du Midi
Hermance, CH-1248 Geneva, Switzerland
Tel: (022) 751 13 68, Fax: (022) 751 16 31
2 Rooms, Double: CHF 260
5 Suites: CHF 340–CHF 450
Closed: Dec 23 to Jan 6, Credit cards: all major
16 km E of Geneva, Bus: 20 min to Geneva
Romantik Hotels
Canton: Geneva

The Hotel Chalet Swiss is appropriately named— it looks like a charming small chalet one would find nestled in a green meadow rather than a hotel on the outskirts of bustling Interlaken. The façade of the hotel is a wonderful weathered brown wood, a steep-pitched shingle roof, and window boxes of red geraniums. In summer the front yard features a manicured rose garden. Although it looks small, the hotel has 54 guestrooms. Most are in a new annex behind the hotel, pleasant but in the motel style of a three-story building where the rooms either have a deck or a terrace. There is also a cozy bar where guests love to congregate for a drink before dinner to share their day's adventures or enjoy a good book when the weather is chilly. The original house has the reception area, the dining rooms, and our preferred guestrooms. Although facing the street (so a bit less quiet), we would opt for one of the front guestrooms with a balcony that affords a lovely view looking up to the mountains. In addition to being such a pretty hotel, the Chalet Swiss has great warmth of welcome. Many staff members have been greeting returning guests for over 17 years. The owner, René Klopfer, worked at the Chalet Swiss for many years before buying it in 1999. He is now updating it and is restoring the somewhat dated décor in the main house guestrooms to their original, more rustic, chalet ambiance. *Directions:* Follow the road to Unterseen, you will see signs on the road.

HOTEL CHALET SWISS
Manager: René Klopfer
Seestrasse 22, Unterseen
CH-3800 Interlaken, Switzerland
Tel: (033) 826 78 78, Fax: (033) 826 78 70
53 Rooms, Double: CHF 180–CHF 260
Open: Jan to Nov, Credit cards: all major
59 km SW of Bern, Train: 5 min. walk
Canton: Bern

The Hotel du Lac, owned by the Hofmann family for over 100 years, is more French than Swiss in appearance, with a gray mansard roof and pink façade. The hotel is located directly on the banks of the River Aare as it flows between the two lakes of Brienz and Thun. Bedrooms at the back overlook the river—a peaceful scene of boats and swans gliding below—while those at the front are less blessed, with street and mountain views. There are two dining rooms on the river and one, the Restaurant Rivière, is especially appealing with large windows and lovely river views. In recent years, all 40 guestrooms have been refurbished and all now offer modern comfort and a somewhat modern decor. Although the Hotel du Lac is large, the management does discourage conference and group bookings at the height of season, and if you want a convenient base for excursions, it cannot be surpassed. We include the Hotel du Lac especially for those readers traveling by public transportation as the location is so convenient—just steps from where the trains depart for the Jungfraujoch excursion and minutes from the dock where the boats leave for exploring Lake Brienz. *Directions:* From the motorway, exit Interlaken-Ost (east), turn right, and pass the train station. The hotel is behind the station.

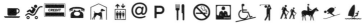

HOTEL DU LAC
Owner: Hofmann Family
Hoheweg 225
CH-3800 Interlaken, Switzerland
Tel: (033) 822 29 22, Fax: (033) 822 29 15
40 Rooms, Double: CHF 190–CHF 300
Open: mid-Mar to mid-Nov, Credit cards: all major
59 km SE of Bern, Train & boat: 100 meters
Canton: Bern

Located on the banks of the Thunner See, the Neuhaus zum See is on Interlaken outskirts next to the golf course in an area called Unterseen. The hotel consists of two sections, the Haupthaus and the Résidence. The Haupthaus is a charming, white Emmental-style farmhouse (dating back to 1861) with an overhanging brown tiled roof and brown and black striped shutters. It sits right on the edge of the lake where there is a small harbor dotted with many colorful yachts. Some guests arrive by boat to enjoy a meal on the terrace shaded by umbrellas. On a sunny day, this is a really fun place to be with all of the merry activity: children playing on the lawn that stretches to the lake and families laughing and enjoying a meal. In addition to the garden dining terrace, there is an attractive indoor restaurant. Upstairs above the restaurant there are some very sweet bedrooms that are prettily decorated with traditional furnishings. Although they cost a bit more, request one with a balcony overlooking the lake. The Neuhaus zum See also has a contemporary annex that is called the Résidence where the reception area and the majority of the guestrooms are located. Although the décor here is pleasant, we suggest you request a room in the Haupthaus since it is right on the lake and has a lot more old-world charm. A local bus can take you to downtown Interlaken, just a few minutes away. *Directions:* Located on the eastern shore of the Lake Thun, next to the golf course.

NEUHAUS ZUM SEE
Owner: Jurgen Ritscha
Seestrasse 121, Unterseen
CH-3800 Interlaken, Switzerland
Tel: (033) 822 82 82, Fax: (033) 823 29 91
40 Rooms, Double: CHF 200–CHF 260
Open: all year, Credit cards: MC, VS
59 km SE of Bern, Train & boat: 5 minutes
Canton: Bern

Iseltwald, one of the cutest of all the villages tucked along the shoreline of Lake Brienz, has the advantage of having its beauty intact since the main highway runs above the town. Quaint wooden homes tucked along the cobbled pedestrian-only streets add to its appeal. Nostalgic steamers stop regularly at the town's dock—making it easy to hop aboard to explore other towns, such as Interlaken and Brienz. A great choice for accommodations is the Hotel Chalet du Lac. The hotel, made from two antique farmhouses, is very pretty with many balconies and windows boxes filled with colorful red geraniums. There is nothing opulent or deluxe about the hotel: rather, it is a sweet, simple, well-managed, family hotel with moderately priced rooms and genuine warmth of welcome. Perhaps what makes this hotel special is that it has been in the same family over a hundred years. Sascha Abegglen, who is the chef in the kitchen, is the 6th generation here. The inn has a large terrace in front where meals are served overlooking the lake, which is the purest one in Switzerland. There is also a restaurant inside decorated with typical light pine furniture. The bedrooms are in two styles. Some are extremely contemporary in décor with modern furniture. Other guestrooms are more traditional in style with light pine furniture. If you want to splurge, ask for the room overlooking the lake with the canopy king-sized bed. *Directions:* On the lake.

HOTEL CHALET DU LAC
Owners: Sascha Abegglen & Susanne Frewein
CH-3807 Iseltwald, Switzerland
Tel: (033) 845 84 58, Fax: (033) 845 84 59
21 Rooms, Double: CHF 180–CHF 200
Open: Mar to Nov, Credit cards: all major
25 km SE of Lucerne, Train: 10 min. Taxi
Canton: Bern

The Landgasthof Ruedihus is the perfect Swiss inn, exactly what I'd always hoped to discover, but had almost decided did not exist except in my dreams: a cozy, flower-laden chalet, nestled in a lush meadow, backed by mountains and brimming inside and out with antique charm. This tiny chalet, dating back to 1753, is fashioned entirely of wood, darkened through the years and decorated with both carved and painted peasant designs. Two rows of small bottle-glass windows stretch across the front of the house, highlighted by boxes of red geraniums. Inside, the romance continues—every room is a dream. Appropriate country antiques are used throughout. Most of the bedrooms have genuine antiques, and those that do not, have beautifully crafted reproductions. Some of the bedrooms have a view of the mountains, but because of the authentic nature of the building, some rooms have small windows peeking out from under the deep eaves. However, no matter which bedroom you choose, if you enjoy an old-world ambiance, you will be happy—each one is enchanting. Although there are only ten bedrooms, the inn has its own well-equipped kitchen, and excellent meals are served in the intimate dining room. Note: Reservations are handled by the Waldhotel Doldenhorn—see next listing. *Directions:* After passing the center of the village, you will find the inn on the right-hand side of the street.

LANDGASTHOF RUEDIHUS
Owner: René Maeder
CH-3718 Kandersteg, Switzerland
Tel: (033) 675 81 82, Fax: (033) 675 81 85
10 Rooms, Double: CHF 240–CHF 260
2 Suites: CHF 300–CHF 320
Restaurant closed Wed
Open: all year, Credit cards: all major
45 km SW of Interlaken, Train: 2 km
Swiss Historic Hotels
Canton: Bern

The Waldhotel Doldenhorn is beautifully positioned at the end of the Kandersteg Valley, with the wooded mountains rising precipitously behind the hotel. There are two sections to the hotel, the main building and an adjacent chalet (where the guestrooms are less expensive). Registration is in the main hotel. Steps lead up to a reception area opening onto an attractively decorated lounge with dark paneling, handsome striped fabric on high-backed chairs, and intimate groupings of leather chairs. Beyond the lounge is the Grüner Saal, an elegant, rather formal, dining room with green-striped draperies framing large windows, silver chandeliers, and tables properly set with pretty linens and fresh flowers. The Restaurant Burestube is a wood-paneled dining room with rustic wooden chairs and milk-glass lamps hanging from the decoratively paneled wood ceiling. Each of the bedrooms is individually decorated, many with lovely antiques. One of the more expensive but especially lovely rooms is 109, a spacious bedroom with beautiful antique furniture and a pretty view. Anne and René Maeder also own the Landgasthof Ruedihus across the road. The Ruedihus exudes a rustic ambiance, while the Doldenhorn displays a more formal charm. The hotel also has a wellness center with fitness room, three saunas, whirlpool, indoor pool, beauty treatments and solarium. *Directions:* After passing the town center, you will find the hotel on the left-hand side of the street.

WALDHOTEL DOLDENHORN
Owners: Anne & René Maeder
CH-3718 Kandersteg, Switzerland
Tel: (033) 675 81 81, Fax: (033) 675 81 85
34 Rooms, Double: CHF 240–CHF 550
Restaurant closed Tue
Closed: Apr & Nov, Credit cards: all major
45 km SW of Interlaken, Train: 2 km
Canton: Bern

I visited the Chesa Grischuna for inclusion in the first edition of our guide to Switzerland and 12 years later the vivid memories of that visit lingered with such pleasure that I knew if the hotel still existed, I would want to include it. The season was different, winter's cozy blanket of snow having given way with spring to clusters of brightly colored flowers, but the interior was as I remembered—romantic and warm. Mellow, weathered paneling enriches most of the public rooms, while antique furnishings and accents of copper pieces and artistic flower arrangements blend beautifully. All the rooms have been renovated and the bedrooms achieve the country feeling, utilizing charming provincial wallpapers and matching fabrics, traditional Swiss furniture, exposed beams, and gently sloping floors. Some of the bedrooms are small, but all are nicely decorated. The dining room, with a country-formal atmosphere, is exceptional in cuisine and service. The personality of the staff matches the character and charm of the inn. The Romantik Hotel Chesa Grischuna never disappoints us—it always remains a favorite. *Directions:* From Landquart, exit the highway and take the road in the direction of Davos. Once in Klosters, after passing the old church, take the next right in the direction of the train station. The hotel is in the center of the village.

ROMANTIK HOTEL CHESA GRISCHUNA
Owner: Guler Family
Bahnhofstrasse 12
CH-7250 Klosters, Switzerland
Tel: (081) 422 22 22, Fax: (081) 422 22 25
7 Rooms, Double: CHF 220–CHF 480
3 Suites: CHF 340–CHF 580
Closed: mid-Oct to mid-Dec & mid-Apr to Jul
Credit cards: all major
40 km E of Chur, Train: 200 meters
Romantik Hotels, Swiss Historic Hotels
Canton: Graubunden

The Romantic Seehotel Sonne has a superb location—just 10 minutes from Zürich yet in a tranquil setting right by the lake. If you arrive by car, it offers the convenience of easy access and free parking. If you are using public transportation, trains run every 30 minutes directly from the Zürich airport to a station within walking distance of the hotel; plus trains run every 15 minutes to downtown Zürich. Sightseeing boats dock just steps from the hotel and you can hop aboard a ferry to explore the towns around the lake, including of course Zürich. This picturesque hotel dates back to the 15th century with one remaining tower to hint of its early heritage. Today, it provides every modern comfort but still retains its old world hospitably. The owners and the staff go out of their way to be sure their guests receive the finest service and you are welcomed as a cherished friend it in a private home. The individually decorated guestrooms are furnished in a contemporary style enhanced by cheerful, warm color schemes. The prime bedrooms are those with a view of the lake. Original art and sculptures are displayed throughout, including paintings by Andy Warhol. There are two excellent restaurants, plus a sensational ballroom with an exquisite frescoed ceiling that harks back to the age of nobility. You can relax after a day of sightseeing at the hotel's spa and wellness center. *Directions:* From Zürich follow the street by the lake until Küsnacht. The hotel is located after the second traffic light.

ROMANTIK SEEHOTEL SONNE **New**   **Cover painting**
Owners: Catherine & André Grüter
Seestraße 120
CH-8700 Küsnacht am Zürichsee, Switzerland
Tel: (044) 914 18 18, Fax: (044) 914 18 00
37 Rooms, Double: CHF 240–CHF 400
3 Suites: CHF 480–CHF 580
Open: all year, Credit cards: all major
5 km S of Zurich, Train: 500 meters
Romantik Hotels, Swiss Historic Hotels
Canton: Zurich

The Hotel du Lac Seehof is in Küssnacht, a small town on Lake Lucerne and a stop for many of the steamers that ply the lake. The hotel is ideally situated directly on the waterfront where the boats dock and serves as a popular luncheon spot. The town of Küssnacht is bustling with tourists, but there is a feeling of tranquility in the oasis of the hotel's terrace restaurant, which is very popular with day-trippers from Lucerne. The hotel has been in the Trutmann family for five generations and is now managed by Albert Trutmann and his attractive wife, Joan. Albert Trutmann lived in the United States for a number of years, speaks perfect English, and understands American tastes. Joan hails from Tahiti and has added her exotic island touch with the Blue Lagoon conservatory on the waterfront. In inclement weather guests dine inside in a series of attractive dining rooms. The food is excellent, with fish being featured on the menu. Upstairs, all the bedrooms, found off broad corridors, have simple decor and spotless shower rooms. Several have a traditional piece of furniture. *Directions:* From Zürich exit the N4 at Küssnacht and follow signposts to the lakefront and ferry.

HOTEL DU LAC SEEHOF
Owners: Joan & Albert Trutmann-de Brath
Seeplatz 6
CH-6403 Küssnacht, Switzerland
Tel: (041) 850 10 12, Fax: (041) 850 10 22
14 Rooms, Double: CHF 190–CHF 230
Closed: Nov, Credit cards: all major
13 km NE of Lucerne, Train: 1 km
Canton: Schwyz

The Hotel Angleterre & Residence is a relatively small, deluxe hotel with a wonderful location facing Lake Geneva in Ouchy, the colorful waterfront of Lausanne. The hotel brims with personality, as it is not within one structure, but instead made up of six buildings. They range in age from a French-style mansion, dating back to the 18th century with some magnificent frescoes, to the latest part of the hotel that is quite contemporary. The reception area is housed in a separate building exuding a warm welcome with sunlight streaming through walls of glass. Like the exteriors, the furnishings within vary dramatically. Each part of the hotel has its own style of decor, so guests can choose whatever they fancy—from ultra modern to English cozy. However, no matter which guestroom you choose, the decoration is done in excellent taste and the quality of every detail is absolutely top of the line. Adding greatly to the pleasure of staying at the Angleterre & Residence is the friendliness and exceptional service of the well-trained staff. The hotel has many of its own amenities including a swimming pool, but a great bonus of the Hotel Angleterre & Residence is that it is a "little sister" to the adjacent grand, opulent Beau Rivage Palace. You can freely go next door to enjoy the use of its indoor swimming pool, fitness room, tennis courts, and spa facilities. *Directions:* Located on the street that runs along Ouchy's waterfront

HOTEL ANGLETERRE & RESIDENCE
Manager: Yves Chavaillaz
Place du Port 11, Ouchy
CH-1005 Lausanne, Switzerland
Tel: (021) 613 34 34, Fax: (021) 613 34 35
75 Rooms, Double: CHF 340–CHF 495*
*Breakfast not included: CHF 27
Open: all year, Credit cards: all major
60 km NE of Geneva, Train 5 km
Canton: Vaud

For a moderately priced place to stay in Lausanne, the family-run Hotel du Port is a real winner. This is not a deluxe hotel with antique ambiance, opulent furnishings, and resort amenities. However, for a friendly, sweet, cheerful, small hotel offering fresh and airy guestrooms (some with a view of the lake) that is decorated in a modern style with good lighting and comfortable beds, the Hotel du Port is outstanding. Plus, the location is prime—the hotel overlooks the waterfront of Ouchy, the area of Lausanne that hugs the shore of Lake Geneva. The exterior of the hotel is as cute as can be: a row of three narrow, old-fashioned, attached houses with steep rooflines and windows framed by brightly colored shutters. In front of the hotel there is a street-side café where tables are set under jaunty umbrellas—a favorite spot to have a cup of coffee and watch the ferryboats glide in and out of the harbor. There is a nice dining room; but when the evenings are warm, the favorite place to dine is outside, and the food is delicious (try the fillet of perch with lemon sauce). The Hotel du Port has been in the Nicolier family for over forty years. Serge Nicolier's mother was the original owner. Now he and his wife, Danièle, operate the hotel, assisted by their daughter, Véronique, and their son, Laurent. For parking, there is a public garage nearby. *Directions:* Located on the street that runs along Ouchy's waterfront.

HOTEL DU PORT
Owners: Danièle & Serge Nicolier
Place du Port 5, Ouchy
CH-1006 Lausanne, Switzerland
Tel: (021) 612 04 44, Fax: (021) 612 04 45
22 Rooms, Double: CHF 190–CHF 220*
*Breakfast not included
Closed: Dec 31 to Jan 25, Credit cards: all major
60 km NE of Geneva, Train 3 km
Canton: Vaud

The Hotel des Balances, located on the banks of the River Reuss is a real winner. The hotel's exterior is a bit unusual, but don't let that dissuade you. The riverside view of the building is white, highlighted with window boxes brimming with blue, yellow, and pink petunias. The side of the hotel that faces a small square is totally covered with intricate paintings of angels, columns, warriors, costumed peasants, and flowers. From the hotel entrance, steps lead up to the lobby, which opens into a cheerful lounge with a colorful cluster of chairs and sofas. To the right of the lobby is the banquet room, very attractive with large oil paintings on the walls. French doors from the lounge lead to a balcony overlooking the river. As you enter the hotel, if instead of going up to the lobby you take the steps to the lower level, you will find the restaurant Balances, with a delightful terrace looking out over the river, serving fine food fresh from the local market. The guestrooms were renovated in 2008 and are attractively decorated in pastel hues. The suites have whirlpools and saunas. The choice rooms, of course, are those with a balcony overlooking the river. *Directions:* Coming from Zürich, take the Zentrum exit then make a right at the traffic light. After the bridge make another right and follow the signs.

HOTEL DES BALANCES
Owner: Peter E. Büsser
Weinmarkt
CH-6004 Lucerne, Switzerland
Tel: (041) 418 28 28, Fax: (041) 418 28 38
56 Rooms, Double: CHF 280–CHF 395*
9 Suites: CHF 380–CHF 550*
*Breakfast not included: CHF 27
Open: all year, Credit cards: all major
56 km SW of Zürich, Train: 700 meters
Canton: Lucerne

Although some tourists opt for a hotel with a lakefront setting, my heart remains with the Wilden Mann—an oasis of charm and hospitality snuggled in the ever-so-appealing medieval heart of Lucerne. Artistically arranged antiques of the finest quality are used throughout this delightful small hotel. The bedrooms too are beautifully decorated and each has its own personality. The ambiance is that of a private home rather than a large hotel. There are three dining rooms, each delightful in its own way. The Wilden Mann Stube is a non-smoking, French-style restaurant with rose tablecloths, candlelight, and, in cold weather, a cozy fire. This dining room has a special feature: on one of the walls there are three framed scenes depicting the Wilden Mann as it appeared in the mid-1800s. Upstairs there is another dining area—an outdoor garden terrace where tables are set for dining on warm summer days. However, my favorite place to dine is the Burgerstube, a charming, Swiss-country-style dining room with an ambiance of informality, warmth and wonderful wooden chairs—many of them antiques—set around the tables. *Directions:* Arriving from Interlaken, exit Luzern-Sud. Take the left lane and continue driving to Pilatusplatz (crossing). Pass under the house on the square, taking the lane to the right. After 100 meters turn right (Parkhaus Kesselturm). The hotel is next to this covered public parking.

ROMANTIK HOTEL WILDEN MANN
Owners: Ursula & Charles Zimmermann
Bahnhofstrasse 30
CH-6000 Lucerne, Switzerland
Tel: (041) 210 16 66, Fax: (041) 210 16 29
50 Rooms, Double: CHF 215–CHF 410
1 Suite: CHF 380–CHF 525
Open: all year, Credit cards: all major
56 km SW of Zürich, Train: 500 meters
Romantik Hotels
Canton: Lucerne

The Romantik Hotel Ticino is located right at the heart of the historic section of Lugano on one of its charming little piazzas. Tucked just off the cobbled street, the hotel's entry is cozy and, just beyond, the inn opens up to an inner courtyard, which reflects the hotel's past history as a convent. Upstairs is a quiet guest lounge where you can relax and enjoy an evening drink. Because this is a very old building, bedrooms tend to be on the small side. If you desire more space, ask for a junior suite. My favorite guestrooms are the newly renovated ones. These are very prettily decorated in pastel tones, and have the added bonus of air conditioning. Do not worry about street noise as rooms have double-paned windows and a great many have air conditioning. Just off the lobby is the hotel's restaurant, one of Lugano's most intimate and popular eating spots. As it is a favorite with locals, it is wise to make restaurant reservations when booking your room. The Hotel Ticino is a lovely, very old Tessin house that flourishes under the personal management and care of the gracious Buchmanns—a very special inn. *Directions:* From the autostrada, follow signposts for the center of the town until you see the hotel signpost to your right (before the train station). Continue straight into the pedestrian zone to the first square where you find the hotel on your right.

ROMANTIK HOTEL TICINO
Owners: Claire & Samuel Buchmann
Piazza Cioccaro 1
CH-6901 Lugano, Switzerland
Tel: (091) 922 77 72, Fax: (091) 923 62 78
18 Rooms, Double: CHF 420–CHF 780
Open: Feb to Dec, Credit cards: all major
30 km N of Como, Train: 2-minute walk
Romantik Hotels
Canton: Ticino

The Swiss Chalet was once the family home of the owner, Joseph Seeholzer, and inside this marvelous old farmhouse, their family rooms have been converted to an intimate melange of dining nooks. Guestrooms in the original farmhouse are found at the top of a steep flight of stairs. Tucked under low ceilings, the accommodations are small and simple in comfort and decor. Only a few have a private bath. In a newer, connecting building, a private dining room is found in what was once the house chapel, and upstairs a few rooms have been converted to guestrooms. We ventured to investigate two additional buildings that offer accommodation under the same ownership. The newly built Schloss Hotel across the street has a lakeside garden, antiques, armor, heavy beams, and wonderful large wooden doors that create an appealing, almost theatrical atmosphere. Guestrooms are modern in comfort, richly decorated, and many look out onto the lake. The Château Golden Gate, also newly constructed, is on the hillside above the other two buildings. Again, the use of armor, beams, and heavy doors give a feeling of an old castle. The guestrooms are large, lovely, and many enjoy wonderful views of the lake. There is also a rooftop terrace with spectacular views of the lake and distant mountains. *Directions:* Travel the road east from Lucerne towards Küssnacht. Merlischachen is just 12 km outside Lucerne and the hotel complex is on the main road.

SWISS CHALET, SCHLOSS HOTEL,
  CHÂTEAU GOLDEN GATE
Owner: Joseph Seeholzer
CH-6402 Merlischachen, Switzerland
Tel: (041) 854 54 54, Fax: (041) 854 54 66
71 Rooms, Double: CHF 110–CHF 278
Open: all year, Credit cards: all major
12 km NE of Lucerne, Train: 5-minute walk
Canton: Schwyz

Montreux, a sophisticated, action-filled city with a fancy casino, hugs the shoreline at the east end of Lake Geneva. It's a fun place to visit, but we prefer to stay just a few minutes away in the quiet, elegant suburb of Clarens. Here you find splendid private villas lining the waterfront with glorious views over the lake and beyond to soaring mountain peaks. One of these mansions, L'Ermitage, has been converted into a renowned, gourmet restaurant. It is housed in a pretty, white, two-story home that exudes the ambiance of a French country manor with its steep mansard roof and gabled windows framed by shutters. There is no road between the villa and the lake to disrupt the serenity—only an enticing walking path that traces the waterfront. The owner, Etienne Krebs, is also the chef whose outstanding cuisine has earned his restaurant a coveted Michelin star. Meals are served in a choice of several intimate, pretty dining rooms. However, when the weather is warm, guests love to dine outside on the terrace where they can enjoy a delicious meal while savoring a breathtaking view of the lake. In addition to the restaurant, L'Ermitage has seven individually decorated guestrooms (including three junior suites) that exude softness and old-fashioned appeal—staying here is like being a guest in a private home. For a special treat, ask for a room with a view. *Directions:* Clarens is located about 1 km north of Montreaux, in the direction of Vevey.

L'ERMITAGE
Owners: Isabelle & Etienne Krebs
Rue du Lac 75
CH-1815 Montreux-Clarens, Switzerland
Tel: (021) 964 44 11, Fax: (021) 964 70 02
7 Rooms, Double: CHF 280–CHF 390
2 Suites: CHF 390–CHF 510
Closed: Dec 24 to Jan 26, Credit cards: all major
1 km N of Montreux, Boat: ferry dock 2 km
Canton: Vaud

The Hotel Masson faces onto a road that weaves up into the hills from Veytaux, a town along the shores of Lake Geneva, just south of Montreux. The house dates back to 1829 when it was built as a private mansion, complete with coach house, horse stables, and wine press. There have been many changes over the years but the high ceilings and handsome parquet floors remind one of the past. What you see today is an attractive, rambling, three-story, white house that is adorned by balconies, and windows framed with green shutters. The hotel exudes the friendly, informal ambiance of being in a private home rather than a commercial hotel. The property is owned by Anne-Marie Sèvegrand, whose father owned it before her. Mme. Sévegrand, a gracious, refined hostess, treats guests like returning friends. You enter from the street into a small foyer with a staircase that leads up the next level where you find the reception area, lounge, and dining room. Dinner begins at 7 pm and a delicious, home-cooked, four-course, set-menu dinner is served. A staircase leads up to the individually decorated guestrooms; my favorites are those in the original part of the house. If you want to visit the romantic Castle of Chillon, it is just a 15-minute walk from the hotel. *Directions:* From highway 9, take the Villeneuve exit. Continue west toward Montreux. About 200m after Chillon Castle, take the first road on your right which leads up to the hotel.

HOTEL MASSON
Owner: Anne-Marie Sevegrand
Rue Bonivard 5
CH-1820 Montreux-Veytaux, Switzerland
Tel: (021) 966 00 44, Fax: (021) 966 00 36
31 Rooms, Double: CHF 180–CHF 290
Closed: Nov to 2 weeks before Easter
Credit cards: all major
3 km E of Montreux, 20-min. walk from Montreux, & ferry
Swiss Historic Hotels
Canton: Vaud

The Carina-Carlton sits on the road facing Lake Lugano in the picturesque small village of Morcote, just a 20-minute drive south of Lugano. Across the street from the hotel is an outdoor restaurant perched on stilts over the lake, with flowers and a brightly striped awning adding even further enchantment to this dining haven. An inside dining room has a wood-beamed ceiling, white walls accented by green plants, and Oriental rugs covering its tiled floor. The breakfast buffet is set here but in fine weather guests usually eat on the adjacent patio. The bedrooms in front can be a bit noisy with the traffic on the street below, but they are still my favorites. Quieter rooms are found in the back, many looking out to the small pool snuggled in the upper terrace. I love room 35, a spacious room with excellent lake views. If you really want to splurge, room 45 is very special—a large, bright corner room with two balconies, one looking out over the tiled rooftops to the lake and the other overlooking the pool with a vista to the church. The Carina-Carlton is very convenient as a base in Switzerland's beautiful southern Lake District. You do not need a car—just board one of the ferries that ply the lake to the many quaint lakeside towns. *Directions:* Leave Lugano in the direction of Milan and Morcote is the first exit after the long tunnel. Follow the lakefront road for 5 km to the hotel. There is free parking at either end of the town.

HOTEL CARINA-CARLTON
Owners: Ingrid & Rudolf Tschannen
Via Cantonale
Morcote, CH-6922 Lugano, Switzerland
Tel: (091) 996 11 31, Fax: (091) 996 19 29
23 Rooms, Double: CHF 195–CHF 330
Open: Mar to Nov
Credit cards: all major
6 km S of Lugano, Train: 6 km
Canton: Ticino

Mürren is nestled on a high mountain shelf with the giant peaks of the Bernese Alps across the valley. From the village, massive granite walls drop straight down to the Lauterbrunnen Valley far below. There is no access by automobile—the only way to reach Mürren is by cable car from Stechelberg or by funicular from the Lauterbrunnen station. The Hotel Alpenruh is conveniently located next to the Schilthornbahn cable car, which begins at the valley floor at Stechelberg, stops in Mürren, and continues on to the Schilthorn. The hotel is not old, but is built in an attractive, low-rise chalet style. Wrapping around the front corner of the hotel is a large balcony, a favorite place for guests to gather on a sunny day to relish the view while enjoying a drink or perhaps lunch. Inside, the hotel is tastefully decorated in traditional style. Just to the left of the reception area is a cozy, pine-paneled lounge where guests can relax with a good book on a chilly day. The large dining room has a more modern look, but is softened by peasant-style paintings on paneled walls and brass gas lamp-style light fixtures. The bedrooms are fresh and attractive with typical Swiss pine furniture with a built-in headboard, table, and two chairs. Most of the bedrooms have balconies with glorious views of the mountains. *Directions:* From Interlaken, drive into the valley to Lauterbrunnen-Stechelberg. Park at Schilthornbahn and take the cable car to Mürren.

HOTEL ALPENRUH
Managers: Mr & Mrs Thomas Willem
CH-3825 Mürren, Switzerland
Tel: (033) 856 88 00, Fax: (033) 856 88 88
26 Rooms, Double: CHF 180–CHF 280
Resturant closed Nov
Open: all year, Credit cards: all major
20 km S of Interlaken
Funicular from Lauterbrunnen: 5-min walk
Canton: Bern

Located just beyond the walls of the medieval town of Murten, directly on the banks of Lake Murten, the Hotel Schiff, which opened its doors as a hotel in 1767, enjoys a lovely waterside setting. The hotel is in the capable hands of Stephan Helfer who oversees it with a gracious warmth and astute professionalism. With a multitude of dining rooms, a bar, and evening music, the Hotel Schiff has facilities that cater to groups ranging in size from 2 to 300 people. Often in the summer season you find a group visiting for lunch and a business function taking place, yet even when the place is bustling, the hotel also caters to the individual traveler. The 15 bedrooms are mostly traditional in their decor and many have tall windows that open up to glimpses of the lake through the trees. Rooms 4 and 5 have balconies. Guests can choose between a brasserie, French restaurant, or terrace for evening dining. A few minutes' walk finds you within the medieval walls of Murten. The ferry docks just in front of the hotel, tempting guests to take it to the interesting towns of Neuchâtel and Biel. *Directions:* Leave the Al autobahn at Murten and follow the hotel's signposts. There is plenty of metered parking around the hotel.

HOTEL SCHIFF
Manager: Stephan Helfer
Direkt am See
CH-3280 Murten, Switzerland
Tel: (026) 672 36 66, Fax: (026) 672 36 65
15 Rooms, Double: CHF 170–CHF 230
1 Suite: CHF 240–CHF 280
Open: all year, Credit cards: all major
31 km W of Bern, Train: 10-minute walk
Canton: Fribourg

Le Vieux Manoir is constantly striving to improve its facilities and please its guests, so it justly deserved the very prestigious award of being named Gault Millau's Hotel of the Year 2000 for Switzerland. Located in the quietest of settings on the shore of Lake Murten, Le Vieux Manoir's beautiful exterior of weathered wood, little gables, high-pitched roofs, overhanging eaves, and whimsical chimneys complements an exquisite interior. The spacious bedrooms have either village or lake views, many have terraces, and all have luxurious decor and top-of-the-line marble bathrooms. A sumptuous breakfast buffet is set in the spacious breakfast room ringed by windows looking over the gardens to the lake. The conservatory, where lunch and dinner are served, offers an even more spectacular lake view. Dinner, either à la carte or table d'hôte, is an evening-long affair and if you grow short of conversation, you can always watch the artistry of the waiters as they serve one party after another with ballet-like precision. Of course, there's a high price to pay for such perfection. Le Vieux Manoir is a member of Relais & Châteaux. *Directions:* Exit the A1 autobahn at Murten and follow the hotel's signposts south to the adjacent little village of Meyriez.

LE VIEUX MANOIR AU LAC
Owners: Judith & Martin Müller-Opprecht
Route de Lausanne, Meyriez
CH-3280 Murten, Switzerland
Tel: (026) 678 61 61, Fax: (026) 678 61 62
33 Rooms, Double: CHF 390–CHF 630
Open: mid-Feb to Jan, Credit cards: all major
34 km W of Bern, Train: 1 km
Relais & Châteaux
Canton: Fribourg

As you enter through the Gothic archway into the Chasa Chalavaina, you slip back in time, with every nook and cranny breathing the history of yesteryear. In 1499, when the troops gathered in front of the inn prepared to battle the German Emperor, Maximilian, the Chasa Chalavaina was already at least 200 years old. From the beginning it was designed as an inn, as confirmed by the large stable where the coachmen sheltered their horses after their arduous journeys over the passes. The old stone floor of the entrance hall is worn smooth by the passage of countless guests. The Chasa Chalavaina has been restored with great respect for its past, with thick walls hung with farm instruments, doors with antique iron locks, old beams secured by wooden pegs, carved pine paneling wearing the patina of time, and rustic antiques galore. The inn has maintained the sturdy, simple, clean lines of the past while adding the conveniences of the present day. Delicious, home-cooked meals are served in the simple, pine-paneled dining room. Each of the guestrooms has its own personality: La Palantshotta has pine furniture and a large terrace tucked in under the eaves; La Stuietta, on the first floor, has its own private terrace; La Stuva del Preir has a deck overlooking the square in front of the hotel. The Chasa Chalavaina offers very basic accommodation and simple comfort. *Directions:* Müstair is just before the Italian border, 4 km northeast of Santa Maria.

HOTEL CHASA CHALAVAINA
Owner: Jonni Fasser
Plaza Grond
CH-7537 Müstair, Switzerland
Tel: (081) 858 54 68
15 Rooms, Double: CHF 138–CHF 184
Open: all year, Credit cards: none
73 km NE of St. Moritz
Train to Zernez, 39 km by bus
Canton: Graubunden

The Gasthof Hirschen isn't a fancy, posh hotel, but if you want to stay in a sweet, family hotel, with fabulous food and old-fashioned hospitality, this is a gem. The gasthof, built in the typical chalet style, sits on a corner in the center of the small village of Oey, a town where the Diemtigal Valley begins, a gorgeous valley that has received awards for being one of the most beautiful in Switzerland. The Kunz family has owned the Gasthof Hirschen for over 100 years. They have been farmers in the valley forever and still take their cows up to the high mountain pastures in summer. The latest family members to take over the hotel are an endearing young couple, Anna and Daniel Kunz. Anna is an exceptionally talented chef who uses products fresh from their own farm. Her reputation as a chef is such that the tables at the restaurant are always packed. A specialty of the house is a delicious White Forest Cake, made from Kirsch, cream, and fresh raspberries. Daniel, in addition to working at the hotel, is an active farmer, a professional yodeler, a talented accordion player, a ski instructor, and a champion wrestler (the Swiss version is called Schwingen). There are seven guestrooms (two of these are without private bathroom). Although simple, they are very attractive with wood paneled walls, pine furniture, fluffy comforters, down pillows, and white embroidered curtains. *Directions:* Oey is next to Latterbach.

GASTHOF HIRSCHEN
Owners: Kunz & Mitarbeiter Families
Dorfstrasse
CH-3753 Oey, Switzerland
Tel & Fax: (033) 681 23 23
7 Rooms, Double: CHF 110
5 Rooms with a private bathroom
Closed: mid-Jun to mid-Jul & Nov
Credit cards: MC, VS
7 km S of Spiez, Train: 5 km
Canton: Bern

Schloss Sins has a charming setting in the wooded hills overlooking a tranquil valley far below. Many mighty castles were built in this strategic area to guard the narrow valley. However, the Schloss Sins is a different kind of castle. Not stern or foreboding, but a large, friendly-looking, pastel-beige house highlighted by intricate cream-colored designs and a tall turret, topped by a whimsical steeple. Luckily, you can spot the castle as you drive into town since there are no signs directing you there. With no hint of commercialism, the Schloss Sins is like a private home in the countryside. A large estate surrounds the house where magnificent horses are grazing in the fields. A beautifully manicured garden, complete with lily pond, is highlighted by an adorable, octagonal-shaped teahouse topped by a peaked roof in front of the property. When you enter the main house, there is a reception hall with a vaulted ceiling, slab stone floors, handsome antiques, and a dramatic staircase. The dining room is particularly lovely with hardwood floors in a herringbone design, lovely paneled walls, and a large antique oval table. The guestrooms are tastefully decorated, but splurge and ask for the spacious suite. *Directions:* Paspels is off A13, about 16 km SW of Chur. Take the Rothenbrunnen turnoff off of A13 and take the small road south to Paspels. You will see the hotel to the right as you approach the town.

SCHLOSS SINS
Owner: Corina Barblan Bernasocchi
CH-7417 Paspels, Switzerland
Tel: (081) 650 10 35, Fax: (081) 650 10 34
11 Rooms, Double: CHF 156–CHF 196
Open: all year, Credit cards: all major
110 km SW of Zurich, Train: 2 km
Swiss Historic Hotels
Canton: Graubunden

I fell in love with this charming cluster of neighboring Engadine homes—one rust, one yellow, one mauve—sitting on Pontresina's main road. Once three individual houses dating from the 17th century, the buildings' communicating walls were torn down to accommodate one large hotel. The Steinbock is charming both inside and out. We entered off a garden courtyard terrace where guests were lingering over a late lunch, served by waitresses in handsome Tyrolean costume, into a cozy, welcoming ambiance of old pine and Alpine fabrics. Just off the reception is a lovely lounge, a large, open restaurant used for breakfast as well as dinner for pension guests. There is also a more intimate à-la-carte restaurant. We saw a number of guestrooms, which were all very pretty and simply decorated in light pines with white duvets topping the beds and patterned curtains and chairs. The hotel is owned by the Walther family who also operate the neighboring, very luxurious Walther Hotel, whose amenities such a swimming pool are available to guests of the Steinbock. *Directions:* From St. Moritz drive east on the 27 for 4 km and then south on the 29 for 4 km to Pontresina. The hotel is on the main street on the east side of town.

HOTEL STEINBOCK
Owner: Thomas Walther Family
CH-7504 Pontresina, Switzerland
Tel: (081) 839 36 26, Fax: (081) 839 36 27
31 Rooms, Double: CHF 340–CHF 465*
*Includes breakfast & dinner
Open: all year, Credit cards: all major
8 km outside of St. Moritz, Train to St. Moritz
Canton: Graubunden

On the outskirts of cosmopolitan St. Moritz is a very pretty neighbor, Pontresina, whose buildings cluster on the hillside and look out to a sweeping ring of Alpine peaks. Standing proud above the main street of town, the Walther Hotel, built in a cream stone with a central entry tower and a few ornamental turrets, is as handsome inside as out. From the entryway an impressive wide hallway leads either to a spacious, elegant salon with many clustering seating arrangements or past the inviting hotel bar to a large open restaurant with dramatic high windows. This is the restaurant used for breakfast and pension guests. Step down round the corner to the Stuva Bella and you will enjoy the more intimate and cozy ambiance of the à-la-carte restaurant. I was able to see a number of guestrooms, reached up the grand central staircase. Rooms, which vary in size, look out either to the mountains or to the back hillside (these latter rooms are removed from any street noise). Some bedrooms have a sitting area, others enjoy beautiful pine paneling, and some have private balconies. Number 75 was one of my favorites with very pretty fabric, gorgeous paneling, and a small terrace. The hotel has a wonderful large swimming pool and a fitness and wellness center. *Directions:* From St. Moritz drive east on the 27 for 4 km and then south on the 29 for 4 km to Pontresina. The hotel sits on the main street on the east side of town.

WALTHER HOTEL
Owner: Thomas Walther Family
Hauptstrasse, CH-7504 Pontresina, Switzerland
Tel: (081) 839 36 36, Fax: (081) 839 36 37
68 Rooms, Double: CHF 410–CHF 820*
2 Suites: CHF 770–CHF 1150*
*Includes breakfast & dinner
Closed: Apr 7 to Jun 12, Oct 6 to Dec 11
Credit cards: all major
8 km outside of St. Moritz, Train to St. Moritz
Relais & Châteaux, Canton: Graubunden

Miralago is a tiny hamlet—no more than a cluster of houses. One of the cutest of these is the centuries-old Albergo Miralago. The exterior of the hotel is painted a soft cream that is accented by pretty blue shutters. It is separated from the beautiful lake by a small road and a railroad track where a colorful little Swiss train adds to the scene giving its little "toot-toot" as it passes by. To the side of the hotel is a sweet little terrace with tables set under a vine-covered trellis and planters overflowing with brilliant red geraniums. The immediate impression is that this small inn is very loved since everything is so well kept. Inside, the same cheerful ambiance continues with bouquets of fresh flowers and gifts for sale artistically displayed on an antique dresser. The charming dining room has exposed stone walls, low-beamed ceiling, mellowed-with-age hardwood floors, and rustic farmhouse-style wooden chairs with carved hearts. There is a second gourmet restaurant that is really romantic in a cave-like room with slab stone and arched stone ceiling. The tables are set with checked tablecloths and fresh flowers. There is no electricity—candles on the tables and the chandeliers gently illuminate the room. The owner is the architect who renovated the building and designed the rooms. He must have had fun in the guestrooms since each one is totally different and nice in its own way. *Directions:* Located about 7 km south of Poschiavo, at the south end of Lake Poschaivo.

ALBERGO MIRALAGO
Owners: Béa Krähenbühl & Richard Hunziker
Miralago
CH-7743 Poschiavo, Switzerland
Tel: (081) 839 20 00, Fax: (081) 839 20 01
10 Rooms, Double: CHF 170–CHF 295
Open: Easter to end-Oct & Christmas
Credit cards: MC, VS
40 km SE of St. Moritz, Train: 3 km
Canton: Graubunden

The Rote Rose (along with the Guesthouse Engelfrid), is the perfect inn with a superb setting on the knoll of a vineyard-laced hill. Guestrooms are housed in neighboring buildings of this beautiful walled village: a meticulously restored, old timbered home—the original Rote Rose, and a magnificent 800-year-old home—the Engelfrid. Every one of the rooms is a prize, decorated with exquisite antiques, and the favorite, the Hexenkuche (Witch-Kitchen) is dramatic, spacious with a canopy bed overlooking the countryside. The inn's best feature, however, is the owner herself, Christa Schäfer. Europe's finest hostesses, she is now joined by her son, Frank and his wife, Dorina, and together they make an incredible team! And as if this is not enough to win your hearts, the walls of the inn are filled with the paintings of the renowned rose artist, Lotte Günthart, Christa's mother. Lotte Günthart's contribution to the world of roses has been so significant that a beautiful, California red rose is named for her. The Rote Rose has no restaurant, but breakfast is a delicious, bountiful offering of fresh breads, rolls, cheeses, yogurts, fruits and beverages. *Directions:* From Zürich airport follow the signs to Schaffhausen and exit at Bülach/Dielsdorf (West). From Dielsdorf, look for a sign for Regensberg and turn left up the hill. Turn right onto the cobblestone road. Drive through the Krone gate opening, turn right, and the inn is the second driveway on the right.

ROTE ROSE & ENGELFRID
Owner: Christa Schäfer
CH-8158 Regensberg, Switzerland
Tel: (044) 853 10 13, Fax: (044) 853 15 59
5 Rooms, Double: CHF 220
4 Suites: CHF 270–CHF 410
5 Studios with kitchenette, monthly from CHF 1700*
*Studios rented by advance reservation only
Closed: Feb, Credit cards: MC, VS
19 km N of Zurich, Train: 2 km, Airport: 20 min
Canton: Zurich

The setting of the Gasthaus zum Gupf epitomizes Appenzell. Perched on the top of the highest rolling Alpine peak, this lovely timbered farmstead looks across the farmland of Appenzellerland to the distant Austrian and German peaks and to the glistening waters of the Bodensee. The Gasthaus zum Gupf boasts a justifiably serious restaurant with an exceptional menu featuring fresh produce and animals from the farm. There are two main dining rooms, the cozy Gupf Stube and the very elegant Alpstein Stube, and in warm weather tables are set on the outdoor terrace. The Gupf Stube, the smaller of the two restaurants, has a backdrop of light pines and looks out through delicate lace curtains to the surrounding countryside. The Alpstein Stube is more formal in its furnishings and has direct access to the incredible wine cellar. For the lucky few there are also six guestrooms upstairs—three singles, two doubles, and one suite, all with modern furnishings and commodious private bathrooms. The suite (room 5) overlooks the front acreage and enjoys the luxury of a sitting area and separate bath. Room 6, a double room, also overlooks the front, and room 7, a smaller double room, looks out through an angled ceiling window to views across Appenzellerland. Thanks to a Swiss friend for this recommendation! *Directions:* Located at the end of a single-lane road at the top of the town of Rehetobel, which is about 10 km east of St. Gallen.

GASTHAUS ZUM GUPF
Owner: Klose Walter
Gupf 20
CH-9038 Rehetobel, Switzerland
Tel: (071) 877 11 10, Fax: (071) 877 15 10
5 Rooms, Double: CHF 240
Closed: Mon & Tues weekly, Feb & 2 weeks in summer
Credit cards: all major
10 km E of St. Gallen, Train to St. Gallen
Canton: Appenzell, Interior Rhodes

I have to thank Benno Meisser of the Hotel Meisser in Guarda for recommending this little gem of a hotel. At the end of a 13-kilometer unpaved road lies the village of S-Charl, a little piece of paradise tucked up against the towering Dolomites along a cascading river, right next to the Swiss National Park. The Ustaria (Restaurant) and Pensiun Crusch Alba & Alvetern is located within three of the village's only ten buildings. The cream-stucco houses are adorned with subtle exterior stenciling and wooden shutters in the lovely Engadine style. I was honestly surprised at the quality of accommodation and the dining options in the middle of what seemed like nowhere. Furnishings throughout reflect the style of the region, with lots of pine and plump duvets topping the beds. Modern bathrooms are gorgeous with hand-painted tiles. Bedrooms in the main house are the nicest, while four simple, rustic rooms with washbasin only are found in another building, Alvetern, which also houses a cozy stube offering light meals such as soups. The main restaurant for pension guests and the à-la-carte restaurant are both found in the main building and are lovely. A third charming building contains a large sitting room for guests. *Directions:* Traveling the 27 northeast from Zernez towards the Italian border, turn south at Vulpera following signs to S-Charl. You will travel along a challenging, unpaved road for 13 km (20 minutes) to the road's end.

CRUSCH ALBA & ALVETERN
Owner: Sutter Family
CH-7550 S-Charl, Switzerland
Tel: (081) 864 14 05, Fax: (081) 864 14 06
21 Rooms, Double: CHF 105–CHF 180
Open: Jun 1 to Oct 20, Credit cards: all major
14 km E of Scuol, Train: 14 km
Canton: Graubunden

The Fletschhorn is a haven of tranquility set on a forested hillside just outside Saas Fee overlooking the most breathtaking Alpine views. Yet this is far more than a hotel in a stunning location—it is a veritable haven for those who like their food not only to taste good but also to look good. Markus Neff, who was awarded "chef of the year" in 2007, and staff ensure that each dish looks like a stunning jewel: ravioli with truffles and mushrooms, lobster with white beans and seagrass, and a raspberry tart covered in a cloud of spun sugar were all outstanding. Small wonder that the Fletschhorn is one of the top eight restaurants in Switzerland. The same creativity displayed in the food is also found in the bedrooms, which come in three categories—double rooms, junior rooms and panorama rooms. Junior rooms are spacious affairs with open-plan bathrooms cleverly incorporated into the design of the room and balconies offering panoramic views. Double rooms are smaller by comparison and more basic in their layout. Three panorama rooms (31, 34 and 35) boast fantastic views of the waterfalls and Alpine valley. Vivid colors and modern furnishings create a dramatic basis for the ever-changing collection of art that adorns the walls and open spaces. A 20-minute stroll from the heart of town. *Directions:* From Brig take the Zermatt road, branching to Saas Fee. In town, park in lot A, call the hotel and the hotel's free electric shuttle will come get you.

FLETSCHHORN
Manager: Charlie Neumiller
CH-3906 Saas Fee, Switzerland
Tel: (027) 957 21 31, Fax: (027) 957 21 87
13 Rooms, Double: CHF 330–CHF 550
Closed: May to mid-Jun & Nov, Credit cards: all major
30 km SE of Zermatt, Train: call for free pick-up
Canton: Valais

Nestled in a high mountain valley beneath a glacier and towering mountain peaks, Saas Fee is a traditional mountain village that has become a lively holiday resort. At the heart of the action you find one of its first hotels, the Romantik Hotel Beau-Site, a solid stone building constructed in 1893. The Zurbriggen family bought the hotel in 1944 and Urs is the third generation of his family to manage it. In more recent years the hotel has undergone a complete renovation that shows off the old stone walls and woodwork. This is particularly noticeable in the high-ceilinged public rooms—the sitting room with its exposed stone walls and heavy pine beams and the dining room all decked out with dark wood and furnished with intricately carved, old-world Swiss chairs. The hotel is a complete resort, with children's playroom, large swimming pool, and spa facilities. Bedrooms come in all shapes and sizes from simpler twin-bedded rooms to a grand suite with intricately carved furniture. Room 26 is an especially attractive suite and room 1893, the year of the hotel's origins, is termed the Honeymoon Room. The hotel's broad terrace is a popular gathering spot serving traditional Swiss fare. *Directions:* From Brig take the Zermatt road, branching to Saas Fee. Arriving in town, park in parking lot A, unload your bags, call the hotel, and by the time you have taken your car to the parking garage the hotel's cart will be there to meet you.

ROMANTIK HOTEL BEAU-SITE
Owners: Marie-Jeanne & Urs Zurbriggen
CH-3906 Saas Fee, Switzerland
Tel: (027) 958 15 60, Fax: (027) 958 15 65
32 Rooms, Double: CHF 260–CHF 510
4 Suites: CHF 390–CHF 630
Closed: mid-Apr to mid-Jun, Credit cards: all major
30 km SE of Zermatt, Train: call for free pick-up
Romantik Hotels
Canton: Valais

Beautiful with its soft-yellow façade dressed with pretty shutters, the Grand Hotel Bella Tola is terraced on the hillside, fronted by a pretty garden and lawn, and looks out to the magnificence of the surrounding peaks and plunging valley. It is elegant and the Buchs-Favre family exude friendliness and hospitality. Bedrooms come in three categories: "classic", smaller tailored rooms with shower; "romantic", larger rooms furnished with lovely antiques accompanied by large bathrooms and balconies; and "superior", the same as romantic but a little larger. I was able to see every room, and noted all-too-many favorites: from 301, a lovely top corner room, to 306 with its own balcony, and 308, a smaller but charming corner room, to room 307 whose bathroom window gives a peek at the Matterhorn. New in 2005 was the hotel's spa and wellness area. In summer breakfast is served in the historical dining room and for dinner you can choose between French cuisine in the conservatory or traditional Swiss fare in the cozy stubli. The village of St. Luc clings to the side of the valley, with skiing being the premier draw in winter and hiking in summer. Guests often take the funicular up the mountain to the observatory, and one of the most popular walks takes you to scale models of the planets. *Directions:* From Lausanne take the A9 south, then east to Sierre and follow signs along the Val d'Anniviers, winding up the mountain for 20 km to St. Luc.

ROMANTIK GRAND HOTEL BELLA TOLA
Owners: Anne-Françoise & Claude Buchs-Favre
Rue Principale, CH-3961 Saint Luc, Switzerland
Tel: (027) 475 14 44, Fax: (027) 475 29 98
32 Rooms, Double: CHF 340-CHF 4801, Suite: CHF 550*
2 Apartments: CHF 531-CHF 648 daily*
*Includes breakfast & 5-course dinner
Open: Jan to Apr & mid-Jun to mid-Oct
Credit cards: MC, VS
22 km S of Sierre, Train to Sierre, 60-min bus to St. Luc
Romantik Hotels, Swiss Historic Hotels, Canton: Valais

What a surprise it was after visiting Meierei Landgasthof on the edge of Lake Saint Moritz to walk into the Hotel Eden and find it is owned by the same family. The son, Maurizio, is busy managing the Meierei while his sister is busy at the Hotel Eden. Both seem to have the same cordial management style that is so frequently reflected when family is at the front desk. Although under the same ownership, there is no competition since each is entirely different. Whereas the Meierei Landgasthof is rustic in decor and well known for its restaurant, the Hotel Eden, which is well located in the heart of Saint Moritz, is a city hotel and serves only breakfast. As you enter the Eden, throw carpets warm the expanse of floor and straight ahead is an atrium, a sunny place to relax and enjoy the offering of afternoon tea. On your right is an old-fashioned, intimate parlor, furnished with rather formal antiques. Breakfast is served in a spacious downstairs dining room where each morning a bountiful buffet is artistically presented on an antique sleigh. The bedrooms are individual in decor and vary in size, decor, and view. Some are very motel-like and others have light knotty-pine furnishings. Room 138, a corner room with a bay window overlooking the lake, is particularly attractive. *Directions:* From the center of the village roundabout, access the hotel through the street in the direction of the parking garage. Continue straight, passing the cinema, and keep to the right.

HOTEL EDEN
Owner: Jehle-Degiacomi Family
Via Veglia 12
CH-7500 Saint Moritz, Switzerland
Tel: (081) 830 81 00, Fax: (081) 830 81 01
35 Rooms, Double: CHF 190–CHF 438
Open: Dec 15 to Mar 15 & Jun 10 to Oct 16
Credit cards: MC, VS
63 km SW of Scuol, Train: 1 km
Canton: Graubunden

From outside, the Hotel Languard looks like a typical patrician residence of wealthy Engadines with the lovely, regional, painted façade. Inside, this small family-owned and family-managed hotel has a warm country ambiance. Beyond the reception desk is an especially bright and cheerful breakfast room with large sunlit windows overlooking a panorama of Lake Saint Moritz. Here the theme is rustic country, with wooden pine tables and quaint carved wooden chairs. The bountiful breakfast buffet is laid out each morning on a fabulous, 17th-century carved wedding chest. There are only 22 guestrooms, each individually decorated, but all maintaining the same country feel with pine paneling and pine furniture. The large and very attractive corner rooms are the most expensive. Especially outstanding is room 9, which has not only handsomely carved antique wood paneling, but also a beautifully painted ceiling. There are splendid views of the lake and mountains from many of the rooms and a few even have a small balcony. The Hotel Languard is directly across a small square from the Hotel Eden. Both are small, personalized, family-run hotels. The Languard has a country ambiance, while the Eden is more formal. *Directions:* It is easy to get lost in the maze of one-way streets at the heart of town. Don't get discouraged—it is a small town and you will eventually arrive at Via Veglia.

HOTEL LANGUARD
Owner: Giovanni Trivella Family
Via Veglia 14
CH-7500 Saint Moritz, Switzerland
Tel: (081) 833 31 37, Fax: (081) 833 45 46
22 Rooms, Double: CHF 180–CHF 572
Open: Jun to Oct & Dec to Apr
Credit cards: all major
63 km SW of Scuol, Train: 1 km
Canton: Graubunden

Although the address is Saint Moritz, the Meierei Landhotel is across the lake, with a pretty view back over the water to town. The hotel is actually an old farm whose origins date back to the 17th century when it was owned by a bishop. It was here that produce for the bishop's table was grown, tithes collected from the surrounding peasants, and beds kept ready for visiting dignitaries of the church. When the Degiacomi family bought the property, it had fallen into sad disrepair. They converted one wing into a very popular restaurant—a favorite place for those hiking around the lake to stop for lunch. The original part of the hotel is a white-stucco, two-storied building with brown shutters. The old restaurant wing, wrapped in weathered brown shingles, blends in very well. On sunny days, the most popular spot to dine is on the outdoor terrace, which is protected from the wind by a wall of glass. The main activity of the Meierei Landhotel is its restaurant, but there are also ten bedrooms furnished in a rustic pine decor. As you approach the main entrance, there is a children's playground to the right and an enticing corral with ponies. If you want to go into Saint Moritz for shopping, it is a pleasant 20-minute walk. Saint Moritz-Bad is also a 20-minute walk by a different path that loops around the lake. *Directions:* Take the Seepromenade on the northwest side of town (opposite the train station) around the lake.

MEIEREI LANDHOTEL
Owner: Maurizio Degiacomi
Via Dim Lej 52
CH-7500 Saint Moritz, Switzerland
Tel: (081) 833 20 60, Fax: (081) 833 88 38
10 Rooms, Double: CHF 178–CHF 488
Restaurant closed Mon
Open: Dec to Apr & Jun to Oct
Credit cards: all major
63 km SW of Scuol, Train: 1 km
Canton: Graubunden

Palazzo Mÿsanus, a handsome, white stucco building perfectly located in the heart of Samedan, is one of the many charming old Engadine homes that line the narrow streets of this colorful town. The handsome building dates back to the 16th century when it belonged to the aristocratic Mÿsanus family. It changed hands many times over the years and during its final days, was a residence hall for the nearby university. The building was recently bought and restored with meticulous care to maintain its outstanding architectural features. In 2003 it was opened as a hotel by your delightful hostess, Monika Martin. You enter though an arched doorway into a very modern foyer. Modern black sofas and metal chairs are softened by potted plants and colorful traditional floral paintings on the walls. The reception area leads into the breakfast room that doubles as a bar in the evenings where live music is frequently the highlight. Here again, you find modern furniture, but the old world ambiance is evident in the vaulted ceilings. The guestrooms vary in style of décor. Those with a modern décor have light wood floors, white upholstered chairs, white duvets on the beds, and modern paintings on the walls. My favorite rooms were those with mellow, antique wood paneled walls and ceilings. *Directions:* Located about a block form the central square.

PALAZZO MÿSANUS
Manager: Monika Martin
Crappun 26, CH-7503 Samedan, Switzerland
Tel: (081) 852 10 80, Fax: (081) 852 10 79
16 Rooms, Double: CHF 180–CHF 260
2 Suites: CHF 360–CHF 385
Open: Dec to mid-Apr & Jun to mid-Oct
Credit cards: MC, VS
74 km SE of Chur, Train: 2 km
Swiss Historic Hotels
Canton: Graubunden

The Domaine de Châteauvieux is just a 15-minute drive from the Geneva airport, a convenient hotel choice for a first or last night in Switzerland, or as a hub from which to explore the Lake Geneva area. It is difficult to comprehend that you are only a few miles west of a large city as you approach this 15th-century stone manor snuggled on a gentle knoll of a hill laced with vineyards. You enter through the front gates into a courtyard with an antique wine press surrounded by an abundance of bright flowers. Inside the Domaine de Châteauvieux there is a tasteful array of antiques gracefully intermingled with new furnishings and bouquets of fresh flowers to give a feeling of coziness and warmth. The emphasis is on truly gourmet dining. In the summer, meals are served out on the terrace overlooking the vineyards. On chilly days, meals are served in a very attractive dining room brimming with old-world ambiance. The hotel is owned by Philippe Chevrier, a superb chef who has justifiably earned two stars from Michelin for his fine restaurant, and his wife Magali, an extremely gracious hostess. The hotel is an excellent choice for those seeking both fine food and excellent accommodations. *Directions:* Leave Geneva airport to the west in the direction of St. Genis. At Meyrin turn south and travel the few kilometers to Satigny.

RELAIS & CHATEAUX DOMAINE DE CHÂTEAUVIEUX
Owners: Magali & Philippe Chevrier
Peney-Dessus
CH-1242 Satigny, Switzerland
Tel: (022) 753 15 11, Fax: (022) 753 19 24
12 Rooms, Double: CHF 315–CHF 455
1 Suite: CHF 680
Closed: Apr 11 to 20, Jul 25 to Aug 10 & Dec 20 to Jan 6
Credit cards: all major
4 km W of Geneva airport, Train: 1 km, free pickup
Relais & Châteaux, Canton: Geneva

The Rheinhotel Fischerzunft is beautifully situated along the banks of the Rhine. The ferry leaves only a few steps from the hotel, making it a most convenient choice if you want to explore the river or just watch the boats go by. As you enter the hotel, an elegantly furnished dining room is to the left, and a sophisticated lounge furnished in muted colors to the right. There is a small staircase just off the hallway leading to a few guestrooms, each individually decorated—but all with a more modern, artistic decor. The rooms in front are termed suites and are the only rooms that face the river. Two of the suites are on the first floor and at water level, so views out the windows give the impression of being on a boat. There is only one suite on the second floor with views out through the dormer window. Until a century ago, the building used to house a fishermen's guild. It was converted to a restaurant and about 50 years ago it was expanded into a simple hotel. In recent years the hotel was purchased by the very talented Mr. Jaeger and Mrs. Zwesper, who renovated the entire building—their exquisite taste is responsible for making the hotel so remarkably attractive. The outstanding, subtle, and fascinating Oriental flavors of the Fischerzunft's "East meets West" cuisine attracts guests from all over the world. *Directions:* The hotel is on the road that hugs the north side of town, on the west side of the river.

RHEINHOTEL FISCHERZUNFT
Owners: André Jaeger & Jana Zwesper
Rheinquai 8
CH-8200 Schaffhausen, Switzerland
Tel: (052) 632 05 05, Fax: (052) 632 05 13
10 Rooms, Double: CHF 280–CHF 440
Restaurant closed Mon & Tues
Open: all year, Credit cards: all major
45 km N of Zürich, Train: 2 km
Relais & Châteaux
Canton: Schaffhausen

We have received nothing but letters of praise for the Hotel Alpenrose, a long-time favorite in our guide. Michel Von Siebenthal and his wife, Carole, do an excellent job of carrying on the tradition of hospitality established by Michel's parents. Although it has grown from a simple ski resort to a prestigious Relais & Châteaux hotel, the Alpenrose maintains the same warmth of welcome and value for money that it did when it was a much simpler property. Of course, it goes without saying that the food is delicious, whether you enjoy it in the delightful dining room or on the lovely terrace. Bedrooms generally are spacious affairs with lovely terraces or balconies enjoying stunning Alpine views across village rooftops. Several less expensive rooms face the street and are ideal for those who wish to experience this fine hotel and its delightful cuisine but who cannot afford a luxurious room. Whether you come to ski or to walk in the mountains, you will be enchanted with this lovely hotel. *Directions:* Schönried is 7 km north of Gstaad. Parking is in either the hotel's garage or an adjacent parking lot.

HOTEL ALPENROSE
Owner: Von Siebenthal Family
CH-3778 Schönried, Switzerland
Tel: (033) 748 91 91, Fax: (033) 748 91 92
12 Rooms, Double: CHF 190–CHF 550
2 Suites: CHF 550–CHF 800
1 Cottage: €1000 daily
Restaurant closed Mon & lunch Tues
Open: Dec to Oct, Credit cards: all major
7 km N of Gstaad, Train: 1 km
Relais & Châteaux
Canton: Bern

Scuol, an enchanting village located in the scenic Engadine Valley, is built on a hill that drops down to the rushing river, the Inn River, which is crossed by a covered bridge. Tall mountain peaks form a backdrop that adds to the striking scene. Due to its thermal waters, Scuol grew in popularity in the late 19th century as a spa. Today, some modern buildings intrude on the town's original medieval character, but once you arrive in the historic center you discover a delightful village with colorfully painted houses, cobbled squares, many flowers, statues, fountains, and a picturesque white church with a clock tower topped by a tall steeple. If you are looking for accommodations, the centuries-old Hotel Engiadina, ideally sitting on a corner in the center of the prettiest part of town, is the perfect choice. It is a very pretty, perfectly maintained, small hotel, in a cream color accented by white trim with Oriel windows. The guestrooms are very attractive with pine furniture and well-appointed bathrooms. Everything is fresh and appealing and top quality. *Directions:* When you arrive in town, look for the tall church steeple and follow signs to the hotel.

HOTEL ENGIADINA
Owner: Barbüda-Giston Family
CH-7550 Scuol, Switzerland
Tel: (081) 864 14 21, Fax: (081) 864 12 45
12 Rooms, Double: CHF 174–CHF 244
3 Suites: CHF 224–CHF 264
Closed: Nov, Credit cards: MC, VS
62 km NE of St. Moritz, Train: 5 km
Canton: Graubunden

Originally a large private residence, the Romantik Hotel Margna was built in 1817 by Johann Josty who took advantage of a prime location, building his home on a small spit of land between two lakes. In the summertime there are countless paths along the lakefront or leading up to imposing mountain peaks, while in the winter this is an Alpine and cross-country skiers' paradise. Johann Josty's manor is now a beautiful hotel with gracious touches of sophistication—warm, cream-colored walls, antique accents such as an old sleigh laden with flowers, and Oriental rugs. There are several lounges, a grill restaurant with an open fireplace, a basement Italian restaurant with "Enoteca" and lounge, a second dining room, the Stuva, a cozy, wood-paneled room original to the hotel, and a new garden terrace that is popular for both breakfast and lunch. The hotel has game rooms, a whirlpool, massage rooms, and steam bath. Each guestroom is delightful but I especially loved number 25, which enjoys views of lake and mountain through three large, arched windows. Golfers will be happy to know that the Margna has its own six-hole course and resident pro. Those on a budget should inquire about the newer wing of less expensive rooms. *Directions:* From St. Moritz travel south to Silvaplana and then 6 km south of Silvaplana cross over to a small peninsula dividing the Silvaplaner and Silser Sees to the tiny hamlet of Sils-Baselgia and the hotel.

ROMANTIK HOTEL MARGNA
Managers: Regula & Andreas Ludwig
CH-7515 Sils-Baselgia, Switzerland
Tel: (081) 838 47 47, Fax: (081) 838 47 48
68 Rooms, Double: CHF 310–CHF 1500*
*Includes breakfast & dinner
Open: mid-Jun to mid-Oct & mid-Dec to mid-Apr
Credit cards: MC, VS
12 km S of St. Moritz, Postal bus from St. Moritz: 12 km
Romantik Hotels
Canton: Graubunden

The village of Sils-Maria is idyllic, nestled on a strip of land dividing two mountain-bound lakes. The Hotel Privata is a charming inn, offering very reasonably priced accommodation and some of the region's most gracious hospitality. Family-run, the pretty, four-story, beige building with brown shutters is located on a small village square. Just to the left of the building is the gathering place for the colorful horse-drawn carriages that take guests into beautiful Val Fex. The hotel is strategically located for hiking—just outside the door, trails lead off in every direction: up into the mountains, into the meadows, around the lakes, and along the rushing creek. This is a pretty inn and I love its comfortable ambiance with crisp white linens, fresh flowers, and endless thoughtful touches. The flagstone entrance with a reception counter opens onto two cozy lounges. A hallway leads to an especially attractive, spacious dining room with windows overlooking the back garden with some lovely sitting places and a sheltered veranda. The dining room has a paneled ceiling, an antique armoire, pine chairs, and fresh flowers everywhere. The dinner is a four-course menu and the food is excellent. Ursula, Dumeng, and their daughters make this a very special place. *Directions:* From St. Moritz travel south to Silvaplana and after 4 km turn left at the traffic sign for Sils-Maria. You will find the Hotel Privata right on the village square.

HOTEL PRIVATA
Owners: Ursula & Dumeng Giovanoli
CH-7514 Sils-Maria, Switzerland
Tel: (081) 832 62 00, Fax: (081) 832 62 01
26 Rooms, Double: CHF 270–CHF 380*
*Includes breakfast & dinner
Open: Dec 13 to Apr 19 & Jun 6 to Oct 18
Credit cards: all major
10 km S of St. Moritz
Postal bus from St. Moritz: 10 km
Canton: Graubunden

From the moment you arrive in Sils-Maria and spot the massive Hotel Waldhaus with its towers, turrets, and crenellated roof dominating the hill above the town, it is immediately apparent that we have deviated from our norm of featuring only small hotels. Inside, the ambiance of grandeur deepens with a spacious reception area that opens onto a stunning drawing room ending in a spectacular bay window looking out to the forest. One lovely room leads to another: cozy sitting nooks, a sweet library, two dining rooms, intimate reading rooms, tearooms, music rooms—all decorated in classic turn of the twentieth century style. Due to the hotel's supreme position overlooking lakes, mountains, and forests, each tastefully decorated guestroom has a view. Incredibly, even with all this grandeur, the Waldhaus exudes the warmth of a small hotel. It has been in the same family since it was built in 1908, the fourth generation maintaining the original standard of hospitality and attention to guests' needs. According to director, Felix Dietrich, the family's policy is to provide five-star hotel amenities and comforts combined with the warmth and welcome of a tiny pension. This, plus a combination of splendor and relaxed friendliness, is precisely what makes this hotel so special. Free pickup for guests arriving by train at St. Moritz station. Free passes to regional buses, trains, and cable cars are included in summer and fall rates. *Directions:* If driving, ask hotel for directions.

HOTEL WALDHAUS
Owners: Maria & Felix Dietrich, and Urs Kienberger
CH-7514 Sils-Maria, Switzerland
Tel: (081) 838 51 00, Fax: (081) 838 51 98
140 Rooms, Double: CHF 510–CHF 925*
10 Suites: CHF 1050–CHF 1480*
*Includes breakfast & dinner
Open: Dec 15 to Apr 15 & Jun 8 to Oct 21
Credit cards: all major
10 km S of St. Moritz, Postal bus from St. Moritz: 10 km
Swiss Historic Hotels, Canton: Graubunden

The Hotel Al Cacciatore is a gem—a tiny hotel that has everything your heart could desire: a quaint village setting, stunning mountain scenery, a delightful restaurant, tasteful decor, and pretty antique furnishings. Adding the final touch of perfection is your charming hostess, Silvia Cafiero, who welcomes guests like friends and lavishes personal attention upon them. Her grandfather came from this tiny village, which she came to love as a child. Many years later, she and her Italian husband, Luigi, left their estate in southern Italy, moved to Soazza, and bought a simple restaurant from one of Silvia's relatives. Then, at an age when most people think of retiring and just enjoying a quiet life, they embarked upon a huge endeavor: totally renovating the property, redoing the restaurant, adding guestrooms, decorating every corner to perfection, and opening a superb little inn. The hotel is housed within a cluster of very old buildings constructed around intimate courtyards. Care was taken to enrich the original architectural features while adding every modern comfort. When the renovation was finished, Silvia decorated the hotel with handsome family antiques and her personal art collection, giving the hotel a warm, homelike ambiance. *Directions:* In the heart of Soazza, which is located just off the A13, 20 minutes north of Bellinzona, en route to the San Bernardino Pass.

HOTEL AL CACCIATORE
Owner: Pia Cafiero Giolo
Piazzetta
CH-6562 Soazza, Switzerland
Tel: (091) 831 18 20, Fax: (091) 831 19 79
17 Rooms, Double: CHF 230–CHF 290
Closed: mid-Jan to mid-Mar, Credit cards: all major
30 km N of Bellinzona, Train: 5 km
Canton: Ticino

Soglio is a stunning hamlet: a cluster of centuries-old, plaster and age-darkened wood houses with stone roofs, perched on a narrow mountain ledge overlooking the splendid Bregaglia Valley, and beyond to soaring, mountain peaks. A tall church spire stretches to the sky and cows graze in lush meadows. The village buildings are rustic farmhouses with one exception—the Palazzo Salis, dating back to 1630, once a magnificent mansion belonging the Salis family, one of the wealthiest, most important families in this region. Today the palace is a small, hotel that abounds with character and offers modern comforts. The moment you enter, the clock turns back to another era with thick walls, slab stone floors, vaulted ceilings, beams, and carved-wood paneling. There is almost a museum quality to the house with its many fascinating oil portraits and marvelous centuries-old furniture. The guestrooms vary in style. My favorites, those furnished with antiques, cost a bit more, but the romantic furniture whisks you back to the time the palace was in its prime. One of my favorites, room 9, has a small sitting area, ceiling and walls of antique-carved paneling, and a queen-sized, four-poster bed. Stay long enough to enjoy the many enchanting mountain paths and breathtaking scenery. An added bonus, the owner, Philippe Cicognani, is a fabulous chef. *Directions:* Soglio is located just north of the Italian border, a few kilometers up a winding road from the 37 motorway.

HOTEL PALAZZO SALIS
Owners: Monica & Philippe Cicognani
CH 7610 Soglio, Switzerland
Tel: (081) 822 12 08, Fax: (081) 822 16 00
16 Rooms, Double: CHF 180–CHF 270
Open: Mar 19 to Nov, Credit cards: all major
60 km SW of St. Moritz
Postal bus St. Moritz to Promontogno to Soglio
Canton: Graubunden

La Soglina is a gem of a hotel in an incredibly picturesque village, high on a shelf-like terrace overlooking the Bregaglia Valley. The hotel is owned by the Nass-Schumacher family. Mr. Nass, originally from Strasbourg, France, is the talented chef in charge of the kitchen. His gracious wife was born in Soglio. The hotel is spread over three buildings in this small village—two stand together at the top and outskirts of town and one is just at its entrance. The reception is located in the newer of the two buildings at the top, along with a recently built restaurant and ten guestrooms. Clean and simple in their decor, the bedrooms are spacious, with Berber-style carpets, whitewashed walls, and sturdy, light-pine furniture. The bathrooms are modern. The restaurant is beautiful with its pine furnishings and carved ceilings. Tables overflow onto an expanse of terrace and enjoy absolutely spectacular vistas. An underground passageway connects the two buildings—the second houses guestrooms and a fitness center with sauna and solarium. Although the rooms are nice and the meals hearty, the outstanding feature of La Soglina is its location. Request one of the most expensive rooms with a view balcony, then settle in for a long stay. You will come home with memories of walks through fields of flowers and mountain panoramas that are almost too perfect to be true. *Directions:* Soglio is located just a few kilometers up a winding road from the 37 motorway.

LA SOGLINA
Owners: E. & R. Nass-Schumacher
CH-7610 Soglio, Switzerland
Tel: (081) 822 16 08, Fax: (081) 822 15 94
33 Rooms, Double: CHF 200–CHF 300*
*Includes breakfast & dinner
Closed: Nov, Credit cards: all major
60 km SW of St. Moritz
Postal bus St. Moritz to Promontogno to Soglio
Canton: Graubunden

The Hotel Krone, a 13th-century residence, is in the fascinating walled medieval town of Solothurn. The cozy exterior leaves nothing to be desired: a pale-pink stuccoed building, muted green shutters, and window boxes overflowing with red geraniums. The location, too, is perfect—facing onto the colorful main square, just opposite Saint Ursen Cathedral. The reception area is more formal than the exterior would indicate, but the dining room has an inviting country-inn atmosphere and fresh flowers are plentiful on the tables. At the top of the stairwell is a large room often used for private parties. There is also a relaxing bar, perfect for a welcome drink. Tables are set outside in good weather for light meals. The bedrooms are all very similar in decor, with copies of Louis XV furniture, which blend nicely with genuine antiques. The more deluxe rooms are especially large and have spacious bathrooms with tubs so big you can almost go swimming in them. Since our original stay at the Hotel Krone, all of the bedrooms have been renovated, and now all of the double rooms are spacious in the old section of the inn. The smaller rooms are in the new addition and are used as singles. *Directions:* Solothurn is located halfway between Basel and Bern on the River Aare and Route 12.

HOTEL KRONE
Owners: Marie-Thérèse & Gerald Dörfler-Aerni
Hauptgasse 64
CH-4500 Solothurn, Switzerland
Tel: (032) 622 44 12, Fax: (032) 622 37 24
42 Rooms, Double: CHF 240–CHF 300
Open: all year, Credit cards: all major
76 km S of Basel, Train: 500 meters
Swiss Historic Hotels
Canton: Solothurn

The Hotel Alte Herberge Weiss Kreuz is located in an attractive village of medieval farmhouses clustered in a barren, but very pretty, area at the north end of the San Bernardino Pass. The hotel is a dramatic white structure made up of three connected buildings with small windows accented by red geraniums. Originally built as a watchtower, by 1519 the Weiss Kreuz had become an inn, accommodating travelers coming over the San Bernardino Pass on horseback. When the road was widened in 1823 to accommodate horse-drawn carriages, business decreased since a competitor's hotel was closer to the new road. The Weiss Kreuz fell into a state of ruin until rescued by an entrepreneur. After total renovation with great care taken to preserve original historic features, the inn reopened in 2000. The exterior looks much as it must have in its prime. However, the architect makes a bold statement inside with startling combinations of the very old and very modern. For example, the bar is in a cave-like stone room but the furniture is chrome. Architecturally, the guestrooms display a charming rustic ambiance. Each is different: some with wood-paneled walls and ceilings, others have thick vaulted walls. However, all feature an ultra-modern bathroom, many separated only by a wall of glass from the bedroom. *Directions:* Splügen is located on the north side of the San Bernardino Pass. From the A13 take the Splügen exit and follow signs to the hotel.

HOTEL ALTE HERBERGE WEISS KREUZ
Owners: Ursula Schwarz & Hans Rudolf Luzi
CH-7435 Splügen, Switzerland
Tel: (081) 630 91 30, Fax: (081) 630 91 34
16 Rooms, Double: CHF 170–CHF 210
Closed: Nov, Credit cards: MC, VS
40 km N of Bellinzona, Train: 5 km
Swiss Historic Hotels
Canton: Graubunden

The Hotel Rheinfels, a beige building with brown shutters, sits directly on the banks of the Rhine as it flows through the storybook-perfect medieval village of Stein am Rhein. In fact, the hotel is so close to the Rhine that the geranium-festooned dining terrace actually stretches out over the water. The restaurant, where you register, seems to be the focal point of the Hotel Rheinfels, but a wide staircase, lined with family portraits, leads up to an attractive lounge decorated with several antique armoires, tables, paintings, and suits of armor. All of the guestrooms are very similar both in decor and size, and all have been completely renovated. Although the bedrooms' built-in furniture is clean and functional, a traditional mood is achieved through the use of floral carpeting in shades of rose with pretty wallpaper and color-coordinated fabrics on the chairs and sofabeds. Every room has its own attractively tiled bathroom. The bedrooms are exceptionally spacious, bright, and cheerful. All rooms but one enjoy windows overlooking the river and it, by contrast, looks out over the medley of town roofs. The family has converted what was their mother's riverside apartment into a spacious rental—an exceptional value. (It even shares a pier with the swans.) *Directions:* Stein am Rhein is approximately 18 km east of Schaffhausen on the Untersee. The Hotel Rheinfels is located right on the water, the first house after the bridge on the left side.

HOTEL RHEINFELS
Owner: Edi Schwegler-Wick
CH-8260 Stein am Rhein, Switzerland
Tel: (052) 741 21 44, Fax: (052) 741 25 22
16 Rooms, Double: CHF 190–CHF 200
1 Suite: CHF 260–CHF 270
Restaurant closed Wed
Open: Mar 10 to Dec 12, Credit cards: all major
18 km E of Schaffhausen, Boat dock: 100 meters
Canton: Schaffhausen

The deluxe Schloss Hotel Chastè is in a tiny village in a gorgeous high meadow of the glorious Engadine Valley, bounded by the soaring peaks of the majestic Dolomites. Completing the idyllic scene is the picturesque Tarasp Castle. Until the turn of the century, the hotel was a farmhouse, and incredibly has been in the same family since it was built in 1480. When Tarasp Castle was being renovated in 1912, Anton Pazeller, the grandfather of the present owner, opened a small restaurant to accommodate tourists coming to see the castle. His grandson, your gracious host, Rudolf Pazeller, trained as a chef and returned home to expand the hotel and add a gourmet restaurant. The façade is in the traditional Engadine style, painted white and accented with intricate designs. Pink geraniums cascade from every window box. Inside, you find beautiful carved-wood paneling and country-style furnishings throughout, which create a charming, rustic ambiance. The bedrooms are individual in decor, but all have a cozy look with furniture made from various woods native to the Engadine. The hotel also has a great spa with sauna and steambath. This is a lovely inn in an idyllic setting. Just steps from the hotel, walking paths lead off in every direction. *Directions:* From St. Moritz, follow the sign for Scuol. Before Scuol, follow the sign for Tarasp-Vulpera, 4 km up the hill. There is a sign for the hotel in Tarasp-Fontana.

SCHLOSS HOTEL CHASTÈ
Owners: Daniela & Rudolf Pazeller
CH-7553 Tarasp, Switzerland
Tel: (081) 861 30 60, Fax: (081) 861 30 61
9 Rooms, Double: CHF 250–CHF 330
8 Suites: CHF 370–CHF 460
Restaurant closed Mon & Tues
Open: Jan to Mar & Jun to Oct, Credit cards: all major
60 km NW of St. Moritz, Train to Scuol, bus to Tarasp
Relais & Châteaux
Canton: Graubunden

If you want to enjoy resort-style living on the lake and still be within an hour of Lucerne by boat or half an hour by car, then the Park Hotel Vitznau might be your cup of tea. It has an ideal, beautiful parklike setting directly on the banks of Lake Lucerne. This is not a rustic hotel in any way. Rather, it is sophisticated with all the amenities that you would expect from a deluxe establishment—a large heated indoor-outdoor swimming pool, beauty spa, sauna, steam bath, table tennis, bicycles, and motorboats for water skiing or excursions. The lakeside setting also allows sailing, swimming, and fishing. The building is like a castle, with turrets, towers, gables, and many nooks and crannies. A beautiful lawn surrounded by gardens runs down from the hotel to the lakeshore where a promenade follows the contours of the lakefront. The setting is one of such bliss that it is hard to believe you are so close to the city of Lucerne. Inside the lobby, the lounge areas and dining room are beautifully decorated with combinations of wood beams, fireplaces, Oriental rugs on gleaming hardwood floors, green plants, and antique accents. *Directions:* From Zürich airport take the highway in the direction of Lucerne, exit at Rotkreuz to the highway Schwyz-Gotthard, then exit in Küssnacht and travel south along the lake to Vitznau.

PARK HOTEL VITZNAU
Manager: Thomas Kleber
Seesstrasse
CH-6354 Vitznau, Switzerland
Tel: (041) 399 60 60, Fax: (041) 399 60 70
101 Rooms, Double: CHF 530–CHF 1800
Open: mid-Apr to end-Oct, Credit cards: all major
25 km E of Lucerne, Boat from Lucerne: 25 km
Canton: Lucerne

L'Ermitage, distinguished as one of the top names in restaurants of the world is located in Vufflens-le-Château, a sweet village tucked among the vineyards that lace the hillsides above Lausanne. Bernard Ravet, owner and renowned chef of L'Ermitage, is assisted by his wife, Ruth, two daughters, Nathalie and Isabelle (both graduates of Lausanne's prestigious Hotel School), and son, Guy, who is also a talented chef. The restaurant has five exquisitely decorated dining rooms exuding the charm and intimacy of a private home. In addition to its superb kitchen, L'Ermitage has a huge cellar featuring an awesome 30,000 bottles of fine wine. Without a doubt, the restaurant is what has made L'Ermitage so famous. In fact, many come to dine without being aware there are also nine bedrooms (including three deluxe suites) for a few savvy guests who can enjoy an exquisite meal accompanied by marvelous wines and retire to their own room after dinner. L'Ermitage, originally the home of a wealthy wine grower, is surrounded by a delightful park, complete with cute duck pond. For guests who want to remember their experience, there is a shop, "Le Vin Vivant" with a collection of gourmet specialties signed by Bernard Ravet, plus a selection of fine crystalware and other gift items. *Directions:* Located 15 kilometers northwest of Lausanne. Exit at Morges from the A1.

L'ERMITAGE
Owner: Bernard Ravet
Route du Village, 26
CH-1134 Vufflens, Switzerland
Tel: (021) 804 68 68, Fax: (021) 802 22 40
9 Rooms, Double: CHF 410–CHF 610
Closed: Aug 2 to Aug 19 & Dec 24 to Jan 15
Credit cards: all major
13 km NW of Lausanne, Train: 5 km
Canton: Vaud

The Hotel Villa Maria, above the Engadine Valley, sits on the road from Bad Scuol as it winds up into the hills toward the picturesque Tarasp Castle. Although the road loops around the hotel, there is an ornately tended garden with decorative gnomes and a "pitch and put" green along the side. The 100-year-old inn, painted a pale yellow with intricately carved wooden balconies and brown shutters, has a Victorian flair which is given a Swiss touch by the traditional boxes overflowing with geraniums hung at every window. Inside, there is a country ambiance—carved pine ceilings, intricate paneling, pine furniture, antiques, and fresh flowers abound. The bedrooms are attractive. All have light-pine furniture offset by the same provincial-print fabrics used in the window coverings. Everything is fresh and new and very pretty. For guests who stay three days, a demi-pension plan is available, with breakfast and dinner included in the room rate. For these guests there is a bright, cheerful dining room overlooking the back garden. In addition, on the street level there is a gourmet restaurant with beamed ceilings, thick planked-wood walls, many antiques, a fireplace, and a charming fondue restaurant off the garden. The Villa Maria is in a wooded area with walking trails feathering off in every direction. *Directions:* Traveling east on the 27, turn south just before Scuol and cross the river to Vulpera.

HOTEL VILLA MARIA
Owner: Erich Jaeger
CH-7552 Vulpera, Switzerland
Tel: (081) 864 11 38, Fax: (081) 864 91 61
15 Rooms, Double: CHF 196–CHF 300
Open: May 20 to Nov & Christmas to Easter
Credit cards: all major
63 km NE of St. Moritz
Train to Bad Scuol then bus to hotel
Canton: Graubunden

Since the turn of the last century Vulpera's spas have been well known due to the village's reputation for its fine water. The town's architecture is mostly contemporary, but the most attractive hotels, such as the lovely Hotel Villa Post, still reflect the nostalgic charm of the Victorian Era. The three-story mansion has a stately, old-world ambiance enhanced by mansard-style roof with perky gables and a cute turret topped by a Swiss flag. Inside there is no hint of the dark furnishings so popular at the time the hotel was built. Instead, there is a bright look with light streaming through large windows and attractive, country-style furniture. Guestroom amenities are the finest quality, light and airy with light wood furniture. Rolf Zollinger has been a Swiss hotelier all of his life and the hotel reflects his professionalism, particularly in the fine restaurant and excellent service. His lovely wife from England, Sally, is also involved in the operation of this family-run hotel, including the responsibility for the stunning gardens where her British flair for flowers is immediately apparent. The most outstanding feature of the Hotel Villa Post—making it stand out from the others in town—is its beautiful grounds. Across from the hotel is a huge park filled with impeccably tended flower beds, fountains, ponds, trees, and pathways. A modern wing is available for small conferences and private parties.
Directions: Upon arriving in town, follow signs to the hotel.

HOTEL VILLA POST
Owners: Sally & Rolf Zollinger
CH-7552 Vulpera, Switzerland
Tel: (081) 864 11 12, Fax: (081) 864 95 85
26 Rooms, Double: CHF 240–CHF 300*
*Includes breakfast & dinner
Closed: Easter to Jun & mid-Oct to mid-Dec
Credit cards: all major
63 km NE of St. Moritz
Train to Bad Scuol then bus to hotel
Canton: Graubunden

Dorly and Urs-Peter Geering are excellent hoteliers, shining lights of Switzerland's most highly regarded profession. The Beau Rivage on the shore of Lake Lucerne is their home, so one of them is always on hand and the warmth they offer guests is echoed by the entire staff from the porter to the maitre d'hotel. To be certain that guests have the opportunity to see everything in the area, the Geerings have arranged for a member of the local tourist office to come several times a week to discuss where to go and what to see. Of course, you must take the ferry to Lucerne and the gondola up to Rigi! However, with the Beau Rivage's unsurpassed lakeside location, it is tempting to while away the hours soaking in the view of the boat activity on the mountain-backed lake, taking dips in the pool, and lunching on the shaded patio. Naturally, you should request a bedroom with a lake view—some have large terraces, others snug balconies. However, you get the best value for money in the spacious rooms under the eaves (no balcony or terrace). *Directions:* From Zürich exit the A4 at Küssnacht and follow the signs along Lake Lucerne, where you find the Hotel Beau Rivage on your right.

HOTEL BEAU RIVAGE
Owners: Dorly & Urs-Peter Geering
Gottardstrasse 6
CH-6353 Weggis, Switzerland
Tel: (041) 392 79 00, Fax: (041) 390 19 81
41 Rooms, Double: CHF 270–CHF 440
Open: Apr to Oct, Credit cards: all major
20 km E of Lucerne
Train to Lucerne & boat to Weggis
Canton: Lucerne

The Hotel Alte Post, an old coaching inn, is a charming country hotel on the road between the international resort of Gstaad and the magnificent lake district of Interlaken. Its terraced back faces the rushing waters of the River Simme. You enter the hotel from the street into a small, informal entry. On one side is a simple country restaurant decorated with pine tables and lovely painted beams and on the other side is a more formal restaurant, elegant in decor. At the back of the inn is a very informal dining area whose tables are set against windows with views of the river. When the weather cooperates, tables are also set outside on a terrace. Nine of the hotel's ten guestrooms are located on the top floor (the other is on the floor below). All are very rustic in their decor, with wood-paneled walls and ceilings and country antiques—very reminiscent of a country "ferme auberge". The sound of the road traffic is diminished by the time it reaches the top floor and any sound that could be heard is drowned out by the rushing river. Six of the bedrooms have a private bathroom with shower, two have a private bathroom with tub, and two are equipped with a sink only. The rooms are comfortably furnished and very reasonable in price. First-class cuisine is prepared by the owner and chef, Herr Brazerol. *Directions:* Weissenburg is right on the river, approximately 20 km east of Spiez and Lake Thun. The Alte Post is on the main road.

HOTEL ALTE POST
Owners: Mr & Mrs Franz Brazerol
CH-3764 Weissenburg, Switzerland
Tel: (033) 783 15 15, Fax: (033) 783 15 78
10 Rooms, Double: CHF 100–CHF 170
Restaurant closed Wed & Thur
Closed: Apr & Nov, Credit cards: all major
30 km NE of Gstaad, Train: 10-min walk
Canton: Bern

When at the end of the 19th century word spread of the incredible beauty of the Alps, sporty travelers began to find their way to Wengen. At that time Wengen was merely a cluster of wooden farmhouses clinging to a mountain shelf high above the Lauterbrunnen Valley. In 1881, Friedrich and Margaritha Feuz-Lauener (great-grandparents of the present owner Paul von Allmen) gambled on tourism and built the Alpenrose, the village's first hotel. Through the years, the hotel has expanded, but the traditional warmth of hospitality remains. Paul and his gracious Scottish wife, Margaret, make all guests feel very special. The lounges and dining rooms are cozily decorated and have been recently remodeled in the beautiful Alpine style using old wood. The dining room is large and becomes a meeting place where everyone has their own table for dinner each night—a time when guests share their day's adventures and often become friends. Paul von Allmen is the chef and the set dinner menu features good home cooking. Most of the bedrooms have been completely renovated and are fresh and pretty with light-pine furniture. Request a south-facing room with a balcony to capture the splendor of the Jungfrau. *Directions:* Cars are not allowed in Wengen. A hotel porter meets guests at the station or if you have just a little luggage, you might want to walk the short distance to the hotel. A town map is available at the train station.

HOTEL ALPENROSE
Owner: Paul von Allmen Family
CH-3823 Wengen, Switzerland
Tel: (033) 855 32 16, Fax: (033) 855 15 18
50 Rooms, Double: CHF 228–CHF 402*
*Includes breakfast & dinner
Open: mid-Dec to mid-Apr & May to Oct
Credit cards: all major
16 km S of Interlaken, Train: 7-min walk
Canton: Bern

Wengen is one of our favorite towns in Switzerland, and the fact that the village can only be accessed by train makes it even more fun to visit. But, what makes the town so special is its breathtaking view of the Jungfrau. There is always a shortage of good places to stay in Wengen so the Caprice, which opened in 2002, is a welcome addition to the hotel scene. Many of the hotels in town exude a nostalgic, old world appeal. However, if you prefer a contemporary elegance, you will fall in love with the Caprice. From the moment you enter, you will be impressed by the understated, refined décor. There is a fresh, uncluttered look achieved through the use of modern furniture and fabrics in pastel earth tones. The choice of subdued colors is an excellent one since nothing conflicts with the greatest asset of the hotel: its walls of windows that open to an absolutely stunning, mountain panorama. The hotel is owned by Christian Aubert. His talented wife, Monica, did the decorating. She has created an ambiance of simplicity that is softened by the warmth of wood, fine fabrics, soft lighting, and fresh flowers. The dining room, again with gorgeous view windows, is beautiful and the food gourmet. The spacious guestrooms, with carved wood balconies and marvelous views of the mountains, are more traditional in décor with pine furniture that has an alpine flair. *Directions:* When you arrive at the train station, call the hotel. The porter will pick you up.

HOTEL CAPRICE
Owners: Monica & Christian Aubert
CH-3823 Wengen, Switzerland
Tel: (033) 856 06 06, Fax: (033) 856 06 07
15 Rooms, Double: CHF 210–CHF 680
4 Suites: CHF 440–CHF 1110
Open: Christmas to mid- Apr & May to Oct
Credit cards: MC, VS
16 km S of Interlaken, Train: free pick up
Canton: Bern

As your train pulls into Wengen (coming by train is the only access), you will see the Hotel Regina perched on the knoll above the station. If you call ahead, the hotel porter will be there to meet you. I saw one cart pull away brimming with children, parents, luggage, and a dog. When you enter the hotel, you will probably be reminded of one of the British resorts so popular at the turn of the last century. The downstairs has large, rambling lobbies punctuated with small seating areas where chairs encircle game tables, and a huge fireplace surrounded by overstuffed chairs—it all looks very Swiss-British. The Chez Meyer dining room is very special, intimate in size, its walls hung with family photos—generations of Meyers who have operated hotels in Kandersteg and now in Wengen—Switzerland's beautiful mountain towns. Notice the chairs that have brass tags of the 11 family members who are always welcome at the Regina. The decor is lovely, and the Meyer family is extremely gracious and happily welcomes guests who return year after year—a tradition for many. The view from the Regina is so stunning that everything else pales in significance. Ask for a room with a balcony—when you're outside, you feel as if you can touch the mountain peaks. *Directions:* Wengen is 16 km up the valley from Interlaken. Cars are not allowed in this mountain village so you have to park at the train station in Lauterbrunnen and then take the cog train up to Wengen.

HOTEL REGINA
Owners: Ariane & Guido Meyer
CH-3823 Wengen, Switzerland
Tel: (033) 856 58 58, Fax: (033) 856 58 50
80 Rooms, Double: CHF 260–CHF 580
4 Suites: CHF 540–CHF 1450
1 Apartment: CHF 1500-CHF 3500 weekly
Open: Dec to mid-Apr & mid-May to mid Oct
Credit cards: all major
16 km S of Interlaken, Train: 3-min walk
Canton: Bern

In the small town of Worb, just a few kilometers east of Bern, sits the Hotel Löwen. This pretty inn, which dates back to 1547, is positioned at the junction of two busy streets but, even so, radiates an immense amount of charm. Ursula or Hans-Peter Bernhard is usually on hand to welcome guests for the Hotel Löwen is their home, with their family living upstairs. A series of cozy, traditional dining rooms occupies the ground floor—and it is here that breakfast is served. However, during the summer, guests usually eat outside in the shade of the sycamore trees. Just off the garden is a bowling alley and Herr Bernhard is always happy to give a demonstration of Swiss bowling. He is also happy to share his other hobbies: his corkscrew and wine collections. While the restaurant has a list of 50 to 60 wines, Hans-Peter has a far larger selection in his nearby shop. The spotless but simply decorated bedrooms all have small refrigerators containing complimentary beers, water, and snacks. My favorite room was number 14 with its window opening up to the church and its intricate, paper-cut pictures on the walls. The Hotel Löwen is just 200 meters from the train station, making it a perfect location for a day trip to Bern. From Worb the road winds up into the Emmental Valley. Please note smoking is only permitted in one of the lounges. *Directions:* From Bern take the A6 towards Interlaken, exit for Langau and drive 10 km to Worb. The hotel is in the center of town.

☕ ✗ 💳 📷 🐕 @ W ⟁ P 🍴 🚭 ⚜ ⚓ 🧍 🥾 🐎 🐻 ⛷ 🍇

HOTEL LÖWEN
Owner: Hans-Peter Bernhard
Enggisteinstrasse 3
CH-3076 Worb, Switzerland
Tel: (031) 839 23 03, Fax: (031) 839 58 77
13 Rooms, Double: CHF 170–CHF 180
Restaurant closed Sat & Sun
Open: all year, Credit cards: all major
8 km E of Bern, Train: 200 meters
Canton: Bern

The picture-perfect, chalet-style Hotel Bella Vista is a charming family-run hotel that really has it all: outstanding warmth of welcome; a delightful alpine ambiance; moderate rates; comfortable guestrooms; pretty country décor; wonderful home-cooking; and a 5-minute walk into the center of town. And, if this isn't enough, its unobstructed views of the Matterhorn are as good as—or better than—any in Zermatt. If you are looking for sumptuous accommodations with a lavish spa, gourmet dining, and all the amenities of a world class resort, Zermatt has many of these. But, if a simple hotel appeals to you, you can do no better than the Bella Vista. The inn has been in the same family for two generations. It was built by the parents of Bernadette Götzenberger, who since 1978 has been running the hotel with her husband, Franz, a keen climber who will share tips on exploring the spectacular countryside, and, if his schedule permits, will pack his rucksack and be your guide. Each morning begins with a bountiful buffet breakfast with freshly-pressed orange juice, fifteen kinds of home-made jam, hot-from-the-oven brioche, and flaky butter croissants. A delicious supper, with a set menu, is available (for guests only) five nights a week. Local Valais wines, chosen from local vintners, are also available. *Directions:* From the phone board at the train station, call the hotel and someone will pick you up.

☕ 🏂 💳 ☎ 🐕 ♨ @ W 🍴 🚭 ♿ 🧍 🚶 ⛷

HOTEL BELLA VISTA
Owners: Bernadette & Franz Götzenberger
CH-3920 Zermatt, Switzerland
Tel: (027) 966 28 10, Fax: (027) 966 28 15
21 Rooms, Double: CHF 188–CHF 264
3 Suites: CHF 230–CHF 350
Closed: May & mid-Oct to mid-Dec
Credit cards: all major
A short walk from the heart of town
Train: free pick up
Canton: Valais

It is not surprising that the Hotel Daniela is so outstanding since the owners, Daniela and Paul Julen, are superb hoteliers who also own and manage the luxurious Julen, just a block away. The Daniela is within easy walking distance to all of the boutiques and restaurants within the village, yet pleasantly secluded from the bustling activity of the downtown area. Newly built in the traditional chalet style with wood façade accented by balconies, the hotel is immediately appealing. When you step inside, there is a charming ambiance of refined elegance. To the left is a pretty sitting area with a delightful bar tucked at the end of the room. A rich breakfast is served in an intimate dining room to the right. The guestrooms (most with balcony) share a similar décor— traditional with lovely fabrics, pretty furniture, and top quality amenities throughout. The double rooms face in the direction of the Matterhorn. Request a third floor room since these are high enough to look out over the rooftops and capture a view of the mountain. If you want to splurge, the suite is attractive with a fireplace for chilly winter evenings. The Hotel Daniela has a huge advantage in being a "sister" hotel of the deluxe Hotel Julen: you can enjoy a serene setting, and yet have access to all the outstanding facilities of the Julen, such as its fine dining and exquisite spa with stunning swimming pool. *Directions:* In Zermatt, call from hotel phone board at the rail station. The hotel will pick you up.

HOTEL DANIELA
Owners: Daniela & Paul Julen
CH-3920 Zermatt, Switzerland
Tel: (027) 966 77 00, Fax: (027) 966 77 77
22 Rooms, Double: CHF 176–CHF 376
2 Suites: CHF 220–CHF 498
Open: all year, Credit cards: MC, VS
A short walk from the heart of town
Train: 5-min walk
Canton: Valais

Sitting high above Zermatt, the Grand Hotel Schönegg has a panoramic view of the towering Matterhorn across the rooftops of the town. In spite of its hillside location you don't have to climb to reach your lofty retreat for the hotel has an elevator, accessed through a grotto-like passageway, which whisks you up from the town. The classic chalet façade is matched by a classic interior, with heavy pine beams and ornate plasterwork ceilings in the public areas and traditional furnishings in the bedrooms. Of course, capturing the view of the Matterhorn is the name of the game in Zermatt and the Schönegg offers many possibilities: from the spacious terrace, the dining room, and a great many of the bedrooms. Bedrooms are found on two floors below and four above the reception area. The majority of rooms enjoy balconies and views of the Matterhorn. The most dramatic is the south-facing suite 604, accessed by its own private stairway and profiting from an expanse of deck. Service and food are exceptional and the price for one of Zermatt's loveliest hotels is surprisingly one of the town's best values. *Directions:* Park you car by the train station in Tasch, take the train to Zermatt, and the hotel's golf cart will be waiting at the station.

GRAND HOTEL SCHÖNEGG
Owner: Metry-Julen Family
CH-3920 Zermatt, Switzerland
Tel: (027) 966 34 34, Fax: (027) 966 34 35
33 Rooms, Double: CHF 290–CHF 580
2 Suites: CHF 467–CHF 834
1 Apartment: CHF 834 daily
Closed: Oct, Nov & May, Credit cards: all major
A short walk from the heart of town
Train: 10-min walk
Canton: Valais

The Seiler family is an integral part of Zermatt. It was back in the mid-1800s when Alexander Seiler ventured into the hotel business with the first hotel in Zermatt—the Monte Rosa. The following generations have continued in the business of hospitality and expanded the family enterprise to include the Mont Cervin Palace, the finest, most elegant hotel in Zermatt. As you enter the hotel it is hard to believe that such a chic resort could be situated in a mountain village. The ceilings are high, with lovely paneling in some areas and wood beams in others, and there are Oriental carpets, fine antique furniture, and flowers everywhere. Converted from what was once a garden courtyard, the Rendezvous bar is a welcoming place to enjoy a drink. The main dining room, painted in pretty, soft yellow and blue, has a tranquil formality combined with a reputation for gourmet food and exquisite service. You find more casual dining in the pine-paneled bar. Guestrooms are located in four buildings and run the gamut from deluxe Alpine-style apartments to traditional double bedrooms. Naturally, the premier rooms have a heart-stopping view of the towering Matterhorn. *Directions:* The village of Täsch is your final destination. The hotel can reserve covered parking. The staff will take care of your luggage and organize the transfer from Tasch to your hotel, either by taxi or train. Be sure to call ahead for reservations.

MONT CERVIN PALACE
Manager: Kevin Kunz
Bahnhofstrasse 31
CH-3920 Zermatt, Switzerland
Tel: (027) 966 88 88, Fax: (027) 966 88 99
114 Rooms, Double: CHF 550–CHF 930
56 Suites: CHF 980–CHF 4200
Open: Dec to mid-Apr & mid-Jun to end-Sept
Credit cards: all major
In the center of Zermatt, Train: 5-minute walk
Canton: Valais

To stay at the Riffelalp, sitting high on a plateau above the city of Zermatt, is to enjoy an elegant resort oasis and unobstructed views of the Matterhorn in a spectacular Alpine setting. As the name implies, the hotel lies 2222 meters (7290 ft.) above sea level on the southern edge of a plateau, at the heart of the Gornergrat skiing/hiking district. During a renovation the original four-story, cream-stucco hotel was gutted and the ambiance of a gorgeous Alpine chalet was created using beautiful Alpine pines for much of the flooring and walls, and even as the basis for the hand-painted ceilings. The attractive bar with its large open fireplace and many cozy sitting areas invite for a drink before or after dinner. The main Alexander Restaurant has intimate seating areas that are created by partitioning off tables and booths, and tables spill out onto the terrace for summer breakfasts or lunches. The lovely guestrooms, all with modern bathroom conveniences and Jacuzzis, have a beautiful Alpine decor and most enjoy views of the Matterhorn. The pool and spa area St-Trop-Alp, with Europe's highest outdoor pool welcomes you. Once you arrive in this idyllic but isolated setting you will not want to leave so the hotel provides many attractions including an underground bowling alley, winetasting, Swiss cheese and Italian restaurants, guided walking and skiing trips as well as ski-in and ski-out access. *Directions:* Take the 20-minute cog-wheel train ride from Zermatt.

RIFFELALP RESORT 2222M
Manager: Hans Jorg Walther
Riffelalp, CH-3920 Zermatt, Switzerland
Tel: (027) 966 05 55, Fax: (027) 966 05 50
65 Rooms, Double: CHF 570–CHF 1290*
5 Suites: CHF 1220–CHF 2500*
*Includes breakfast & dinner
Closed: mid-Apr to mid-Jun & end-Sep to mid-Dec
Credit cards: all major
Above Zermatt, Train: Cog wheel train from Zermatt
Canton: Valais

A cascade of colorful flowers adorns every inch of the balconies of the Hotel Julen at the height of summer—a lovely sight. This hotel, owned and managed by Daniela and Paul Julen, is well located, just across the bridge and river from the heart of Zermatt. Inside, the decor is surprisingly modern with bold designs and strong colors. Just off the entry, stools around the new bar as well as leather sofas in front of the cozy fireplace attract many guests—the ambiance is one of relaxation and friendliness. Settle on the patio and watch the changing moods of the Matterhorn, enjoy a salad-bar lunch or an à-la-carte dinner in the dining room. Another option is a traditional, romantic meal in the Schäferstube "lamb room", a romantic, old-world dining room. Bedrooms vary in size from elegant suites to more standard twin-bedded rooms. Paneled in 100-year-old spruce wood and furnished with traditional light-pine furniture, each guestroom has green silk drapes and contrasting striped carpets. The three choice rooms (107, 108, and 109) all open onto an expanse of balcony and unobstructed views of the Matterhorn. The fitness center offers everything that you expect to find at a luxurious resort, including a swimming pool with water jets, an incredible weight room, and a sauna. *Directions:* Park your car by the train station in Täsch, take the train to Zermatt, and your hotel golf cart will be waiting at the station.

ROMANTIK HOTEL JULEN
Owners: Daniela & Paul Julen
Riedstraße 2
CH-3920 Zermatt, Switzerland
Tel: (027) 966 76 00, Fax: (027) 966 76 76
27 Rooms, Double: CHF 300–CHF 558
5 Suites: CHF 360–CHF 748
Open: all year, Credit cards: all major
A short walk from the heart of town, Train: 5-min walk
Romantik Hotels
Canton: Valais

The Schlosshotel Tenne, just a two-minute walk from the main Zermatt rail terminal, is one of the few hotels in Zermatt to incorporate into its structure a very old wooden chalet. Part of the hotel is of more modern construction but the old and the new have been blended well. The hotel is owned by an old Zermatt family, the Perrens. The Tenne is managed Sonja whose gracious hospitality makes guests feel very welcome. The hotel has a modern, Swiss art-deco theme—walls, pillars, and carvings all have this motif. In the chalet are five junior-suites termed "rustic" rooms because of their carved blond paneling. Each has a separate sitting room and bedroom. Several face the Matterhorn with the Gornegrat cog railway station in between. All the bedrooms have a bathroom with whirlpool tub. The hotel offers a generous buffet breakfast with champagne. There is no restaurant for dinner but guests can walk to a number of restaurants from the hotel. Ask about the great skiing packages. *Directions:* Park you car by the train station in Tasch and take the train to Zermatt. Opposite the train station in Zermatt, you will see the arched sign for the Schlosshotel Tenne, next to the Gornegrat cog railway station.

SCHLOSSHOTEL TENNE
Owner: Sonja Biner-Perren
CH-3920 Zermatt, Switzerland
Tel: (027) 966 44 00, Fax: (027) 966 44 05
35 Rooms, Double: CHF 220–CHF 380
Open: Dec to Apr & Jun to Oct
Credit cards: all major
At the heart of Zermatt, Train: 50 meters
Canton: Valais

The Hotel Monte Rosa is a must when evaluating the hotels of Zermatt. How could you possibly not consider the original hotel in Zermatt, one that is so intricately interwoven with the history of this wonderful old village? The members of the Seiler family who own the Monte Rosa are descendants of Alexander Seiler who waved goodbye on July 13, 1865, to the famous Englishman, Edward Whymper, as he began his historic climb to become the first man to conquer the Matterhorn. Back in the 1800s, when Edward Whymper was asked about the best hotel in Zermatt, he always replied, "Go to the Monte Rosa—go to Seiler's". The answer has not changed over the past century. There are now several Seiler hotels on the hotel scene, but it is still the Monte Rosa that best captures the nostalgia of the old Zermatt. It is not just the romance that makes this inn so special—it also has delightful old-world lounges, such as the pine-paneled Whymper Room and the traditional billiard room. The charming guestrooms are all tastefully decorated in an old-world style. Each bedroom is lovely in its own way, with fine furnishings accented by pretty, color-coordinated fabrics. The service is refined and reflects the best in Swiss tradition and hospitality. Guests loyally return year after year to experience this exceptional hotel. *Directions:* Park you car by the train station in Täsch, take the train to Zermatt, and your hotel electric car will be waiting at the station.

SEILER HOTEL MONTE ROSA
Manager: Martin Sonderegger
Bahnofstrasse 80, P.O. Box 220
CH-3920 Zermatt, Switzerland
Tel: (027) 966 03 33, Fax: (027) 966 03 30
47 Rooms, Double: CHF 270–CHF 830
Open: mid-Dec to mid-Apr & mid-Jun to mid-Oct
Credit cards: all major
In the center of Zermatt, Train: 5-minute walk
Swiss Historic Hotels
Canton: Valais

The Claridge Hotel Zurich is a real charmer, an appealing country inn away from the bustle of the city, yet within easy walking distance of the heart of Zürich. Lacy trees frame the yellow façade whose small-paned windows are enhanced by off-white shutters. A gay yellow-and-white striped awning forms a cozy canopy over the front entry. From the moment you enter, you are surrounded by a homey ambiance—nothing commercial, just comfortable chairs, antique chests, Oriental rugs, lovely paintings, and sunlight streaming in through the many windows. The bedrooms are a special surprise. Each seems so large as to almost be a suite, with plenty of space to relax and read or write letters. All the rooms even have a computer work station with office software, highspeed internet access, internet TV and radio, air conditioning. The cozy Orson's Restaurant, Lounge & Bar was newly designed by famous architect lady Pia Schmid. It serves Mediterranean specialties. The ACE restaurant specializes in local Swiss fare. In warm weather, meals are served in a delightful little garden tucked to the side of the hotel. In the summer snacks, cocktails and teas are served on the terrace: to see and to be seen. Beat Blumer owns and personally manages the Claridge. *Directions:* From the train station, cross the Limmat River on Bahnhofbrücke, turn right on Hirschengraben, which becomes Zeltweg after it crosses Rämistrasse, and then turn left on Steinwiesstrasse.

CLARIDGE HOTEL ZURICH
Owner: Beat Blumer
Steinwiesstrasse 8-10, CH-8032 Zürich, Switzerland
Tel: (044) 267 87 87, Fax: (044) 251 24 76
31 Rooms, Double: CHF 220–CHF 480*
8 Suites: CHF 390–CHF 650*
*Breakfast not included: CHF 24
Open: Jan 05 to Dec 18, Restaurant closed Sun
Credit cards: all major
City center near the Museum of Fine Art
Train: 500 meters, Tram 150 meters, Canton: Zurich

We discovered this charming boutique hotel when taking an evening stroll up from the river. Enchanted just by peeking through windows, we knew our brazen efforts were rewarded when we entered the lobby. The Hotel Kindli, once a 16th-century townhouse, retains the warmth and character of a private home. Decorated throughout in Laura Ashley wallpapers and fabrics, the guestrooms are rich and handsome in their furnishings. The setting, on cobbled streets at the heart of the pedestrian district, affords quiet and a wonderful central location. Rooms open to the sounds of footsteps on cobbled streets and the bells of St. Peter's. Since it was evening and many guests had already checked in, we felt fortunate to see even a sampling of rooms. All the rooms have private bathrooms and open off lovely quiet corridors. A circular stair of beautiful pink marble winds up through the center of the home (they also have an elevator). Everything here is tasteful and English-country, yet if you are not attracted by the rooms, you might simply find yourself a patron of the wonderful Restaurant Kindli, which is cozy and inviting. *Directions:* Located on a pedestrian area just up from the river off the Limmat Quai on the east side. Ask for directions as to where to park and how to unload your luggage.

HOTEL KINDLI
Owner: Gisela Lacher
Pfalzgasse 1
CH-8001 Zürich, Switzerland
Tel: (043) 888 76 76, Fax: (043) 888 76 77
21 Rooms, Double: CHF 400–CHF 440
Open: all year, Credit cards: all major
At the heart of town, Train: 5-minute walk
Canton: Zurich

A small hotel more than 400 years old, the Romantik Hotel Florhof is located on the north side of the River Limmat on a quiet street that twists up from the little squares and alleys of old Zürich. Providing a tranquil oasis from the bustle of activity, but close enough for you to walk to all major attractions such as the art museum and the university, the Florhof is more like a residence than a hotel. Having been totally refurbished in 2000, it is elegant, yet comfortable and in keeping with the style of this lovely old patrician home. The outside is painted a pretty gray-blue, and there is an intimate patio at the rear—perfect for summer dining. The entry is warmed by richly paneled walls, dramatic flower arrangements, and a marvelous old blue-and-white rococo tile stove. Just off the lobby is a cozy dining room where you can enjoy delicious, market-fresh cuisine. Beautiful guestrooms are all elegantly similar, decorated in either a blue, red, or green color scheme mixed with rich creams, and have handsome antiques. Perhaps the greatest asset of the Florhof is the graciousness of its enthusiastic hosts, Brigitte and Beat Schiesser. Having traveled extensively, they have now chosen to settle in Zürich and make this charming inn their home. *Directions:* From the train station, cross over the Limmat River on Bahnhofbrücke, turn right on Hirschengraben and then left on Florhofgasse just before the Kunsthaus.

ROMANTIK HOTEL FLORHOF
Owners: Brigitte & Beat Schiesser
Florhofgasse 4
CH-8001 Zürich, Switzerland
Tel: (044) 250 26 26, Fax: (044) 250 26 27
35 Rooms, Double: CHF 360–CHF 380
2 Suites: CHF 510–CHF 610
Restaurant closed Sun & Bank holidays
Open: all year, Credit cards: all major
Walking distance of heart of Zürich, Train: 10 min walk
Romantik Hotels, Canton: Zurich

The Hotel zum Storchen is absolutely wonderful, offering the professional service of a grand hotel but with a truly personal touch. Under Joerg Arnold's direction, the staff not only serves graciously but seems to anticipate one's needs. Guests enjoy the most sophisticated luxuries in modern bedrooms, all beautifully decorated in rich fabrics of reds, blues, and creams that complement the handsome walnut and mahogany furniture. A few rooms deserve special mention: Room 323 is a favorite, a large corner room with an expanse of river view through French windows, and 521, although a standard room, enjoys a private terrace overlooking the rooftops of town. The Storchen Bar is a cozy place to settle for a drink and accompanying piano music. The dining room is elegant, with an excellent menu and wonderful views (weather permitting, tables are set on the geranium-adorned terrace). The dining room is also the stage for a breakfast feast of juices, breads, meats, cheeses, cereals, and yogurts. Recent renovations have dramatically enhanced the entry and lobby of the hotel. Zürich is one of Europe's most elegant cities, and the Zum Storchen affords a comfortably elegant base. *Directions:* From the Lucerne highway follow Zürich City/See signs and turn left before the bridge.

HOTEL ZUM STORCHEN
Manager: Joerg Arnold
Am Weinplatz 2
CH-8001 Zürich, Switzerland
Tel: (044) 227 27 27, Fax: (044) 227 27 00
65 Rooms, Double: CHF 550–CHF 800
Open: all year, Credit cards: all major
On the banks of the River Limmat, Train: 1.5 km
Canton: Zurich

Hotel Descriptions

Index

Index 275

KAREN BROWN wrote her first travel guide in 1976. Her personalized travel series has grown to 17 titles, which Karen and her small staff work diligently to keep updated. Karen, her husband, Rick, and their children, Alexandra and Richard, live in a small town on the coast south of San Francisco.

CLARE BROWN was a travel consultant for many years, specializing in planning itineraries using charming small hotels in the countryside. Her expertise is now available to a larger audience—the readers of her daughter Karen's travel guides. When not traveling, Clare and her husband, Bill, divide their time between northern California, Colorado, and Mexico.

JUNE EVELEIGH BROWN hails from Sheffield, England and lived in Zambia and Canada before moving to northern California where she lives in San Mateo with her husband, Tony, their German Shepherd, and a Siamese cat.

JANN POLLARD, the artist of all the beautiful cover paintings in the Karen Brown series, has studied art since childhood and is well known for her outstanding impressionistic-style watercolors. Jann has received numerous achievement awards and her works are in private and corporate collections internationally. She is also a popular workshop teacher in the United States, Mexico and Europe. *www.jannpollard.com.* Fine art giclée prints of her paintings are available at *www.karenbrown.com.*

BARBARA MACLURCAN TAPP, the talented artist who produces all of the hotel sketches and delightful illustrations in this guide, was raised in Sydney, Australia where she studied interior design. Although Barbara continues with architectural rendering and watercolor painting, she devotes much of her time to illustrating the Karen Brown guides. Barbara lives in Kensington, California, with her husband, Richard, and is Mum to Jono, Alex and Georgia. For more information about her work visit *www.barbaratapp.com.*

Seehotel Sonne, Küsnacht am Zürichsee

Romantik Hotels & Restaurants – Arrive, Relax, Enjoy!

At Romantik Hotels & Restaurants we invite you to arrive, relax and enjoy. Among our more than 200 Romantik Hotels you can find historic country inns, opulent estates and elegant city mansions in 11 European countries. We invite you to indulge in regional cuisines, discover award-winning restaurants or simply relax in one of our beautiful spas. We offer true Romantik hospitality, outstanding cuisine and a historic environment steeped in tradition. In Switzerland over 25 Romantik Hotels & Restaurants are awaiting you. For more information and availability go to www.romantikhotels.com.

Romantik Hotels & Restaurants are about personal service, attention to detail and true hospitality.

ROMANTIK
HOTELS & RESTAURANTS
INTERNATIONAL

We look forward to your visit.
Romantik Hotels & Restaurants GmbH & Co. KG
Hahnstraße 70, 60528 Frankfurt, Germany

Fon: +49 (0) 69/66 12 34-0
Fax: +49 (0) 69/66 12 34-56

info@romantikhotels.com

www.romantikhotels.com

Karen Brown's World of Travel

**A FREE KAREN BROWN WEBSITE MEMBERSHIP
IS INCLUDED WITH THE PURCHASE OF THIS GUIDE**

$20 Value – Equal to the cover price of this book!

In appreciation for purchasing our guide, we offer a free membership that includes:

• The ability to custom plan and build unlimited itineraries
• 15% discount on all purchases made in the Karen Brown website store
• One free downloadable Karen Brown Itinerary from over 100 choices
• Karen Brown's World of Travel Newsletter—includes special offers & updates
Membership valid through December 31, 2009

To take advantage of this free offer go to the Karen Brown website shown below and create a login profile so we can recognize you as a Preferred Customer; then you can utilize the unrestricted trip planning and take advantage of the 15% store discount. Once you set up an account you will receive by email a coupon code to order the free itinerary.

Go to ***www.karenbrown.com/preferred.php*** to create your profile!

Karen Brown's
2009 Readers' Choice Awards

Most Romantic
Landgasthof Ruedihus
Kandersteg

Warmest Welcome
Rote Rose & Engelfrid
Regensberg

Greatest Value
Hotel de Moiry
Grimentz

Splendid Splurge
Schloss Hotel Chasté
Tarasp

Be sure to vote for next year's winners by visiting
www.karenbrown.com